if that
ever happens
to me

STUDIES IN SOCIAL MEDICINE

Allan M. Brandt & Larry R. Churchill, *editors*

if that ever happens to me

MAKING LIFE AND DEATH DECISIONS AFTER TERRI SCHIAVO

LOIS SHEPHERD

The University of North Carolina Press

Chapel Hill

© 2009 The University of North Carolina Press
All rights reserved
Designed by Richard Hendel
Set in Quadraat and Scala Sans
by Tseng Information Systems, Inc.
Manufactured in the United States of America

The paper in this book meets the guidelines for
permanence and durability of the Committee on
Production Guidelines for Book Longevity of the
Council on Library Resources.

The University of North Carolina Press has been a
member of the Green Press Initiative since 2003.

Library of Congress Cataloging-in-Publication Data
Shepherd, Lois L., 1962–
If that ever happens to me : making life and death
decisions after Terri Schiavo / Lois Shepherd.
   p. ; cm. — (Studies in social medicine)
Includes bibliographical references and index.
ISBN 978-0-8078-3295-0 (cloth : alk. paper)
1. Schiavo, Terri, 1963–2005. 2. Terminal care.
3. Right to die. 4. Euthanasia. I. Title. II. Series.
[DNLM: 1. Schiavo, Terri, 1963–2005. 2. Euthanasia,
Passive—ethics. 3. Decision Making—ethics.
4. Enteral Nutrition—ethics. 5. Life Support Care—
ethics. 6. Persistent Vegetative State. 7. Withholding
Treatment—legislation & jurisprudence.
WB 65 S548t 2009]
R726.8.S4755 2009
179.7—dc22   2008045187

13 12 11 10 09   5 4 3 2 1

To my husband, Paul,

and my children, Max,

Summer, and Charlie,

whom I trust and love

with all my heart.

CONTENTS

ACKNOWLEDGMENTS

Many thanks to

The library faculty and staff at the Florida State University College of Law, especially Mary McCormick, Trisha Simonds, Marin Dell, Margaret Clark, Anne Bardolph, Robin Gault, Faye Jones, and Jon Lutz. You are extraordinary. Your research and acquisition skills are positively gymnastic.

Larry Churchill, for inviting me to write this book. It has been a challenging and rewarding endeavor.

Kathy Cerminara, of Nova Southeastern University Law School, for her amazing grasp of end-of-life law and her willingness to share it so readily in answer to my e-mails with the subject line "quick question—," although there are really no quick answers in this field.

Kenneth Goodman and the University of Miami Ethics Programs, for helping to obtain the trial transcript of the original 2000 hearing before Judge George Greer.

Both Professors Cerminara and Goodman, for their incredible Web site that posted resources on the Schiavo case as the controversy unfolded.

Aline Kalbian and John Corrigan, of the religion faculty at FSU, for their encouragement and advice.

My editor at the University of North Carolina Press, Sian Hunter, for helping shape this book and for all her insights.

Norman L. Cantor, Professor Emeritus of Rutgers School of Law, whom I've joined on several panels to discuss the Schiavo case and other end-of-life problems. While Professor Cantor and I come out differently on so many issues, his work and his conversation always push me away from too-easy answers. And he is an example to all scholars in the passion and compassion he brings to these problems.

My husband, Paul Shepherd, novelist and editor extraordinaire, for reading and editing countless drafts and for having the nerve to be the harshest but most loyal of critics.

The Florida State University College of Law, for its generous research support, and those at the Center for Biomedical Ethics and Humanities at the University of Virginia, especially Margaret Mohrmann, for believing in this project.

if that
ever happens
to me

In the early months of 2005, Theresa Marie Schindler Schiavo, known as "Terri," captured the national public spotlight—but she did not know it. Nor, at age forty-one, had she known anything of her previous fifteen birthdays. She was in what doctors call a persistent or permanent vegetative state. When patients are in a vegetative state, doctors believe they cannot experience life in any way—that they are completely unconscious. When the condition is properly diagnosed as permanent, there is no evidence that the patient can ever regain any consciousness; after fifteen years, the chance of recovery, even slight recovery, is most accurately described as zero.

While Terri's husband and her parents were initially in agreement about her care, through the years they became sharply and bitterly divided. In 1998, eight years after the collapse that caused Terri to enter a vegetative state, her husband, Michael Schiavo, began a long court battle to remove her feeding tube. Without it, Terri would certainly die. Yet Michael insisted that this—death rather than life in a permanent vegetative state—was what Terri would want.

Her parents, Robert and Mary Schindler, disagreed. In court, they argued that Terri would not have wanted the feeding tube removed. When that argument failed, they challenged the diagnosis that she was in a permanent vegetative state. Then they argued, as you are allowed to do in court, "in the alternative." That is, even if Terri *was* in a permanent vegetative state and *at one time* would have wanted to have the feeding tube removed, as a Catholic, she would have changed her mind when Pope John Paul II spoke on the general issue in 2004. These are some of the main arguments that the Schindlers made, but there were many others. Over seven years, the Schindlers exhausted every avenue of relief in the courts. Many of their methods were unconventional, and some were even of questionable propriety. But while their activities in court granted them some delay in the removal of Terri's feeding tube—which over the seven-year battle was twice removed only to be reinserted—the courts gave them no ultimate relief. Circuit court judge George Greer in the initial hearing of 2000 agreed with Michael Schiavo that Terri would want the feeding tube removed, and neither that court nor any other would upset that ruling.

Beginning in 2003, the Schindlers turned to the legislative and executive branches of government. They also garnered substantial media attention and the support of various religious and disability rights groups. The tactic here was somewhat different. While the Schindlers continued to disagree with Michael about what Terri wanted and her medical condition, a new focus became whether it was *morally right* to cause someone's certain death by failing to provide the basic necessities of food and water.

In Florida, these efforts paid off. In October 2003, the Schindlers received a reprieve through special legislation under which the Florida governor, Jeb Bush, ordered the reinsertion of Terri's feeding tube after it had been removed. When that law was declared unconstitutional the following year by the Florida Supreme Court, the Schindlers and their supporters sought federal action. Appealing to President George W. Bush and the federal legislature, they were successful in achieving extraordinary legislation to force federal court review of the case. But the federal courts did not go along, refusing to revisit the issue of Terri's condition or her wishes. All legal means to block the removal of Terri's feeding tube had now been exhausted.

Terri died on March 31, 2005, thirteen days after her feeding tube was removed. Throughout these days, cable news programs provided continual updates of Terri's condition and the activities of protesters outside the hospice where she lived. They supplied endless commentary and debate among clergy, politicians, and medical and legal experts. And they reported how even in Terri's last days, her husband and parents publicly fought—over visitation rights, cremation versus burial, and the location of Terri's remains.

Choosing Sides

The story of Terri Schiavo is not a simple one. Yet during the controversy surrounding the removal of her feeding tube, people of all kinds—politicians, religious leaders, physicians, bioethicists, legal experts—made emphatic statements about the facts and offered even more certain opinions about what should be done. Some who protested the removal of Terri's feeding tube insisted, contrary to the opinions of medical experts who had examined her, that she was not in a permanent vegetative state but in a newly recognized condition called a "minimally conscious state." In fact, Senator (and doctor) Bill Frist, then Senate majority leader, was willing to state his medical opinion on this issue after viewing a few minutes of videotape of Terri. Similarly, others declared that removal of her feeding tube would amount to "starvation" and that starving someone to death was morally wrong. Many argued that when a person like Terri has not placed her wishes in writing, feeding tubes should never be removed. In the words of conservative bioethics commentator Wesley Smith, "casual conversations"—statements like "I wouldn't want to live like that," which a person might utter after seeing a relative in the hospital—should not be the basis of a "death order."[1] On the personal front, Michael Schiavo, Terri's husband, was openly accused of being a liar and a cheat. These were the perspectives shared by the parents of Terri Schiavo and their supporters—politicians seeking conservative support, many newscasters, right-to-life groups, and some disability rights groups.

Those who supported the removal of Terri's feeding tube spoke just as certainly in their views. According to this group, the removal of feeding tubes in situations like Terri's is not cruel starvation but a constitutional right. Feeding tubes, they insisted, are just like ventilators—advanced, intrusive medical treatment that people have an absolute right to refuse. So anxious were some of them to point up that Terri's case was beyond hope that they dismissed the very idea that a "minimally conscious state" might exist for any patient, characterizing this new category of patient condition as a political rather than a scientific discovery. But most important to commentators who supported removal of the feeding tube was the fact that Terri didn't want to live this way: a court had clearly determined what her wishes were after a full and impartial hearing and according to proper legal standards—and not just one court but many (Internet blogs put the number at twenty) accepted that conclusion. In the end, according to this view, Terri's right to refuse medical treatment was supreme and was dutifully honored by a beleaguered husband and a courageous judge.

Those who study and comment on law tended to fall into the latter camp. Part of their support for the courts' decisions to allow the removal of Terri's feeding tube came from support more generally for the rule of law. Following the rule of law means that rather than throwing such decisions to the political winds, existing legal precedents and statutes are allowed to govern, and recognized, fair, and open processes to determine their application are followed. The Schiavo case erupted at a time when the judiciary was already under attack by conservative politicians and commentators who accused judges of using their positions on the bench to impose their liberal beliefs upon the American public. When the courts permitted the removal of Terri's feeding tube, critics rallied around the case with even greater charges of "judicial activism." The criticisms carried the threat of action. During this time, a number of legislative proposals were introduced at both the state and federal levels to restrict or otherwise affect judges' decision-making powers.

This context helped shape the response of legal academics to the Schiavo controversy, which tended, during its pendency, to be driven by concern for the independence of the judiciary and continued respect for the rule of law. A nearly singular response issued: the courts had followed the law, and the law was good. This support for the judiciary might have appeared weakened by admitting to any uncertainties or concerns about the law generally or its application in Terri's case.

And so it appeared, from the politician to the protester and from the clergy member to the legal academic, that there were only two sides to the Schiavo case. And in a way, there were. Either the feeding tube would be removed and Terri would die, or the feeding tube would stay in place and Terri would live. But the issues involved in this case were more complex and more subtle than either side would admit, and each side made some compelling points.

This is not a "red state/blue state," conservative/liberal, Republican/Democrat issue. It is not as simple as pro-life versus pro–personal liberty. It's not a matter of choosing sides and you're done, although that's how the politics appeared to play out and the media chose to spin it.

What we lost in the Schiavo case is an appreciation for the uncertainties and doubts that these kinds of cases necessarily entail, and acceptance of the fact that despite such uncertainty and doubt decisions must be made. By failing to appreciate these complexities, we have not advanced our understanding of how best to handle end-of-life decisions. The Schiavo case brought only polarized—and ultimately false—clarity: one clear vision for conservatives and another clear vision for liberals.

Inspired by the case, conservatives have been seeking revision of state laws to make sure the "next Terri Schiavo" does not die. They are also seeking to change public attitudes about feeding tubes in general—to get more people to view them as morally necessary, for themselves and for their family members. The upshot, if they are successful, is less freedom in the future to decide what we would like done for ourselves and our loved ones. And this "we" includes "them," the conservatives themselves, although it's not clear that they appreciate this. They want to insist that we can all protect our individual freedoms by providing written instructions ahead of time in a "living will," but the evidence so far about living wills shows that they cannot by themselves guarantee that we will get what we want (and not get what we don't want) in terms of life support.[2]

Liberals, in the face of this threat to individual choice, risk digging in their heels and hanging on to existing laws without reflecting on their possible weaknesses. Many legal commentators and medical ethicists during and immediately after the Schiavo case, and still today, insist that there was nothing new about the case. The law and ethics in this area, they repeatedly stated, have been long settled. Often they referred to the earlier famous cases of Karen Ann Quinlan in 1976, a young woman in a permanent vegetative state whose parents sought and won removal of her ventilator, and Nancy Cruzan in 1990, also in a permanent vegetative state whose parents sought and won removal of her feeding tube. Those cases created new law and ushered in new medical practices. But not Schiavo—that episode, according to these commentators, was essentially legally and ethically insignificant, merely a political circus stirred up by rabid conservatives.

Framing the Questions

But the case of Terri Schiavo is increasingly significant, both from a legal and an ethical perspective. As will be explained more fully in the coming chapters, there are weaknesses in existing law and many issues that are left to be decided. Perhaps to the liberal's surprise, our current legal system actually gives insufficient respect to a person's wishes in certain circumstances. Many states require that individuals' wishes be proved by such a high standard of evidence before life support can be removed that patients are more likely to have their wishes ignored rather than honored when they are in a permanent vegetative state.

Moreover, many legal and ethical issues are not or should not be considered settled, a point made clear when the Schiavo case is studied in its multifaceted dimensions. When a large number of Americans, a vocal media presence, and a majority of two legislative bodies are saying, "Wait a minute—" because they are uncertain or confused or unhappy about how end-of-life decisions are being made, then it is not enough to say, "We [meaning the legal and medical establishments] settled that issue years ago." As law and ethics scholar Rebecca Dresser has written, "[P]erhaps the public response was not so surprising. Over the past three decades, clinicians and legal authorities have constructed a basic approach to treatment decisions for incapacitated patients, but as the passions this latest case unleashed suggest, this approach is both unfinished and vulnerable to challenge."[3]

While liberals are not antifamily any more than they embrace a "culture of death," as they are sometimes charged, during the Schiavo case they rarely were willing to engage in a careful discussion about how certain we should be of a patient's wishes before removing life support, or about the role of the family, or about the appropriateness of making quality-of-life decisions and the need to protect vulnerable individuals.

It might appear that we are at a crossroads in end-of-life law. Will we follow a path toward more restrictions on the removal of life support in the name of valuing all life, especially vulnerable life? Or will we strengthen a commitment to personal choice and expand what is commonly referred to as a "right to die" — to include physician aid in hastening death, for example?

More likely, we will choose neither but continue an uneasy balancing act between the two. When what is at stake is described in such polar and oversimplified terms (for which constitutional interpretation is partly to blame), the lines to be drawn will never be satisfactory.

But it may be possible to frame these issues in a way other than a preference of life over choice, or choice over life, or some uneasy balance or trade-off between the two. In this book, I suggest such a reframing of the issues — one that places primary importance on respect and care for the patient and the patient's family. Preservation of the patient's life and deference to the patient's choice will still be important, but building on a foundation of respect and care enriches our understanding of what is at stake in these matters. We have to think about "respect" more broadly than simply as respect for patient self-determination or choice; we must also include respect for the individual human life — are we making decisions to benefit this person, or others? Is the patient's privacy being protected? Similarly, we have to think about "care" in terms other than simple labels, such as the labeling of nutrition and hydration as "basic care," a term that gained a certain traction during the Schiavo dispute. Sometimes, as we'll see, feeding tubes can actually cause a patient more pain and suffering with little or no benefit—and then it doesn't look like "care" at all.

"Respect" and "care" change the focus from what people have a right to—a right to live? A right to die?—to how we must act responsibly in our regard and treatment of them. Rights still matter, but as we'll see, legal rights tend, often for good reason, to be rather thin and often incomplete and inadequate, although they are important and at times determinative and completely necessary.

End-of-life law and ethics are due for a reexamination. The Schiavo case makes that abundantly clear. More was lost, after all, in the political and cultural battle surrounding the case than an appreciation for complexity and the necessity of making decisions in conditions of uncertainty: Terri Schiavo herself was lost. She became a pawn in the pursuit of larger agendas—agendas involving traditional and religious values, or the protection of people with disabilities, or libertarian notions of freedom of choice, or sometimes, even worse, individual politicians seeking a spotlight.

It is true that the political exploitation of the Schiavo case—in the federal Congress, at least—appeared to backfire. When a memo identifying the Schiavo case as one from which Republicans could benefit politically was traced to Senator Mel Martinez's office, he incurred swift and universal public condemnation. His general counsel, who admitted authorship of the memo, immediately resigned. Bill Frist has since publicly acknowledged that he made a mistake in pushing through special legislation authorizing federal court review of the case; some political commentators claim that Frist's involvement in the dispute—in particular, his "diagnosis" of Terri—severely diminished his chances of a 2008 presidential bid.

Polls have consistently shown that the American public thought the U.S. Congress had no business getting involved in the controversy. According to one CBS News poll conducted in March 2005 (during the flurry of federal activity to "save" Terri), 82 percent of those surveyed believed that Congress and the president should stay out of the Schiavo dispute. Another CBS News poll showed that 74 percent of respondents thought the federal legislation was passed to advance a political agenda.[4] Candidates for the 2008 presidential election avoided taking firm positions on the extraordinary actions taken by Congress and the president in 2005 although repeatedly pressed to do so early in their campaigns.

This apparent calming of the waters should not be interpreted as a sign that the fundamental issues of the case are settled. While political motivation to become entangled in such individual matters may have waned, we as a society must still grapple with how best to approach—legally and ethically and practically—the sorts of questions raised by Terri's case. They are not going to go away.

A Strategy from Here

This book has several aims. The first is to provide an explanation of what happened and why in the battle over the removal of Terri Schiavo's feeding tube. To some extent, the facts are disputed. For example, was Terri in a permanent vegetative state or not? Could she be fed by spoon or straw? And if so, what then? At times, in the telling of the story of Terri Schiavo, I will have to choose which version of the facts is most credible, but I will explain why I believe those facts to be more credible than the alternative story. At other times, while I will acknowledge there to be a dispute about the facts, I will argue that which version of the facts one chooses to believe is not crucial to how one should assess the decisions made in the Schiavo case. While the facts have been set out in numerous books, articles, and television programs, the telling of them has more often than not been marred by hasty research, polemical characterizations, and crucial legal inaccuracies.

A second aim of the book is to see what we can learn from the Schiavo controversy in the larger context of the law, ethics, and culture of end-of-life decision making. In particular, the Schiavo case raised these questions:

—How much do we know about the permanent vegetative state, and how strong was the evidence that Terri Schiavo had no hope of ever recovering consciousness? Because of recent reports about new scientific evidence regarding the vegetative state and other disorders of consciousness, the subject of Terri's condition is given a separate chapter immediately following this introduction, before the book delves into the facts about Terri's medical treatment and life support (chapter 2) and the law as it relates to the permanent vegetative state (chapter 3).

—In order to withdraw life support, how much and what kinds of evidence must be brought forward regarding the wishes of a formerly competent patient? Should we insist on a living will before we allow life support to be withdrawn? Chapters 4 and 5 explain how our current legal standards of evidence in this area hinder us in making accurate legal decisions for the permanently vegetative patient and, more particularly, why we should not expect living wills to solve this problem.

—How do we determine who should speak for the incapacitated patient in making decisions to refuse treatment, and how do we protect patients from surrogates making decisions in their own rather than the patient's interests? In chapter 6, I'll discuss both the weaknesses and strengths of relying on surrogate decision making and how we might better take into account the full spectrum of the interests of everyone—especially those of the patient.

—Should the quality of life of the patient factor into decisions to allow the removal of life support? Should the condition of the patient serve as a limit on when life support can be removed—for example, would it/should it have made a difference if Terri Schiavo were minimally conscious, or merely profoundly disabled? Chapter 7 argues that we can better respect and care for both the profoundly disabled and those in a permanently vegetative state if we appreciate their differences. Considerations of quality of life cannot always be avoided.

—Are feeding tubes different from other forms of life support, because feeding represents a basic form of care? Chapter 8 challenges the idea that tube-feeding and even hand-feeding always represent a form of care and finds that too often we think about care from the perspective of the caregiver rather than of the cared-for.

— *Does the law give enough protection to human life? Should our right to life be protected as much as our right to die? Should it be protected even more?* In chapter 9, I argue that a narrow "rights" approach too often fails to capture what is at stake in these cases. Our laws and practices do need changing—but more deeply, and foundationally, than a simple rights approach can capture. In chapter 10, I'll describe an alternative approach that emphasizes respect and care and explore how this new approach might be applied to different types of patient conditions, including the terminally ill, profoundly disabled and never competent, minimally conscious, and permanently vegetative.

My position on Terri's case should be made clear at the outset. I think she should have been allowed to die. In fact, I think she should have been allowed to die years before the final removal of her feeding tube and without an extended court battle over her wishes. Not only do I think her feeding tube should have been removed, but I think that even if she could have been forced to reflexively swallow food, she should not have been fed by hand, either.

In the past, I have taken strong positions in favor of disability rights and against a right to physician aid in hastening death (sometimes referred to as physician-assisted suicide). How can I now argue for allowing Terri Schiavo to die? Isn't starvation or, more accurately, dehydration a cruel way to end a life? Doesn't our failure to nourish mean that we are not properly caring for a patient?

No, to both questions. With respect to Terri, she could not experience dehydration, just as she could not experience anything. Properly respecting and caring for her as a patient meant caring for her body by keeping it clean and neat, protecting her privacy, respecting her wishes if they could be discerned, and, most important, treating her as a person rather than as an object. These do not, though, lead to an assumption that she should have been maintained in a state of biological life so long after the person who really was Terri Schiavo had been gone.

Do I come to the conclusion that Terri should have been allowed to die because the evidence was so overwhelming about what her wishes were? No. In fact, I think we don't really know what Terri would have wanted. Some evidence exists about what she wanted, but when we review the testimony at trial (chapter 4), we'll find it's not nearly as clear as we might like to think it was.

Instead, I come to this conclusion because people in a permanent vegetative state have no present interest in continuing to live. They can experience nothing in this world, or even in the most inner world of their minds, and they never will. That means that if their lives are continued indefinitely, it is done so only for other people, not for them. They become an instrument, a mere object, for others to do with what they like. The exception would be if a person had made known his or her wish to continue to live in that condition. This was not the case with Terri Schiavo, which is not surprising, considering that studies show that the great majority of Americans would not want their own lives continued in a permanent vegetative state.

Some argue that if we remove feeding tubes from people like Terri, it would be easier to remove feeding tubes and other life support from people who might still have some consciousness or who might wake up from a coma. They fear we would be starting down a slippery slope where we might eventually wind up removing tubes from people who are profoundly disabled but not in a permanent vegetative state. This is apparently what concerned a number of disability rights groups, who vigorously joined the Schindlers' fight to prevent removal of Terri's feeding tube.

I would like to make clear my support for the protection of people with disabilities and for the provision of the utmost respect and care for such individuals, especially the profoundly disabled. Over the years, I have found myself in alignment with disability advocates on many issues. For example, I have written elsewhere of our shared concern that calls to respect "dignity" in dying may signify an intolerance for certain conditions (and the people who live with them) that might seem undignified—conditions such as dependence on others for bodily care or incontinence.

But I part company with them on the Schiavo case. Here, I think their "slippery slope" concerns were misplaced and some of their tactics were worse—that even they were exploitative of Terri. People in a permanent vegetative state can be distinguished from people with profound disabilities—that distinction is consciousness, or the potential for consciousness. By adopting at times in the Schiavo controversy a clearly distorted view of the facts (for example, in a joint statement they suggested that Michael Schiavo improperly denied rehabilitation for Terri and made up evidence of her wish to die after winning a malpractice lawsuit),[5] disability rights groups have hurt their credibility. Of more concern, by failing to distinguish people in a permanent vegetative state from people who are profoundly disabled, I think they have done a disservice to the latter, who are conscious and therefore have present needs and desires that we should work diligently to meet.

It is for these reasons, all of which will be explored more fully in this book, that I have argued elsewhere for a presumption in favor of discontinuing the tube-feeding of people in a permanent vegetative state.[6] Currently, the law favors continued feeding. I have argued that for people in this unique state, where biological life continues without the capacity for any consciousness, the law should be changed, and that to do so would actually show more—rather than less—respect for them as people.

I know that many will remain unconvinced by this argument, but it is not crucial to agree with me on this point to find value in the discussion that follows, because *no matter what our positions*, we need to reevaluate the moral, legal, and policy reasoning we bring to this debate. In particular, we need to discard the notion that there will be simple solutions to these problems—like recent simplistic appeals to the living will. Further, we need to resist a tendency to rely on stock phrases, like "sanctity of life" or "freedom of choice" or "basic care," that have become slogans in this area. And we must reject the current framing of end-of-life issues as being singularly or even primarily about an individual's rights. In early cases, it was the right to self-determination that gained recognition; during the Schiavo dispute, we heard rhetoric insisting on a right to life. Asking only what a person's rights are will not answer most of the important, practical questions about what should be done in a particular case. Asking about Terri's rights did not really answer what should be done in her case. And that may be why her case is unsettling. Upon close examination—like the examination you will find in this book—we see that we need to keep searching for better understanding of our responsibilities to one another in these contexts, not simply for more expressions of our rights.

1 DISORDERS OF CONSCIOUSNESS AND THE PERMANENT VEGETATIVE STATE

Theresa Marie Schiavo was twenty-six years old when she suffered a cardiac arrest for reasons still unknown. Terri grew up in the suburbs of Philadelphia, Pennsylvania, the oldest of three children. She married her first boyfriend, Michael Schiavo, whom she met in college, and they moved to Florida in 1986. Her family followed them there. Terri worked as a clerk for an insurance company while Michael worked in restaurant management. One early morning in February 1990, Michael awoke, found Terri collapsed in the hallway of their apartment, and called 911. Twelve minutes later, at 5:52, paramedics begin resuscitation efforts and, after several attempts at defibrillation, restored her heartbeat. By this time, her brain had sustained severe injury due to lack of oxygen. She was taken to a local hospital. She never again regained consciousness.

Defining the Permanent Vegetative State

Initially, Terri entered a coma. During this time, she would have looked like she was asleep. A coma resembles sleep because the patient's eyes are closed, but the patient is unresponsive and cannot be roused. A coma is typically a temporary condition; patients who initially enter a coma will either die without ever recovering consciousness, will recover either complete or partial consciousness, or will enter a vegetative state. This, after about a month, was how Terri's coma ended—in a vegetative state.

Drs. Bryan Jennett and Fred Plum adopted the term "persistent vegetative state" in 1972 to describe patients who had, after trauma to the brain, entered a condition of unconsciousness that is marked by periods of apparent wakefulness,[1] where a cycle of "eyes-open, 'wakeful' appearance alternates with an eyes-closed 'sleep' state."[2]

As recently described by Drs. Nicholas Schiff and Joseph Fins, "In all other respects, the vegetative state is similar to coma. Patients in vegetative states demonstrate no evidence of awareness of self or response to their surroundings."[3]

The term has been widely used by those inside and outside the medical community and is incorporated in a number of legal cases and statutes. While originally intended to signal a continuing, or persistent, condition from which recovery may or may not occur, the term has come to be widely used to refer to a permanent—not merely long-lasting—condition. Recently, experts have suggested that, to reduce confusion about the predicted duration of the condition, we should call patients who have *recently* entered the state as "vegetative" and call those patients for whom the condition is considered *irreversible* as "permanently vegetative."[4] In this book, I will, as much as possible, follow this recommendation (language quoted from other texts may still use the term "persistent" or the even more ambiguous "PVS"). How clearly the line can be established between the vegetative state and the permanent vegetative state will be covered later in this chapter. While there are no definite numbers of how many people live in a permanent vegetative state in this country, estimates range from 10,000 to 25,000 adults and 6,000 to 10,000 children.[5] Approximately 4,200 new cases of vegetative state are diagnosed each year in the United States.[6]

There is some concern that the use of the term "vegetative" is demeaning because it suggests that the person is something less than a person, a mere "vegetable." I am sympathetic to this argument. We need to understand and appreciate that all people, no matter their condition, *are* people and should be treated with respect and care. However, the terminology has become so widespread, with no alternative yet achieving any significant use, that to use a different term would cause confusion. My intention is to use the term itself with care—indeed, one concern I'll raise throughout this book is that too often, people living in these highly dependent states too easily become objects or curiosities.

Diagnosis and Misdiagnosis

Recently—since Terri died, in fact—a number of scientific studies and articles have revealed new insights into the vegetative state and a related but very different condition, the minimally conscious state. Some of the popular press accounts of this research appear to cast doubt on issues highly relevant to the resolution of the Schiavo case and might appear to validate the concerns voiced by those who opposed the removal of Terri's feeding tube. A reader of these accounts is led to wonder: can doctors adequately distinguish between patients with no consciousness and patients with some, even if minimal, consciousness? How reliably can doctors tell which patients have no hope of returning to consciousness and which have some potential of doing so? Is there really a *complete* loss of consciousness in vegetative patients?

The story of Terry Wallis—which hit the national news around the same time as Terri Schiavo's case—is an especially alarming case of misdiagnosis. Following a severe traumatic brain injury, Wallis was diagnosed as permanently vegetative in 1989. He was discharged to a nursing home and, despite reported observations from his family that he could follow simple commands, was never reevaluated by a neurologist. His father's requests for further evaluations were denied as too expensive and unhelpful.[7] Nineteen years later, Wallis experienced a sudden, meaningful recovery that appeared miraculous. After nearly two decades of silence, he began speaking.[8] In fact, a *New Yorker* article explained that when a medical researcher needed Wallis's social security number in 2005 to help him receive assistance, Wallis himself provided it.[9] Studying the brain imaging results from special MRI techniques performed on Wallis, researchers have hypothesized that his brain developed "new connections between surviving neurons" that help explain his recovery.[10] In other words, decades after entering what now clearly was not a permanent vegetative state but instead a minimally conscious state, Terry's brain structures experienced new, unexpected growth that may help explain his recovery. Wallis appears to have transitioned from an initial coma, to a vegetative state lasting less than a year, to minimal consciousness and then ultimately, years later, emerged from a minimally conscious state. As Dr. Joseph Fins writes, "Wallis's story is a cautionary tale."[11] It reveals both the real possibility of misdiagnosis (some estimates put the error rate of diagnoses of minimally conscious patients as in a permanent vegetative state as high as 30 to 40 percent) and the consequent neglect of misdiagnosed patients, who are denied rehabilitative therapy as futile and given only "custodial care."[12]

It is a horror we can all imagine. The parents of Terri Schiavo, like the family of Terry Wallis, insisted that she showed signs of consciousness, tracking objects with her eyes and following commands. Terri also was considered a hopeless case soon after she transitioned from her original sleeplike coma to a state of unconsciousness with sleep-wake cycles. Her parents have written that two weeks after Terri's collapse, her doctors told them that she was "PVS" and that she was "never going to get any better."[13] She also, like Terry Wallis, received this grim diagnosis long before the medical community was aware that the early vegetative state could be a transitional condition to the minimally conscious state.[14] Could she have also suffered from misdiagnosis and neglect?

The answer to that question, in short, is no. Nothing medical research has revealed since Judge George Greer's original order in 2000 to remove Terri's feeding tube has raised any real doubts about her diagnosis (vegetative state) or her prognosis (permanence of the vegetative state with no reasonable hope of recovery of any kind or degree). (The evidence about Terri's condition will be covered later.) What the new research does reveal about other cases, however, is important to various issues discussed in this book.

Some people who work or study in the field of medical ethics have reacted to the new research into disorders of consciousness with disbelief and uneasiness—suspicious that the research may be motivated by a desire to diminish our rights to refuse treatment. A few whom I personally know were quick—too quick—during the pendency of the Schiavo dispute to dismiss the idea of the minimally conscious state as not a "real" diagnosis but something essentially "made up," a category that was spliced so thinly from the condition of the permanent vegetative state that it was morally irrelevant. To them, the recently identified category served only to create doubt about the appropriateness of the removal of life support from patients who had no hope of any meaningful interaction with the world. Fins, an expert who has written extensively on vegetative and minimally conscious states, decried a similar reluctance to reckon with the minimally conscious state expressed in an e-mail forum of bioethicists. In an article in the *American Journal of Bioethics*, he writes, "Many of our colleagues cannot imagine life in a state of diminished consciousness and want to 'protect' patients and families from the horrors of severe brain injury. So disposed, they preclude the possibility that some patients may recover. . . . It is the mirror-image of those who sought to impose their religious beliefs on Terri Schiavo. Instead of imposing our views on families touched by severe brain injury, it is best to simply share what is known, and perhaps more critically at this early juncture, *what is not known.*"[15]

This chapter will examine what we know and are learning about the permanent vegetative state and the minimally conscious state and also the new, promising techniques to distinguish between the two. It will also review the evidence about Terri Schiavo's condition.

Living Persons

One thing that is absolutely clear is that people in a permanent vegetative state are living. They are not dead under our current medical and legal understandings of death, which are the same because the legal definition of death draws from medical knowledge and practice. Despite a number of media references (even in such prestigious newspapers as the *Wall Street Journal*)[16] that described Terri Schiavo as a "brain dead" woman, she was by all reasonable standards a living person during the controversy that surrounded her, mainly because her brain stem, which controls autonomic responses such as respiratory and cardiac activity, was still functioning. Someone who is brain dead is dead just like someone whose heart has stopped beating, but because the brain dead person's breathing is maintained by a ventilator (to preserve organs for transplantation, for example), doctors cannot use signs of cardiopulmonary function to determine whether death has occurred.[17] Brain function must be tested instead. If the ventilation of the brain dead patient were stopped, the patient's breathing would also stop and ultimately so would the patient's heart. Terri Schiavo could breathe on her own, without mechanical assistance, and was therefore, by all pertinent definitions, clearly a living, breathing person.

While not always appreciated during the Schiavo controversy, this distinction between permanent vegetative state and brain death is important. The duties we owe to the dead are weaker than those owed to the living. Indeed, our duties to the dead are often carried out because of concern, sympathy, and respect for the living—loved ones of the deceased. When people are alive, like Terri Schiavo was during the fight over her feeding tube, we owe them respect and care, beginning with as clear an understanding as possible of their situation.

Absence of Awareness

While people in a permanent vegetative state are not dead, their senses are absent—all of them. They have a "complete unawareness of the self and the environment."[18] In the short video clips that appeared on television and on the Web site that Terri's parents maintained throughout their fight, Terri's eyes appeared to be following a balloon, and she seemed to be smiling in response to her mother's presence. But those tapes showed deceptively edited moments taken from hours and hours of videotaping in which Terri's eyes wandered without purpose, without seeing, and in which her mouth might have appeared to show all sorts of expression, although they were not expressions relating to anything going on around her. Such "activity" is consistent with the diagnosis of a vegetative condition. According to expert Dr. Bryan Jennett, "What characterizes the vegetative state is the combination of periods of wakeful eye opening without any evidence of a working mind either receiving or projecting information, a dissociation between arousal and awareness."[19] Patients in a vegetative state exhibit some movements that may make them appear to be conscious. They may have startle reflexes, where the body reacts to a sudden stimulation. This is understandably very disconcerting to those around them.

Jennett provides this description: "The limbs are usually spastic and they may move in a nonpurposeful way and there may be groping movements. A grasp reflex may be set off by contact with bedclothes, the nasogastric tube or the hand of an observer and these may be misinterpreted as indicating voluntary movements or meaningful responses, especially by relatives seeking evidence for recovery. However, careful observation reveals no consistent movements that are voluntary or learned, or a response to command or mimicry."[20]

In addition, Jennett writes, "[m]ost patients show some response to painful stimuli. A stimulated limb may withdraw or there may be a generalized movement of all four limbs, sometimes accompanied by facial grimacing and perhaps a groan. There may also be a rise in respiratory and pulse rates and in blood pressure. It is generally held that these responses are all at a reflex level and do not indicate that pain is being experienced on a conscious level."[21]

The report of Dr. Jay Wolfson, one of the independent guardians ad litem assigned by the court to protect Terri's interests, reveals some of the difficulty laypeople have in comprehending the condition of the vegetative patient. Wolfson is not a medical doctor but a professor holding both a doctorate in public health and a law degree. He concluded in 2003, after reviewing the entire court file to date as well as clinical and medical records, that "highly competent, scientifically based physicians using recognized measures and standards have deduced, within a high degree of medical certainty, that Theresa is in a persistent vegetative state. This evidence is compelling."[22]

He also visited Terri almost daily for a month and observed nothing to call that conclusion into doubt. And yet he poignantly wrote in his report: "This having been said, Theresa has a distinct presence about her. Being with Theresa, holding her hand, looking into her eyes and watching how she is lovingly treated by Michael, her parents and family and the clinical staff at hospice is an emotional experience. It would be easy to detach from her if she were comatose, asleep with her eyes closed and made no noises. This is the confusing thing for the lay person about persistent vegetative states."[23]

For family members who love the patient, who seek any sign that the person they love is still able to perceive them, it can be very difficult to accept that the movements of the vegetative patient do not signal understanding or perception.

The Minimally Conscious State

Terri's parents claimed that she was not in a vegetative state but rather in the recently recognized condition known as the minimally conscious state. Between 112,000 to 280,000 people in the United States are estimated to live in a minimally conscious state.[24] The critical difference between a minimally conscious state and a permanent vegetative state is that a patient in the former condition shows some level of cognitive function, while a diagnosis of permanent vegetative state means there is *no* evidence of cognition. The responses of a person in a minimally conscious state may be as simple as any intelligible verbalization or any purposeful behavior—such as reaching for objects—or any appropriate affective response to stimuli or the visual tracking of moving objects. Often such responses are inconsistent and infrequent, making it difficult to distinguish between the purposeful activity of a minimally conscious person and the random movements of the vegetative patient and requiring serial examinations by a properly trained neurologist.

Dr. Joseph Giacino explains disorders of consciousness as falling along a continuum. He places minimally conscious patients at "an intermediate point along a continuum of consciousness that includes those in vs [vegetative state] on one pole, and those who consistently exhibit meaningful behavioral responses on the other." Until recently, he writes, the category of minimally conscious patients "was indiscriminately lumped together with patients in vs and coma."[25] This lumping together has contributed to a high rate of inaccurate diagnoses in the past—the case of Terry Wallis being one such example.

In recent years, careful efforts by experts have produced consensus about the characteristics that distinguish the minimally conscious state from the vegetative state. The resulting publication of diagnostic criteria should reduce the risk of misdiagnosis in the future.[26]

Distinguishing between patients in a permanent vegetative state and those who are minimally conscious is critically important in considerations of whether life support might be removed or whether it should be continued (the ethical and legal implications are discussed more fully in chapters 7 and 10). But present consciousness versus no present consciousness is not all that distinguishes these diagnoses; the prognosis of these two categories of patients can also be widely divergent. Experts have recently determined that while the person who has been correctly identified as being in a permanent vegetative state has no reasonable hope of recovery of any kind, the prognosis of the patient in a minimally conscious state is more open. While a minimally conscious state may be permanent, it may also be transient, and late recoveries, like that of Terry Wallis, can occur. "Emergence" from the minimally conscious state occurs when the patient exhibits consistent and reliable interactive communication (such as responding to simple questions) or functional use of two different objects (such as bringing a comb to the head).[27] A patient in a vegetative state that has not yet been determined to be "permanent" may sometimes emerge into a minimally conscious state and then emerge further from that condition into one of severe disability or some higher level of recovery. Age (increased age decreases the probability of recovery) and cause of the patient's vegetative condition are two factors that appear to influence the potential for recovery.[28]

Diagnostic Practices

How can doctors tell when a patient is in a vegetative state and when the patient is minimally conscious? The diagnosis is made through clinical observation—in other words, by doctors examining the patient. Experienced physicians are needed, and the patient must be observed over a prolonged period of time, with the doctor checking visual, auditory, and physical systems of the patient. Doctors performing these examinations attempt to get the patient to respond to various simple requests. They look for any sign that the patient understands these requests or attempts to perform the act requested. They also look for spontaneous action on the part of the patient that signals something more than mere reflex, such as visually following an object or another person around the room. Review of nurses' notes and interviews of people who maintain close contact with the patient over time are also important, because patients with disorders of consciousness other than the vegetative state can exhibit signs of consciousness at certain times and then none at others.[29]

There is no diagnostic test, such as a brain scan or blood test, that can definitively determine when a vegetative state, as opposed to some other condition, exists. But it is true that over time, the lack of function in the higher brain of the patient in a permanent vegetative state reveals itself in an atrophy of brain tissue. This is another piece of information that might be considered in a diagnosis. Evidence of a progressive diminishment in brain tissue would be consistent with a diagnosis of a permanent vegetative state. A scan of Terri Schiavo's brain showed that by 1996, six years after she had entered a vegetative state, "much of her cerebral cortex [was] simply gone and [had] been replaced by cerebral spinal fluid."[30] After her death, an autopsy confirmed this conclusion. In fact, her brain weighed half that expected of a person her age. (The autopsy also confirmed that Terri was blind; contrary to the impression given by the famous videotape of her mother's visit, Terri could not see Mary Schindler in the room beside her.)[31]

Certainly, there have been cases of misdiagnoses—doctors make errors—but these errors do not appear (at least not now) to be the result of poorly defined or uncertain criteria. Rather, such misdiagnoses seem to result from a problem of application—such as when the diagnosis is made by doctors who have little experience with such patients or when the diagnosis is made too quickly after the patient's injury, or in a single visit, rather than through serial examinations. In other words, the differences between a permanent vegetative state and a minimally conscious state should be discernible with proper clinical examinations by knowledgeable and experienced physicians.

"Late Recoveries"

Media reports have for years overstated the potential for late recoveries from a permanent vegetative state, when actually the reported cases involved patients who were misclassified. When in 1994 the Multi-Society Task Force on PVS, comprised of five American medical societies, reviewed thirty media reports of alleged late and unexpected recoveries from either a prolonged coma or a vegetative state, the task force found no truly amazing recoveries from permanent vegetative state. In fifteen of the cases, recovery had in fact occurred prior to the recommended period for determining permanence. Nine of the cases were definitely not vegetative and another four only possibly vegetative. The two remaining cases appeared (on the basis of the limited information available) to be truly vegetative; each of these recovered five months after a nontraumatic injury— later than expected, but not much later.[32]

The task force also considered medically verified late recoveries but found similar problems with the data. Again, some of the alleged late recoveries appear to have been late discoveries of recoveries that had actually taken place before the recommended guidelines for determining permanence (which the task force placed at three months for nontraumatic injury, such as lack of oxygen following cardiac arrest, and twelve months for traumatic injury, such as a head injury from a car accident). Furthermore, at the time the task force investigated these stories of late recoveries, diagnostic criteria for the minimally conscious state had not yet been established, leaving open the possibility that these patients were misclassified early on—being minimally conscious rather than vegetative. The task force recognized, however, that a rare late recovery is possible, explaining that "like all clinical diagnoses in medicine, [diagnosis of a permanent vegetative state] is based on probabilities, not absolutes." In those rare instances where a late recovery may have occurred, "recovery" was almost always to a condition of very severe disability, such as a minimally conscious state or slightly better.[33]

New Research

But that was the task force speaking in 1994. Are its conclusions still valid? Now we have new brain imaging and brain stimulation techniques. Are late recoveries more probable now? A *New Yorker* article entitled "Silent Minds" by Dr. Jerome Groopman in the fall of 2007 could well have alarmed readers that the entire field was in disarray and every patient's condition a scientific mystery. The article recounts this remarkable tale from neuropsychologist Joseph Giacino:

> He recalled making rounds with two eminent neurologists and stopping by the bedside of a woman who had had a brain hemorrhage. The neurologists examined the woman, who lay with her eyes half closed and did not respond to the doctors' commands. The neurologists concluded that she was in a vegetative state. "So I sort of sheepishly said, 'Let me show you what happens when we stimulate her,'" Giacino recalled. He had been using a technique called "deep-pressure stimulation," which involves squeezing a patient's muscles with force and precision. Giacino started with the woman's face and worked his way down to her toes, pinching her muscles between his fingers. As he explained, the nerve endings of the muscles send impulses to the brain stem, which relays them to other brain structures and rouses the patient to consciousness. "I did a cycle of deep pressure stimulation, and within a minute or so she was talking to us," Giacino said. "The neurologists were flabbergasted." The woman was able to say her name and her husband's name, and answer simple questions, such as "Is there a cup at your bedside?" After a few minutes, however, she became unresponsive again.[34]

What do we take from this story? Like with many media reports about disorders of consciousness, it is difficult because we have to be careful we do not read the story to mean far more than it actually says.

At the same time, we should not dismiss the possibility of real gains being made in the treatment of disorders of consciousness.

The reporting of this story gives the impression that this patient was *actually diagnosed* as being vegetative—or that she would have been if these neurologists had been her doctors—and that the prognosis would have been of a permanent vegetative condition. But on more careful reading, we realize we're told that the neurologists examined her briefly at her bedside and "concluded that she was in a vegetative state." No respectable neurologist would presume to make a diagnosis of vegetative state without more thorough and repeated observations, a review of the medical record, and so on. I don't doubt that these neurologists were flabbergasted by what they saw—it *was* surprising—but I do doubt that a diagnosis of vegetative state would have been made so cavalierly. At the same time, the story does give us a glimpse of a new therapeutic technique that reveals promise for certain patients, like Giacino's, who have, as the article explained later, what is called a "drive disorder," preventing the patient from being able "to speak, move, or, possibly, think, unless physically stimulated—by touch." (Another promising technique being investigated by medical researchers is deep brain electrical stimulation, involving the implantation of electrodes within the central thalamus of minimally conscious patients.)[35] The story also reveals how easy it would be to miss the abilities this patient did retain were she considered a hopeless case, living in a nursing home, and her abilities given only cursory regard.

But Groopman's article recounted another astonishing story about a patient who *was* considered vegetative by skilled experts under accepted guidelines. With this patient, the surprise came from the results of new brain imaging technologies. A young British neuroscientist, Dr. Adrian Owen, compared the brain scan results of the vegetative patient when asked to "imagine playing tennis" with the brain scans of healthy volunteers asked to perform the same task. The same patterns of activity revealed themselves on the scans, suggesting that the patient had purposefully responded to and completed the researcher's request. Other explanations for this pattern of brain activity were excluded by further comparisons between the brain activity of the supposedly vegetative patient and the healthy volunteers when they were asked to "just relax" from the requested imagination exercise and when asked to perform another exercise, "imagine visiting the rooms of your home." The researchers concluded in their own report of the studies that "although it is almost certainly the case that similar fMR [functional magnetic resonance] imaging responses will not be found in most patients who meet the clinical criteria for being in a vegetative state, there is little a priori reason to suppose that this is the only patient for whom this will be the case."[36] In other words, if brain imaging scans combined with imagination exercises revealed the misdiagnosis of this patient, we would be foolish to think there were no others.

And, indeed, while not as remarkable as the Owen "tennis imagining" patient, other recent studies using brain imaging have identified some patients who had shown no outward signs of responsiveness—and had therefore been diagnosed as being in a vegetative state on the basis of clinical observation—but who may have "islands" of cognitive function of some level, observable only through images of the brain. In several studies, certain speech-processing networks appeared to still be functional in some patients diagnosed as in a vegetative state. To conduct these studies, patients' brains were observed with respect to how they responded to their own name (a powerfully evocative stimulus), to intelligible versus unintelligible speech, and to ambiguous speech (where words such as "bark" or "creek/creak" are contained in sentences). Parallel studies with healthy subjects have revealed neural activity in certain parts of the brain when given such prompts; the vegetative patients were tested to determine if their brains showed the same sorts of patterns of activity. Some of them, it turned out, did.[37]

Researchers are quick to point out the caveats and limitations, though. For one, this evidence of brain activity in response to speech does not necessarily mean that the patients actually understand language (Owen's patient aside). What looked like a response in these patients' brains may have been on the order of mere reflex. As one researcher has written, "[P]rocessing is not consciousness."[38] Moreover, these positive results of brain activity took place in patients who had not been in a vegetative state for very long—not long enough to have been classified as *permanently* vegetative under the established criteria. In fact, it appears that the patients who did show signs of some speech processing networks began showing outward, behavioral signs of response (that a physician might observe) during the period *after* the brain imaging studies and *before* the time they would have been diagnosed as permanently vegetative in the absence of such signs.

In other words, brain imaging may be helpful in identifying patients who are transitioning from a vegetative state to a minimally conscious state but do not yet show outward signs of progress. In fact, this was also the case with Owen's tennis-imagining patient. The brain imaging scans were conducted five to six months after the patient's traumatic brain injury. Clinical guidelines preclude identifying the patient as "permanently vegetative" before twelve months following traumatic injury. By eleven months, the patient was exhibiting behavioral signs of consciousness—specifically, visual tracking—suggesting that at the time the brain scans were performed, the patient was transitioning from a vegetative state to a minimally conscious state.[39] As of this date, there do not appear to be *any* cases in the scientific literature in which brain imaging revealed the existence of consciousness—or even intact speech processing networks—in a person diagnosed as being in a permanent vegetative state according to existing clinical criteria, nor would such recovery be expected. Recent studies have, however, given us some hope that with quicker and more appropriate care—or with the application of newer therapeutic techniques—following brain injury, the chances of recovery, of some sort, for some patients, may be greater.

In addition to their promise in aiding future diagnosis of brain-injured patients, brain imaging studies highlight the uncertain boundaries between science and philosophy. If machines can pick up brain activity in response to certain stimuli (visual images, spoken words), does that—"brain activity" in and of itself—constitute consciousness or, if not consciousness as we have understood it, some other morally relevant experience? In the past—and particularly in discussions of law and ethics—we've expected more, some meaningful awareness of the self and the world and some ability to interact with the world, even if in a rudimentary way. And awareness and interaction are what appear to matter to families confronting questions about continuing or discontinuing life support—and to patients contemplating such issues beforehand. While advanced technology and further study promise to aid in determining what parts of a patient's brain continue to function and to what degree, it will not answer the fundamental questions of what kind and amount of functioning are important and how long to wait for its return, or the additional question of important *to whom*—the patient prior to injury, his family and caregivers, society at large? To be sure, we will be better able to *apply* our answers to these questions with the aid of scientific innovations that allow doctors to more accurately determine a patient's degree of function or probability of return of function, but these questions are not medical or scientific ones.

What brain imaging and other scientific advances may mean for the future is that law and ethics might rely less on medical or scientific categories and definitions ("permanent vegetative state," for example) and might instead delve deeper into questioning what are the basic qualities in life that matter, such as the ability to respond to the environment, to experience emotion, to interact with other living beings. In the past—and even now, as the brain imaging science is in its infancy—we've been able to use these medical and scientific concepts as convenient shorthand for what is important. We may not be able to for long.

Many living will forms and state statutes, for example, refer to the persistent or permanent vegetative state and were drafted before the "minimally conscious state" entered the medical lexicon in 2002. Where does that leave the minimally conscious patient today—with a living will that doesn't apply, or with one that should be broadly construed to include the patient's current condition? Where does it leave the surrogate decision-maker when the relevant state statutes recognize the surrogate's authority to withdraw life-sustaining treatment in the permanent vegetative state and terminal conditions only? This is a new frontier in end-of-life law—and it's far from certain where we will end up.

Treatment Decisions

Does the promise of better understanding of the vegetative state and other disorders of consciousness mean that we ought to pursue caution and patience for decades? No. If we refuse to make treatment decisions, including those with life-and-death consequences, based on what science may promise in a distant future, we will fail in our duties to the permanently vegetative patient while also holding the family hostage to distant hopes that rob them of life in the present. As with other medical decisions, many of which involve risks of life and death, we can accept that we are making the *best decision* that we can under the *current conditions*. This should be preferred to a requirement that we only make decisions that we *know* are the right decisions. How tempting it is to refuse to decide unless we can be certain we make right decisions, but refusing to decide is still a decision.

What we can expect and require are more early attempts at therapy, more accuracy and testing when making diagnoses, waiting more appropriate lengths of time (which may change as our knowledge of disorders of consciousness improves), and devoting more of our resources to make these things possible. The beauty of greater insight into disorders of consciousness is that treatment avenues and appreciation of care become paramount. We have exciting new promise that those in the early stages of a disorder of consciousness may recover and that those recoveries can be more successful than we had thought. For the minimally conscious, those who show some—any—signs of interaction with those around them or their environment, we ought to regard their conscious abilities with considerable humility: we know too little. And we have to make sure that politics—whether driven by predispositions to expand the classification of the minimally conscious and reduce the class of patients understood as permanently vegetative, or vice versa—doesn't influence the development of clinical guidelines or their application in particular cases.

Mixing Politics and Medicine

In the Schiavo case, as in other contested cases involving patients in a permanent vegetative state, moral opposition to the withdrawal of nutrition and hydration appears to have motivated a number of medical professionals to submit affidavits on behalf of the Schindlers asserting evidence of Terri's consciousness. The late Dr. Ronald Cranford, a medical pioneer in this field brought in for a second hearing in the Schiavo case, has pointed out that

> [n]one of these medical professionals (including internists, rehabilitationists, speech pathologists, and others) who submitted these multiple sets of affidavits over the years at the behest of the Schindlers had ever personally examined the patient, reviewed the medical records in any detail, considered the medical opinions of the consulting neurologists, nor looked at the CT [computed tomography] scans or EEG's [electroencephalograms]. They instead relied on the brief videotapes showing Terri apparently interacting with her parents and noting that Terri could handle her own secretions. A few of these medical professionals did go to the bedside with the Schindler family to make observations about Terri's apparent interactions with her family but none performed a complete neurological examination.[40]

This sort of ideologically motivated testimony is unfortunately not uncommon, although courts appear to be able to sort it out. Cranford explains:

> In almost every vegetative case before the courts, there almost always has been medical testimony attempting to refute the diagnosis of the vegetative state, with doctors and others arguing that the patients had some features outside of the vegetative state (e.g., Nancy Cruzan "eating bananas," and Joelle Rosebush covering her private parts with a gown when she was not only in a permanent

vegetative state but also quadriplegic). This kind of conflicting testimony first appeared in a major right to die dispute in the case of Paul Brophy, a Massachusetts fireman in a permanent vegetative state (1985), long before the minimally conscious state was established in the medical literature. These medical opinions have ranged from the plausibly persuasive to the absurd, but ultimately none of them has been successful in confusing the courts. Usually trial court judges have easily recognized the deficiencies of these highly questionable medical opinions and have had little difficulty in determining the correct neurological diagnosis.

Politics, ideologies, or other motivations can similarly skew medical findings in the other direction, as the botched case of Haleigh Poutre reveals. This Massachusetts case, which followed on the heels of Terri's death, involved an eleven-year-old girl who had been the subject of repeated battering and had entered what doctors believed to be a vegetative state. In fact, only *eight days* after she had entered the hospital in a condition of unconsciousness, her doctors declared her vegetative state to be permanent. The state of Massachusetts, through its Department of Social Services, won temporary custody of Haleigh and sought to remove her from all life support. Although not the explicit motive for the state's petition, if Haleigh died, her stepfather, accused of beating Haleigh, could have been charged with murder. The department's petition was successful in lower court and affirmed by the state supreme court. But the day after the court's decision, it became apparent that Haleigh was not permanently unconsciousness; in fact, she was not even unconscious at that moment! Two years later, she has recovered some speech and also communicates through a keyboard; ABC News reported that she might be well enough to testify against her stepfather.[41]

A rush to diagnosis, such as Haleigh's, raises concerns about the validity of doctors' expertise—and sometimes their motives. In order for family members, the patients' medical caregivers, and courts to determine what should be done regarding the continuation or discontinuation of life support for individuals with severe brain damage, there must be consistent care and attention—devoid of ideological, political, or financial concerns—placed on both the diagnosis and the prognosis of these patients. Then again, we must realize that the kind of mistakes made in the cases of Terry Wallis and Haleigh Poutre—mistakes that can be explained in large part by undue haste—were not made in Terri Schiavo's case.

Terri's diagnosis was not rushed; her condition was continually reevaluated; she was clinically examined by at least six reputable neurologists with substantial experience in this area; results of repeated CAT scans and EEGs were consistent with the diagnosis. Fins, in a 2007 article in the journal *Neurology* discussing the mistakes of the Wallis case, makes clear that the Schiavo case was very different: "The Schiavo case was contested against unimpeachable evidence that she could never recover. In that case, the science was clear: Recovery from vegetative state (VS) produced by anoxic brain injury categorically does not occur 15 years after injury. Such a VS is permanent and immutable with widespread neuronal loss and degeneration of the brain."[42]

The new science, unfortunately, had nothing to offer Terri Schiavo. While we must be aware of it as we consider the future of end-of-life decision-making law and ethics, it should not factor into evaluations of the Schiavo case.

LEGAL AND POLITICAL WRANGLING OVER TERRI'S LIFE

Before it was all over, Terri's parents and husband would accuse each other of outright lying, trying to make money from Terri's plight rather than looking out for her interests, and even bearing responsibility for Terri's condition. With respect to the latter, the Schindlers, some years after Terri's cardiac arrest, accused Michael Schiavo of having physically abused her during their marriage, possibly even strangling her on the night she collapsed. There is no evidence of this. Three separate inquiries by the state attorney's office, two of them at Governor Jeb Bush's request, found a "complete absence of evidence that Terri's collapse was caused by anyone's criminal actions"; the final report of the prosecutors suggested the inquiry was motivated by disagreement with the court's decision to allow Terri's feeding tube to be removed rather than by any "objective consideration of the evidence."[1] Michael Schiavo, for his part, came back with an accusation of his own: Bob Schindler, through his teasing and belittling of Terri as an overweight teenager, was to blame for her excessive dieting and eating habits and ultimately for her cardiac arrest and resulting vegetative state.[2]

It may be surprising, then, that before Terri's cardiac arrest, Michael Schiavo had gotten along very well with his in-laws, including Terri's younger brother and sister. Michael and Terri had moved from the Philadelphia suburbs to St. Petersburg, Florida, in anticipation of the Schindlers' move and lived for a while in the Schindlers' condominium. Bob, who had worked in industrial sales and owned a heavy equipment business, and Mary, a homemaker, would later join them in Florida.[3]

In the months following Terri's collapse, Michael Schiavo and Terri's parents, especially Mary Schindler, were active partners in her care. The Schindlers had no objection to Michael's guardianship over all Terri's affairs, including her health care decisions. In fact, Michael moved in with them again, and in September 1990, about six months after Terri's collapse, they brought her home to be cared for. After three weeks, however, she was returned to a skilled care facility because her family found it difficult to meet all her needs. According to an independent guardian ad litem later appointed by the court to represent Terri's interests, in these early years of Terri's vegetative condition, "[t]here is no question but that complete trust, mutual caring, explicit love and a common goal of caring for and rehabilitating Theresa, were the shared intentions of Michael Schiavo and the Schindlers."[4]

Terri received aggressive rehabilitative therapy and even an experimental stimulator implant in her brain, for which Michael took Terri to California for several months in late 1990. Yet despite all efforts, periodic medical examinations revealed no improvement.

Insertion of the Feeding Tube

The device whose removal years later would provoke such divisive debate was inserted during the early days of Terri's treatment with little fanfare. Those retelling Terri's story—her husband, her parents, her guardian ad litem, and others—say very little about the initial decision to provide Terri with artificial nutrition and hydration. Her feeding tube appears to have been inserted as a matter of course as her state of unconsciousness dragged on.

This lack of detail or drama surrounding the insertion of the feeding tube is understandable. First, the fact that a feeding tube is physically inserted does not mean that the tube must remain in place until the patient either resumes eating by mouth or dies. While at one time there was some debate over whether an ethical or legal distinction could be made between withholding and withdrawing life-sustaining treatment, this issue has been settled and was not challenged by those opposing the removal of Terri Schiavo's feeding tube. The clear consensus in the medical and legal fields is that there is no reason to treat these acts differently and actually good reason to treat them the same—if it were more difficult to withdraw treatment than to withhold it, families and physicians may hesitate to try a treatment for fear that they would not be able to discontinue it if the patient did not improve. With respect to Terri Schiavo, then, the decision to insert a feeding tube would not have seemed momentous and irreversible at the time.

Moreover, Terri's situation was one in which a feeding tube was eminently appropriate. The PEG (percutaneous endoscopic gastrostomy) tube is a simple, inexpensive feeding and hydration device inserted by only minimally invasive surgery that could supply Terri with needed sustenance until she could recover and eat on her own—still in these early days a possible outcome that everyone hoped for. The PEG tube was invented for just such short-term use. It was first developed in 1979 to provide nutrition and hydration to an infant with a swallowing impediment that would in fairly short order be corrected.

In recent years, use of the PEG tube has expanded from its original application in emergency situations involving younger patients and is increasingly seen used in elderly residents of nursing homes and individuals with advanced dementia. As discussed more fully in chapter 8, many studies have found that this has led to an overuse of feeding tubes, often with no benefit—and with real harm—to the patient. Financial incentives in the form of higher insurance reimbursements for residents with feeding tubes and quicker feeding times (because a nursing assistant can more quickly hook up a tube than hand-feed a resident) may be fueling this practice, along with sometimes overzealous nursing home supervision by state regulators.

While the Schiavo case may have repercussions for the future use and misuse of feeding tubes in these populations, Terri's situation was very different. The feeding tube would and did extend her life—without it, her health would have suffered and she may have died within weeks of her collapse because she could not be effectively hand-fed in her unconscious state. Because her prognosis was uncertain in these early weeks, a failure to insert the feeding tube would have been inappropriate.

Medical Malpractice Lawsuit

As Terri's condition continued, without change, her physicians became more convinced that it was permanent. Michael Schiavo, by most accounts, had not yet accepted this fact when in 1992 he initiated a lawsuit against the physicians caring for Terri before her collapse. This included Terri's primary care physician (who settled out of court for $250,000) and the OB-GYN who had been treating her for infertility. Michael alleged that Terri's doctors should have inquired into her dietary habits when she reported to them that she was missing her menstrual period—a common result of excessive weight loss. Terri had been heavy as a teenager, weighing at one time as much as 250 pounds. She had lost as much as 100 pounds before she met Michael and continued to lose weight after their marriage. In 1990, she weighed approximately 110 pounds.[5]

Terri may have been bulimic—an eating disorder characterized by binging on large quantities of food and then vomiting—and in the lawsuit, Michael alleged that Terri's cardiac arrest was caused by a potassium imbalance linked to her bulimia and other dietary habits, mainly drinking large quantities of iced tea, which has a diuretic quality.

Professor Jay Wolfson's report to the court describes this theory of Terri's collapse:

> Sodium and potassium maintain a vital, chemical balance in the human body that helps define the electrolyte levels. The cause of the imbalance was not clearly identified, but may be linked, in theory, to her drinking 10–15 glasses of iced tea each day. While no formal proof emerged, the medical records note that the combination of aggressive weight loss, diet control and excessive hydration raised questions about Theresa suffering from Bulimia, an eating disorder, more common among women than men, in

which purging through vomiting, laxatives and other methods of diet control becomes obsessive.[6]

The autopsy performed after Terri's death could not confirm bulimia as the cause of her cardiac arrest, which still remains somewhat of a mystery. A jury, however, found that Terri's OB-GYN was negligent in failing to diagnose her condition. The case resulted in an award of $300,000 for Michael Schiavo for his loss of Terri's companionship and $750,000 for her care and guardianship costs. The jury's award would have been much larger had it not found Terri to be largely responsible for her condition.

The money awarded for Terri's continued care was placed in a trust. An independent trustee was responsible for the funds, over which Michael Schiavo had no control. He would, however, stand to inherit the money if Terri died. By the time her situation garnered national media attention (between 2003 and 2005), there was very little left of this money. Michael's potential inheritance could not have credibly influenced any decisions he made at that time about whether the feeding tube should stay in place or be removed, and, in fact, years earlier when Michael sought original court approval for removal of the feeding tube, he formally offered to donate to charity any remaining amount of Terri's award if the Schindlers would withdraw their objection to the termination of artificial nutrition and hydration.[7]

Falling Out

It was around the time of the resolution of the medical malpractice lawsuit that Michael Schiavo and Mary and Robert Schindler fell out of friendship. The cause of this falling out is a matter of great disagreement. In 2000, Judge George Greer would write the following about the cause of the falling out that took place in 1993: "While the testimony differs on what may or may not have been promised to whom and by whom, it is clear to this court that such severance [of the friendship] was predicated upon money and the fact that Mr. Schiavo was unwilling to equally divide his loss of consortium award with Mr. and Mrs. Schindler. The parties have literally not spoken since that date."[8]

What caused such bitter animosity is not really relevant to the legal and ethical questions explored in this book. At the same time, the feud between Michael Schiavo and the Schindlers became a very public matter and influenced people's views about who was really looking out for Terri's interests and who was motivated by their own interests. Michael Schiavo claimed that Bob Schindler, Terri's father, a businessman experiencing financial troubles at the time, demanded a portion of the money right after the trial for the Schindlers' own benefit. The Schindlers claimed that Michael had promised to use the money for rehabilitation for Terri but then later refused to do so. Neither of these versions has, to my mind, ever carried a strong ring of truth. With Michael's version, we have to ask why Mr. Schindler, on good terms with Michael up to this point, would all of a sudden think he was being cheated when Michael wouldn't share his malpractice award. And in assessing the Schindlers' version, we have to acknowledge that Terri had not lacked rehabilitation for want of money—her medical expenses were covered by insurance, and her own trust account from the lawsuit could have been used for rehabilitation services. Moreover, according to independent investigation, Terri did receive "regular and aggressive physical, occupational and speech therapy" through 1994.[9]

According to Michael Schiavo's book, he and the Schindlers at one time talked about building a large house in which they would all live, with special facilities where Terri could be taken care of by a nursing staff. In September 1990, the Schindlers and Michael brought Terri home but found caring for her overwhelming and beyond their abilities. If building a house had indeed been discussed at one time as a potential outcome of a successful malpractice suit, then we can more easily understand an angry response from Mr. Schindler when it became clear that Michael was not going to pay for it. The Schindlers had been in financial difficulties for a number of years and were, at the time of the malpractice award, living in a small condo. This version also jibes with the Schindlers' version that Michael was refusing to use the award for Terri's rehabilitation, understood broadly.

No matter what the true story was behind their dispute, in the years that would follow, the Schindlers repeatedly charged that Michael Schiavo was motivated by money to end Terri's life. The trial court found no basis for these charges and would not remove Michael as Terri's guardian although repeatedly requested to do so on the grounds of conflict of interest. In fact, in its original order, the trial court explained that both Michael Schiavo and the Schindlers could be understood as having a conflict of interest regarding the decisions made for Terri. If the Schindlers were able, through legal maneuvering, to keep Terri alive long enough so that Michael Schiavo would seek a divorce, then they, rather than Michael, would stand to inherit from Terri's estate. The Schindlers also sought Michael's removal as guardian on the basis that he was not properly caring for her and, in later years, on the grounds that he was living with another woman, Jodi Centonze, whom he called his "fiancée" and with whom he had had two children. (After Terri's death, Michael married Jodi.)

The courts repeatedly concluded that Michael Schiavo had been appropriately attentive to Terri's care. Guardian ad litem Jay Wolfson in his 2003 report says, "[Michael's] demanding concern for [Terri's] well being and meticulous care by the nursing home earned him the characterization by the administrator as 'a nursing home administrator's nightmare.' It is notable that through more than thirteen years after Theresa's collapse, she has never had a bedsore."[10]

Removing the Feeding Tube

In 1998, eight years after Terri's cardiac arrest, Michael Schiavo asked the court to remove her feeding tube. Because Terri had not designated anyone to make health care decisions for her in the event of incapacity, this job fell by law to Michael Schiavo. (The Florida surrogacy rules will be discussed in more detail in chapter 6.) Under Florida law, a surrogate can authorize the removal of a patient's life support if the patient is in a permanent vegetative state and removal is what the patient would want. While Michael Schiavo had by this time concluded that Terri would not want to continue living in her current condition, he knew her parents disagreed. Even though court approval is not necessary under Florida law to remove life support, Michael Schiavo petitioned the local court for its approval. Had Michael not asked for a court to review the issue, the Schindlers could have. They still believed that treatment was possible, that even without consciousness Terri's life should be preserved, and that Michael was failing to act responsibly as her guardian by seeking removal of the feeding tube.

The case was assigned to circuit judge George Greer, who had served as judge in the probate division since elected in 1992. Before that, Judge Greer was a zoning and land use attorney and county commissioner. A Republican and Southern Baptist, he was not the sort of figure one would expect to draw ire from pro-life and religious right groups, though he would do that and more—including calls for impeachment and even death threats—as he saw the case through seven years of permutations.

Although Michael Schiavo's petition was filed in May 1998, it was not until January 2000 that a hearing was held to determine whether the feeding tube might be removed. During this time, a guardian ad litem was appointed (the second of three ultimately assigned to the case) to represent Terri's interests. Richard L. Pearse Jr.'s report was not filed until December 1998 and then was challenged by Michael Schiavo's attorney as reflecting the guardian ad litem's personal bias against removing feeding tubes in these kinds of situations. Pearse's report concluded that Michael Schiavo's testimony alone would not be sufficient to meet Florida's evidentiary requirements regarding Terri's wishes, in large part because of his apparent conflict of interest as the potential heir to Terri's estate (consisting at this time of at least $700,000 from the malpractice case). His report did advise the court that should it find that there *was* sufficient evidence that Terri would have wanted the feeding tube removed, then it should be withdrawn.[11] Judge Greer rejected the suggestion that Pearse was biased, as nearly everyone who might serve in this role would have some feelings about the issue. He noted instead that Pearse's recommendation was, in his own words, a "close call" and that Pearse did not have the same evidence available to him that the court did as a result of the hearing.[12]

On the basis of this evidence, Judge Greer determined that Terri Schiavo was "beyond all doubt . . . in a persistent vegetative state" and that the medical evidence "conclusively establishes that she has no hope of ever regaining consciousness."[13] A CAT scan revealed that "to a large extent her brain ha[d] been replaced by spinal fluid."[14] Terri's abnormal EEG was also consistent with the diagnosis of persistent vegetative state, although it is a less specific test. An expert witness in the case, Dr. James Barnhill, testified that the probability that Terri could become conscious again was "zero." At the hearing, the Schindlers did not formally dispute that Terri was in a persistent vegetative state nor offer a medical expert's testimony about her condition. They nevertheless repeatedly attempted to introduce evidence (some of which was admitted) about what various individuals, like Mary Schindler, observed as purposeful behavior on the part of Terri.

In addition to determining that Terri was in a permanent vegetative state, Judge Greer also found that there was clear and convincing evidence that removal of the feeding tube was the decision Terri Schiavo herself would make if she were competent. He based his decision on statements reportedly made by Terri to Michael Schiavo, his brother Scott Schiavo, and his sister-in-law Joan Schiavo (his brother Bill's wife). Terri had told them of situations in which she would not want to continue living during discussions they'd had in connection with the death of Michael Schiavo's grandmother, the dependency of Terri's uncle on her grandmother, and television movies and reports about people on life support.

The Schindlers' Reaction

Over the next year, the Schindlers appealed this decision without success. In April 2001, Terri's feeding tube was clamped.

The Schindlers now took a different tack; Michael, they argued, had given false testimony. They filed a new legal action, in a different division of the circuit courts, based on their discovery of a new witness. They claimed that a former girlfriend of Michael's (it was now eleven years after Terri had entered a permanent vegetative state) reported that Michael had told her that he and Terri had never discussed what Terri's wishes would be in her present condition. Later, the appellate division of the courts would note that the complaint did not include an affidavit signed by the former girlfriend. It only included affidavits from Bob Schindler and a private investigator, which, strangely, were "acknowledged" before a notary, rather than "sworn to," as is the normal procedure. In addition, the complaint itself bore unusual characteristics. It appeared to have been prepared by a lawyer, but no lawyer had signed it; it was signed only by Mr. and Mrs. Schindler. The appellate court noted, "Oddly, in the acknowledgment, the notary affirmatively states that the Schindlers did not swear to the facts of the complaint under oath."[15]

The Schindlers' complaint urged that Terri's life was in imminent danger. Judge Frank Quesada, the judge to whom this new lawsuit was assigned, received the legal pleadings in the afternoon and convened an emergency hearing for that evening. Following the hearing, he granted the request for an injunction so that further facts in the case could be developed.

Although unorthodox, and even suspect, the Schindlers' strategy paid off. Through a series of motions and two additional reviews at the appellate level, this request by the Schindlers meant that the feeding tube was reinserted until Judge Greer could hold a new hearing. The appellate court did not allow a rehearing on the issue of the credibility of the witnesses in the original hearing, which is what the Schindlers had sought, but the Schindlers did manage to raise doubts about Terri's prognosis through the affidavits of several licensed physicians. The new hearing would explore again evidence of her condition.

Dr. Fred Webber was particularly instrumental in persuading the appellate court to give the case a new hearing. He claimed that Terri had "a good opportunity to show some degree of improvement" if treated with a "cardiovascular medication style of therapy."[16] The sort of "improvement" alluded to in his affidavit was "speech recovery, enhanced speech clarity and complexity, release of contractures, and better awareness of the patient's surroundings." Although the appellate court expressed skepticism, it determined that Florida's default position in favor of life meant that a sufficient question had been raised as to whether the order to withdraw nutrition and hydration should stand.

At the hearing, the Schindlers would have to show that new medical treatment offered significant promise of improving Terri's condition in order for the feeding tube to remain in place. Five doctors gave expert testimony—two chosen by Michael Schiavo, two by the Schindlers, and one by the court. Curiously, Webber did not appear as one of the doctors chosen by the Schindlers. Judge Greer also viewed four and a half hours of videotape footage of Terri Schiavo, select portions of which would later repeatedly air on national television. Following the hearing, Judge Greer ruled that "the credible evidence overwhelmingly supports the view that Terry Schiavo remains in a persistent vegetative state."[17] In addition, no testimony was offered that revealed treatment options that would significantly improve Terri's quality of life. The court entered a new order to withdraw Terri's feeding tube. This ruling was affirmed by the appellate court, which stated, "It is likely that no guardianship court has ever received as much high-quality medical evidence in such a proceeding."[18]

When the Schindlers appealed to the Florida Supreme Court, the court declined to review the decision.

Terri's Law

Because the second hearing on Terri's condition revealed no reasonable possibility for improvement, Terri's feeding tube was removed a second time on October 15, 2003. The Schindlers and their many supporters among right-to-life and disability rights groups asked the Florida governor and legislature to intervene. Besieged by over 100,000 e-mails, as well as letters and telephone calls, the Florida legislature rushed through special legislation specifically to cover Terri's case. The legislation allowed Governor Bush to issue a "stay" of the court's order to withdraw the feeding tube and permitted the governor to order the tube's reinsertion. Specifically, the law allowed the governor to prevent the withholding of nutrition and hydration from a patient if, as of October 15, 2003,

(a) that patient has no written advance directive;
(b) the court has found that patient to be in a persistent vegetative state;
(c) that patient has had nutrition and hydration withheld; and
(d) a member of that patient's family has challenged the withholding of nutrition and hydration.

This narrow description covered Terri's case and only Terri's case, and the legislation aptly became known as Terri's Law.[19]

In effect, this meant that Governor Bush was named Terri's surrogate but without the restrictions contained in the already established laws and regulations that govern surrogates—the most important of which is that surrogates' decisions must be ones patients would make for themselves if they could.

Terri was transported by ambulance to a nearby hospital to have her feeding tube reinserted on October 21, 2003. According to the *St. Petersburg Times*, Governor Bush had some difficulty at first in finding a doctor who was willing to comply with his order. In fact, Terri's longtime physician, Dr. Victor Gambone, resigned rather than reinsert the feeding tube.[20]

The actions of the Florida legislature and governor had no precedent. The closest parallel was a Virginia dispute in the late 1990s over the fate of Hugh Finn, a former television newscaster whose feeding tube was removed at the request of his wife several years after a car accident had left him in a permanent vegetative state. Twenty members of Virginia's legislature adopted an "informal declaration" (of no specific legal consequence) relating to Finn's case, asserting that "food and water" should never be withdrawn from patients when doing so would cause their death. The governor of Virginia also stepped in, filing a lawsuit to prevent the removal of Finn's feeding tube, but it was unsuccessful. As compared to the intervention of the Florida governor and legislature in the Schiavo case, state involvement in Hugh Finn's case was brief, ineffective, and relatively mild.

In the one-day debate over Terri's Law, Florida legislators appeared largely out of their depth, both in their knowledge of existing Florida law and constitutional precedent and in their understanding of the medical and other facts surrounding the case. There were, for example, numerous comments by legislators supportive of Terri's Law that the videos shown of Terri clearly revealed that she was not in some sort of "coma." Debate on the floor was intense, including both political grandstanding and emotional, sometimes even tearful, goodwill. The New York Times reported that "[m]any lawmakers drew on their own religious beliefs and experiences with death, sometimes choking up as they described the drawn-out illness of a parent or spouse."[21]

The legislation was peculiar in the narrowness of its scope—applying only to Terri Schiavo. But Florida senate president Jim King had balked at the idea of adopting broader legislation. King was the original sponsor of Florida's statutory framework on end-of-life issues. While ceding to mounting pressure to respond to the Schiavo situation, he did not want whatever passed to be a complete undoing of the law he had earlier guided through the legislature. According to news reports, King hit upon the idea of a "stay" as he huddled with advisers and staff. He apparently asked those around him, "Because a governor can grant a stay of execution in a death penalty case, might he also be given such authority in the Schiavo case?" According to his communications director, when King asked this question, "Everybody kind of looked at each other. Was this something we could do?" King called the governor, and the bill began to take shape. It was passed the next day. The analogy of the governor's intervention to a "stay of execution" would be picked up by Schindler supporters to argue that Terri should at least be given the procedural protections and mercy that are given to death row inmates.[22]

Later, King said he regretted his vote in favor of Terri's Law and that it was one of the worst he had ever cast. At the time, though, he was visibly moved by the case and explained that he had to act to save Terri in the face of doubts about the process. He urged everyone to fill out a living will to avoid a situation like Terri's and even handed out living will forms to fellow legislators on the floor of the senate.

Michael Schiavo immediately challenged Terri's Law. His attorneys, now aided by the American Civil Liberties Union, argued that the special legislation violated the separation of powers of the Florida Constitution and Terri's individual privacy rights. In contrast to the previous Schiavo litigation, this was not between Michael Schiavo and the Schindlers but between Michael Schiavo and the governor. The case was first heard in the spring of 2004 by Judge Douglas Baird of the Circuit Court of Pinellas County and then went directly to the Florida Supreme Court in the fall of 2004. It was allowed to bypass the intermediate appeals court because it involved a question "of great public importance . . . requiring immediate resolution."[23]

The Florida Supreme Court struck down Terri's Law on two grounds. First, the law usurped the power of the judiciary by nullifying a decision duly made by a court. The law, in effect, selected one particular dispute that the courts had decided and threw out the courts' judgment. Second, Terri's Law was an unconstitutional delegation of legislative authority. It in effect gave the governor the power to decide what the law should be in Terri's case, because it allowed him to order the reinsertion—or, in fact, the subsequent removal—of the feeding tube but provided no standards for that order. He could do whatever he liked. The Florida Supreme Court admonished, "[T]he Act does not even require that the Governor consider the patient's wishes in deciding whether to issue a stay, and instead allows a unilateral decision by the Governor to stay the withholding of life-prolonging procedures without affording any procedural process to the patient."[24]

The circuit court considering Terri's Law had further found the law to be unconstitutional because it invaded Terri Schiavo's privacy interests protected by the Florida Constitution. Unlike the U.S. Constitution, Florida's constitution contains an explicit right to privacy, adopted by the citizens of Florida in 1980: "Every natural person has the right to be let alone and free from governmental intrusion into the person's private life."[25] The opinion of Judge Baird explained how Terri's Law violated this right to privacy:

> By substituting the personal judgment of the Governor for that of the "patient," the Act deprives every individual who is subject to its terms of his or her constitutionally guaranteed right to privacy of his or her own medical decisions. . . . [E]ven in those instances where the desires of the "patient" correspond with the Governor, the Act is still unconstitutional because the Governor is not required to consider, much less act in accord with, those desires. It is the unrestricted power to act, regardless of the individual's right of privacy, which creates this fatal constitutional infirmity on the face of the Act.[26]

Requests for Swallowing Tests

During the challenges to Terri's Law, a number of other developments occurred outside the courtroom. One provision of Terri's Law required the court to appoint a guardian ad litem who would conduct an independent investigation into the case and then report to Governor Bush and the court. The person appointed for this task was Jay Wolfson, some of whose conclusions have already been noted. Overall, his report determined that the courts had acted appropriately and on the basis of sufficient evidence in discerning both Terri's condition and her wishes. His report further revealed that he tried to mediate a resolution between the Schindlers and Michael Schiavo. Under the proposed resolution, Terri would be given swallowing tests and therapy, even though previous attempts at this had failed. While the agreement broke down in the end, his report nevertheless recommended this solution to the governor.

Later, in early 2005, when Terri's Law was struck down, the Schindlers filed their own petition urging that Terri be given swallowing tests and therapy. In so arguing, they invoked a Florida law providing that it is a felony to withhold food from a disabled or vulnerable adult.[27] The Schindlers had also requested similar tests at earlier times, in both 2000 and 2003. Judge Greer denied these earlier requests as well as the one made in 2005, noting that extensive swallowing tests had already been conducted several times, in addition to annual evaluations of Terri's swallowing ability, and that the requests for tests were instead attempts by the Schindlers to relitigate the entire case. (Further discussion about whether Terri could swallow food on her own and, if she could, what that would mean as a matter of law and ethics can be found in chapter 8.)

The Pope Speaks

During the spring of 2004, in the midst of widespread publicity about Terri Schiavo's case, Pope John Paul II addressed the International Congress on Life-Sustaining Treatments and Vegetative State. He declared that artificial nutrition and hydration were not like other medical treatments but constituted "minimal care," "normal care," and "basic health care" (akin to providing cleanliness and warmth). He said that for patients in a permanent vegetative state, the provision of artificial nutrition and hydration is "morally obligatory" and its withdrawal "euthanasia by omission."[28] While not considered official church doctrine, this statement of the pope drew much attention. At the time, the church's policy and the practice of Catholic hospitals in the United States had been to allow family members more discretion to withdraw artificial nutrition and hydration for patients in a permanent vegetative state. This was permitted under the quite liberal policy that artificial nutrition and hydration could be withdrawn from incompetent patients when continued treatment is burdensome to the patient or the patient's family. The pope's statement called that policy into question.

The Schindlers used the pope's statement to request that Judge Greer review his decision about what Terri would have wished. They argued that even if Terri's wishes in 2000, during the original hearing before Judge Greer, were to have the feeding tube removed, those wishes would have changed to follow the pope's directive that patients in a permanent vegetative state should always be fed. Judge Greer denied the request in October 2004, explaining that there was no new evidence about Terri's own religious convictions (for which there was no compelling evidence in the 2000 hearing), nor was there any person who had been a religious adviser to Terri who might shed light on how she would have reacted to the papal announcement. He concluded, "Nothing has changed."[29]

Back to the Legislature

After the Florida Supreme Court struck down Terri's Law in September 2004, the pressure was back on the Florida legislature. A special law directed only at Terri's situation would obviously not work. Sympathetic lawmakers instead focused on developing stricter rules for withdrawing nutrition and hydration more generally. A bill was introduced into the Florida legislature that was drafted with the aid of the National Right to Life Committee, the pro-life and antiabortion advocacy organization. In fact, the bill was introduced in two sessions of the Florida legislature, first in the spring of 2004 when the Florida Supreme Court was still reviewing Terri's Law (when the pressure to "save" Terri was less pronounced) and then again after Terri's Law was declared unconstitutional.

The title of the proposed law was the "Starvation and Dehydration of Persons with Disabilities Prevention Act." It essentially provided (with very narrowly crafted exceptions) that artificial nutrition and hydration would be required for any patient for whom it might provide some benefit unless the patient had previously signed a living will indicating specifically that artificial nutrition and hydration was refused in these circumstances. This bill would have applied retroactively to Terri Schiavo. After amendments, a milder version of the bill passed in the Florida House. Meanwhile, the senate was considering a somewhat different bill that would have prevented the removal of a feeding tube from any person in a permanent vegetative state in the event of disagreement among those who could serve under state law as the patient's surrogate. This bill failed, twenty-one to eighteen, on March 17, 2005, with nine Republican senators siding with twelve Democrats to defeat the measure. As debate on the bill took place, fliers appeared in the Capitol building with pictures of these senators under the heading "Wanted: The Republican 9." The fliers were quickly removed, but security was upgraded as the lobbying and protests intensified. None of the nine moved; the Florida legislature was done.

A National Spectacle

Terri Schiavo's feeding tube was removed for the third time on March 18, 2005. What amounted to a national death watch began to play continually on televised media. The number of protesters outside the hospice where Terri lay grew to the hundreds. Some, including children, were arrested for attempting to bring water to Terri. The Reverend Jesse Jackson would show up a week later to join them in prayer. During this time, Judge Greer was under bodyguard protection, and security was heightened for Michael Schiavo and his family, all whom had received death threats. A North Carolina man was arrested by FBI agents for soliciting the murders of Michael Schiavo (for which he allegedly offered to pay $250,000) and Judge Greer ($50,000). In addition to death threats, Michael Schiavo reportedly received offers of money (of $700,000, $1,000,000, even $10,000,000) to remove himself from the guardianship role in Terri's case, which he turned down. The Schindlers continued to file every conceivable motion, in state and federal courts, to delay or reverse Judge Greer's decision. In a particularly memorable moment, Barbara Weller, one of the attorneys for the Schindlers, came before the television cameras claiming that Terri had said, "Aaaaah . . . ," and then, "waaaa . . . ," in answer to Weller's plea to Terri to say she wanted to live in order to save her own life. Judge Greer dismissed this assertion and others, saying they were attempts to relitigate the case without any real new evidence.

Terri's case now became the subject of hurried and unprecedented involvement by the U.S. legislature, the president, and the federal courts. First, on the date of the feeding tube's removal, congressional subpoenas were issued for Terri Schiavo, her husband, and others involved in the case to appear before the House Committee on Government Reform, which, according to the subpoenas, was conducting "an inquiry into the long term care of incapacitated adults." The idea behind issuing these subpoenas for Terri (and for Michael, who was ordered to bring "all medical and other equipment that provides nutrition and hydration to Theresa Schiavo—in its current and continuing state of operations") was that failing to provide her with artificial nutrition and hydration would constitute a criminal obstruction of justice and contempt of Congress.[30] Judge Greer, however, decided that the subpoenas would not affect the order requiring the removal of the feeding tube and was backed up by the Florida Supreme Court. Legal experts at the time pointed out that Congress had never tried to use its subpoena powers in this way, to override a completely adjudicated legal proceeding. The closest example was a threat in 2000 by several lawmakers to subpoena the Cuban child Elián González during a politically charged custody and immigration dispute. While the subpoenas would have prevented Gonzalez's father from returning the boy to Cuba, they were never delivered.[31]

When the subpoenas failed to work, the U.S. legislature, on March 21, 2005, passed a bill to allow the Schindlers to seek federal review of their case.[32] The bill was called "An Act for the Relief of the Parents of Theresa Marie Schiavo." While many legislators had already left D.C. for the Easter break, a substantial number returned to cast their vote on what would be called the "Palm Sunday Compromise." President Bush cut short a vacation in Crawford, Texas, to return to D.C. so that he could sign the bill immediately after it passed—which, because of rules of Congress, could not occur until a little after midnight on Sunday.

The act required the federal court to review the case *de novo*, meaning that the federal court should ignore the factual findings of the state courts and determine itself what the relevant facts were about Terri's condition and her wishes. But in order for this legislation to "save" Terri, whose feeding tube had already been removed, the federal court would have to decide that the Schindlers were entitled to a temporary restraining order directing Michael Schiavo and the hospice where Terri resided to transport Terri to a hospital for reinsertion of her feeding tube. A temporary restraining order can be issued by a court prior to a full hearing on an issue only when waiting for the full hearing will mean irreparable harm. Apparently, members of Congress voting for the law assumed, or at least hoped, that the court would grant a temporary restraining order and thus order the reinsertion of Terri's feeding tube prior to a full review of the case.

The federal court declined to do that. It decided not to issue a temporary restraining order because the parents of Terri Schiavo could not meet their burden of showing a substantial likelihood of success on the merits of their claim. Because they were now in federal court, the Schindlers had to claim that Terri's constitutional or federal rights were being violated. To do this, they argued that she was being deprived of life without the "due process of law" required by the Fourteenth Amendment to the U.S. Constitution.[33] In deciding not to issue a temporary restraining order, the federal court did not allow a relitigation of the case. Though the court had been directed to review the case *de novo*, it could not ignore the seven-year history of the case in state court; that history and the amount of "due process" that it represented was in fact the issue raised by the Schindlers' claim. The U.S. Court of Appeals affirmed the lower federal court's decision, writing, "[W]e are called upon to make a collective, objective decision concerning a question of law. In the end, and no matter how much we wish Mrs. Schiavo had never suffered such a horrible accident, we are a nation of laws, and if we are to continue to be so, the pre-existing and well-established federal law governing injunctions . . . must be applied to her case."[34] The U.S. Supreme Court—as it did several times throughout the Schiavo legal battle—declined to get involved.

Near the End

On March 24, Governor Bush made one last-ditch effort to restore Terri's feeding tube. Through the powers of the Florida Department of Children and Families (DCF) and the Florida Department of Law Enforcement, he ordered investigations into wrongdoing on behalf of Michael Schiavo. Officials at DCF had sought intervention in the case before this time—on the grounds that there were allegations of abuse and neglect that warranted investigating—but they had been unable to convince Judge Greer that their request to intervene was anything but a disagreement with the decision to remove the feeding tube. Judge Greer, in fact, entered an order forbidding DCF from "taking possession" of Terri. A legal technicality, however, left open a window of time in which that order was not effective (the order was automatically stayed upon the filing of an appeal), and during this time, DCF apparently intended to take Terri from the hospice with the aid of the Florida state police. When made aware of the effect of the automatic stay, Judge Greer canceled it, but not before a squad of state police and DCF officials were en route to the hospice where Terri was cared for, with apparent intention to remove her to a hospital for reinsertion of the feeding tube. Before they arrived, local police told the state agents that they would not allow Terri to be removed without a court order, and state agents then backed down. The *Miami Herald* quoted one official's description of the day's events: "There were two sets of law enforcement officers facing off, waiting for the other to blink." State officials later denied any suggestion that a "showdown" had occurred.[35]

Terri Schiavo died on March 31, 2005. The U.S. public obtained hourly updates by radio, the Internet, and television. The credentials of the "experts" chosen to fill these hours varied widely. As an example of the depths to which such reporting would sink, one cable news channel offered as an expert commentator a young lawyer in New York City who appeared to have no experience in the area, her only relevant credentials being a law degree and her opinion that the "starvation" of Terri Schiavo was outrageous. Cable news show hosts continually made references to starvation, dying of thirst, and what Terri must be feeling.

The last few days of Terri's life were as bitterly contentious as the previous years' fight over the decision to discontinue life support. Michael Schiavo and the Schindler family fought over who would spend time with Terri, the performance of religious last rites, whether she would be cremated or buried, and where her remains would be placed.

A few months after Terri's death, Governor Bush ordered an investigation into the events surrounding her collapse. The cause of her cardiac arrest has never been determined with any certainty, although an autopsy ruled out trauma. The investigation sought by the governor this time focused on whether there had been any delay between the time Michael Schiavo said he discovered Terri's unconscious body and when he called 911. The investigation concluded that there was no evidence of delay and "strongly recommend[ed] that the inquiry be closed and no further action be taken."[36] This was the end of the legal wrangling that had toured every level of the courts, prompted the uncommon intervention of a governor, a president, and state and federal legislatures, and absorbed a nation. The feelings on both sides were expressed with life-and-death urgency. And the facts—of her condition, of the laws that applied, and of what she might have wanted—were drowned in nearly constant misinformation and often given less consideration than mere opinion.

3

IN CONTEXT—
LAW AND ETHICS

Outside of the specially passed laws and particular facts of Terri Schiavo's case, Americans have our history, the foundations of our government, our ethical and moral foundations, and our laws. Indeed, one of the most disturbing aspects of the drama was how readily some of our political leaders wanted to make this case "special," not subject to established rules, not to be guided by orderly judicial process or the benefit of the wisdom from past cases and carefully considered ethical frameworks. This happened partly because thirty-second media images allowed an oversimplification of what the issues really were, as when the leader of the U.S. Senate, himself a doctor, felt capable of making a diagnosis based on a televised videotape of Terri. And it happened partly because when we talk about things like rights, responsibilities, and care, we tend to use the terms loosely, and we don't tend to respect how much and how complexly our rights and responsibilities are bound up in each other's.

In this chapter, I will look at three fundamental legal and ethical questions involved in making decisions about Terri's life and death. The first is: *What were her rights?* Did she have a right to die, or a right to life? Did she have a right to refuse treatment, or to be fed? Are some of these rights more "fundamental" or more established than others? It is important in understanding what was done in her case and what will guide future cases to carefully identify what rights we recognize in this context. Second, I will introduce the problem of *how Terri could exercise these rights when she had no voice.* What rules do we follow and how do we respect patients' rights—especially rights involving *choices*—when someone else has to speak for them and the stakes are high, matters of life and death? Finally, I will consider *what responsibilities grow from our rights and our guardianship of the rights of others.*

Terri's Rights

The right most central to Terri's case is the right to refuse treatment, even when doing so will cause death. Sometimes, especially in early cases of this sort, this right has been referred to as a "right to die." In recent years, the term "right to die" has come to be more heavily associated with the right to hasten one's death with the assistance of a physician—a right that the Supreme Court has explicitly rejected.[1] Instead, what the majority of state courts have recognized, and the Supreme Court has also acknowledged, is the much narrower, yet crucially important, right to refuse life-sustaining treatment, including artificial nutrition and hydration. It began with the case of Karen Ann Quinlan.

In 1975, Karen, age twenty-one, collapsed after a party and stopped breathing for at least two fifteen-minute periods. (The cause of her collapse was never clear; she had apparently eaten nothing for forty-eight hours and had been drinking at the party. There were also early suggestions that Karen had ingested a toxic mixture of drugs and alcohol, but medical reports could not confirm the presence of significant drugs.) She was resuscitated and placed on a ventilator but never again regained consciousness and entered a permanent vegetative state. After several months, her father, believing that she would not want to live in that condition, sought a court order to remove her from the ventilator. At the time, doctors believed that Karen could not breathe on her own and would die without the ventilator. Even with the ventilator, her case was considered "terminal," doctors believing that she would die within a few months no matter what efforts were made to extend her life.

Mr. Quinlan's request was opposed by her doctors, the hospital, the local prosecutor, the state of New Jersey, and a guardian ad litem appointed for Karen. The lower court in New Jersey denied the request, writing in its opinion, "There is a duty to continue the life-assisting apparatus, if, within the treating physician's opinion, it should be done."[2] Dr. Robert Morse, Karen's doctor, testified that medical tradition did not justify removing the ventilator.

But the New Jersey Supreme Court reversed this decision, charting a new legal course for cases of this kind. It found that patients have a right to refuse extraordinary treatment when their cases are judged to be hopeless. No interest of the state in preserving life or protecting medical ethics could "compel Karen to endure the unendurable, only to vegetate a few measurable months with no realistic possibility of returning to any semblance of cognitive or sapient life."[3] The only practical way for Karen's right to be honored, said the court, was to allow her family to render their best judgment about what she would want done. The court also acknowledged that, while this was the first judicial decision of this nature, the practice of terminating or withholding extraordinary treatment in terminal cases was already occurring—outside of judicial review, but in responsible ways and in accordance with the expressed or implied intentions of the patients. Those actions, the court noted, had not diminished "society's reverence for the lives of sick and dying people."[4]

The justices of the New Jersey Supreme Court based Karen's right to refuse treatment squarely on the right of privacy protected by the U.S. Constitution. Other state courts followed this lead in the cases that would immediately follow. The right of privacy is, of course, the right that in the 1960s and 1970s was identified by the U.S. Supreme Court as protecting reproductive freedoms, like contraceptive use and, more controversially, abortion.[5] There is, of course, no explicit right to privacy in the Constitution, as compared to, for example, the clear and express freedom of speech and of the press in the First Amendment, making more specific rights based on the right to privacy vulnerable to charges of judicial activism.

Beginning in the 1980s, there has been a noticeable shift away from reliance on a federal constitutional right of privacy as the source for the right to refuse treatment. A number of state courts recognizing the right to refuse treatment have chosen instead to rely on the right against unwanted intrusions of the body found in the common law (the body of judge-made law ensconced in our history and traditions), explicit rights to privacy in state constitutions (like Florida's), statutory rights, or some combination of these legal sources. The contours of the right, though, in any jurisdiction, don't appear to vary by the source of the right. They do vary by the *standard of evidence required* or the *process* that must be followed—but there is generally a consensus on the following:

- Competent patients have a right to refuse life-sustaining treatment.
- The right includes the ability to refuse artificial nutrition and hydration.
- The right also belongs to patients who are not competent.
- The right of incompetent patients may be exercised by someone they appoint or, in the absence of appointment, by an appropriate family member.
- In order to protect incompetent patients from decisions that don't reflect what they would want or what is in their best interests, the law can insist on a high level of proof about their condition, their wishes, and their interests.

The Cruzan Case

To this date, the U.S. Supreme Court has ruled on only one case that involves withdrawing or withholding medical treatment. In 1990, the justices considered whether another young woman in a permanent vegetative state, Nancy Beth Cruzan, could be removed from life support. She had been involved in a tragic car accident seven years earlier. When her parents became convinced that there was no hope for improvement, they asked that her feeding tube be removed. This would certainly cause her death. The state hospital, where Nancy was cared for, refused. Although a lower court initially sided with the parents, the state of Missouri, at that time under Governor John Ashcroft, appealed. The Missouri Supreme Court reversed, holding that state law allowed removal of artificial nutrition and hydration from a patient in a permanent vegetative state only if the patient *had directly expressed a desire not to be maintained in such circumstances.* Here there was only testimony about what her family thought she would want based on her personality and values and general statements that Nancy had made about not wanting to live in a severely impaired condition. According to the Missouri Supreme Court, this was not enough.

The U.S. Supreme Court deferred to the state on this matter. It upheld Missouri's right to set the bar as to the level and kind of evidence it would accept. While Missouri had adopted more stringent evidentiary requirements than a number of other states—such as New Jersey, which had substantially deferred to Karen Ann Quinlan's father's views about what his daughter would want—these stringent requirements did not violate Nancy's constitutional rights.

Because the Supreme Court upheld Missouri's guidelines about how a right to refuse treatment could be exercised, the Court did not have to directly recognize that a constitutional right existed. The Court instead said that a right to refuse life-sustaining treatment may be *inferred* from some of the Court's prior opinions establishing individual liberties. In these past cases, the Court had recognized constitutional protection against mandatory vaccinations, the forced administration of antipsychotic medications, and involuntary confinement for mental health or behavior modification treatments. The logic of these cases, according to the Court, would embrace a right to refuse "the forced administration of life-sustaining medical treatment, and even of artificially delivered food and water essential to life."[6]

After the case received national attention, two former co-workers of Nancy's came forward and recounted conversations they had had with her in which she said she would not want to be artificially maintained if she had such severe disabilities that she was unaware of the world around her. This additional testimony allowed the lower court to rehear the case and determine, as it had before, that the feeding tube could be removed. This time the state did not appeal, the feeding tube was removed, and Nancy died a short time later.

Responses to the case have varied, which is understandable given that the Supreme Court declined to lay down clear rules in the case and that the justices themselves were split in ways that yielded a majority opinion, two concurring opinions, and two dissents. On the one hand, because the Court affirmed the Missouri court's decision that Nancy Cruzan's feeding tube could not be withdrawn, much commentary at the time expressed fear that states would adopt more stringent rules about withdrawing life support, rules that looked more like Missouri's. This did not happen, and in fact many states in the aftermath of the *Cruzan* case loosened some of their restrictions on the removal of artificial nutrition and hydration.

On the other hand, people who wanted the *Cruzan* case to stand for more power to the individual—by establishing a clear federal constitutional right to refuse life-sustaining treatment—read it that way. For many, it appeared a welcome affirmation of what state courts had been saying for several years. The Florida Supreme Court in its landmark 1990 *Browning* decision cited *Cruzan* as precedent for a right to refuse artificial nutrition and hydration, although the majority opinion had avoided saying precisely that. Part of the confidence in this conclusion came from counting justices: even if the opinion of the Court did not directly identify a right to refuse artificial nutrition and hydration, one could find among the various opinions five justices who were willing to announce its existence.

A number of commentators went further, reading *Cruzan* as establishing an even broader "right to die." When several years later the Ninth Circuit Court of Appeals addressed the argument that terminally ill patients have a right to physician aid in hastening their deaths, that court wrote that "*Cruzan*, by recognizing a liberty interest that includes the refusal of artificial provision of life-sustaining food and water, necessarily recognize[d] a liberty interest in hastening one's own death."[7] The Supreme Court, on appeal, hastened to clarify that "the two acts are widely and reasonably regarded as quite distinct" and "we certainly gave no intimation that the right to refuse unwanted medical treatment could be somehow transmuted into a right to assistance in committing suicide."[8]

The evolution of the right to refuse treatment—recognized first in state courts from a number of different sources and then implicitly recognized ("strongly suggested" are the words the Supreme Court itself would later use)[9] by the Supreme Court in *Cruzan*—has relevance in determining the strength and contours of the right and in understanding the challenges offered by the Schiavo controversy and any future legislative change we may see.

The *Cruzan* case suggested that the right to refuse treatment was in a weaker category of rights than had been originally recognized for the right to abortion in *Roe v. Wade*. Rather than *Roe v. Wade*'s "fundamental privacy right," which states cannot intrude upon without a compelling reason and then in only limited and narrow ways, the right to refuse treatment would be only a "liberty interest" that would be "balanced" against other interests of the state.

Another important distinction should be noted between the early abortion cases and the Court's end-of-life jurisprudence. A number of the abortion cases include expansive language about the importance of a woman's decision to her "autonomy" and "self-determination."[10] In these cases, the Constitution protects important personal decisions rather than simply protects people from unwanted bodily intrusions. But in *Cruzan* and the later Supreme Court cases about hastening death through physician aid, the right to refuse treatment is described as protection against unwanted intrusions into the body. This emphasis on bodily integrity rather than self-determination has allowed the Court to support the right to refuse treatment but to reject a right to physician aid in hastening death. But it may have other implications as well for the future of end-of-life law.

The emphasis on bodily integrity rather than self-determination may permit greater control by the states over end-of-life decisions for formerly competent patients, if they choose to assert it. Lawmakers seeking to tighten standards for removing life support (particularly artificial nutrition and hydration) might require that a patient have made specific references to the life-sustaining treatment in question—to the sort of bodily intrusion that he or she wishes to reject, since it is the patient's right against state intrusions of the body that appears to be constitutionally protected. Or, the treatment might need to be actually burdensome—painful or otherwise causing suffering—before it can be withdrawn. Legal restrictions of this sort may be more likely to pass constitutional muster if the right to refuse treatment is understood only under the narrower basis of protecting bodily integrity rather than under the broader protection of honoring self-determination. By contrast, if the constitutional right were grounded in self-determination, one could make a strong argument that the focus should be on the *condition* that the patient wishes to avoid (for example, living in a permanent vegetative state for years) rather on than the treatment he or she wished to avoid.

The requirement that the patient have identified the kind of treatment rejected (and of particular concern here is artificial nutrition and hydration) is already the law in a small number of states and has recently been considered by more.[11] Such a standard restricts the group of individuals for whom the right to refuse treatment is meaningful. Of course, those state supreme courts relying on *state* constitutional law for the right to refuse treatment can interpret the right more broadly and reject legislation requiring more specific evidence of a patient's wishes before withdrawing life support.

Another way in which the *Cruzan* case might be seen as falling short of providing any sort of robust federal right to refuse treatment is in its application to patients who have never had capacity to make decisions for themselves. In early 2000, the attorney general's office of the state of New York (under Eliot Spitzer) got involved in an end-of-life case involving a terminally ill, profoundly mentally disabled patient. Sheila Pouliot's physicians recommended that she be provided only comfort care in the final days of her life; due to her condition, the administration of artificial nutrition and hydration would cause her severe pain and suffering. Although her family and the hospital's social worker, nursing staff, chaplain, and ethics consultant all agreed that this was the most humane course of action, lawyers from the attorney general's office advised hospital officials that to do so would be illegal. According to them, New York law did not allow anybody—even a court—to direct the withdrawal of life-prolonging measures from a patient who had never been competent. After several months of "intense suffering" on Pouliot's part caused by the forced administration of artificial nutrition and hydration, "with no corresponding medical benefits—beyond prolonging her life," a court ordered discontinuation of treatment over the objections of the attorney general's office.[12] Pouliot's sister later sued the attorney general's office, arguing that Sheila's federal constitutional right to refuse treatment had been violated by the attorney general and his assistant. She lost. In *Blouin v. Spitzer*, the federal appeals court determined that there is no established constitutional right to refuse treatment for someone who has always lacked the capacity to make decisions about medical treatment. *Cruzan*, under this court's 2004 opinion, was limited to individuals who, while competent, expressed their intentions regarding medical treatment.

While the *Cruzan* case is important for understanding whether there may be federal limits on what states can do in regulating end-of-life decisions, patients are going to be most affected by the particulars of state law. And here there is considerable variation concerning under what circumstances and by what procedures life support may be withdrawn—though generally all within the bounds of the consensus described above that recognize a right of patients to refuse treatment. This is also the forum in which right-to-life groups have been working to effect change.

Patients Who Have Lost Decision-Making Capacity

While this chapter so far has focused on identifying and describing the right to refuse treatment, Karen Quinlan, Nancy Cruzan, and Terri Schiavo never, of course, actually refused treatment. They obviously did not have the capacity to do so. Nor had any of them left any written instructions prior to their incapacity, although even if they had, the legal effect of such instructions, as we'll see, is not certain.

The right to refuse treatment is a right that involves making choices and is personal to the individual whose treatment is in question. It is not a right that belongs to the patient's family or physician but belongs uniquely to the individual patient. It's about what that patient would want, the choice he or she would make. When understood literally and narrowly, as the *Blouin* court did in the case of

Sheila Pouliot, this could essentially mean no right for people who have never had the capacity to make decisions. But it's also problematic for people, like Quinlan, Cruzan, and Schiavo, who have lost that capacity. In a way, we are talking about somewhat of a fiction when we talk about those women making choices, exercising their right to refuse treatment, because their wishes cannot really be known with any certainty. So how do we decide what to do in the individual case?

Generally, through statutes or court decisions, states have adopted some means of trying to determine what the formerly competent patient would want. The sanctioned methods are often imprecise and can vary considerably by state. Generally, consideration is given to some combination of at least some of the following: written instructions, if any, that the patient executed while competent; the directions of an individual formally appointed by the patient (a proxy or health care agent); any oral statements the patient might have made, while competent, about what he or she would want; what the closest family members believe the patient would want, based on his or her values and personality. Objective considerations sometimes play a part as well. Some states allow treatment withdrawal on the basis of the patient's "best interests," objectively determined. Interestingly, and in keeping with the idea that the right to refuse involves making a choice, this standard is sometimes justified as being actually subjective—the argument being that the patient would choose, if he or she were able, to do what was in his or her best interests; like most competent patients, the incompetent patient would weigh the burdens and benefits of treatment options in making medical decisions. Other states insert objective criteria into the process by restricting treatment withdrawal to certain medical preconditions—like "terminal condition" or "permanent vegetative state."

In Florida, a surrogate decision-maker can authorize the withdrawal of life support, including artificial nutrition and hydration, from patients in a permanent vegetative state if the decision is "supported by clear and convincing evidence that the decision would have been the one the patient would have chosen had the patient been competent or, if there is no indication of what the patient would have chosen, that the decision is in the patient's best interest."[13]

Michael Schiavo did not pursue a "best interest" standard when he sought to remove Terri's feeding tube: to do so would have required him to show that she was burdened by the medical treatment that continued her life. She was not burdened in any tangible sense—she felt no pain; she was not suffering. Continued life for her was not experienced as a benefit either, but the presumption under the best interests standard is that treatment will be withdrawn only if the burdens outweigh the benefits—a conclusion impossible to reach. Some scholars argue that we should consider the burden of indignity to the person in a permanent vegetative state,[14] but as disability rights groups and others have pointed out, considering a person's dignity in making life and death decisions has pernicious implications for people with disabilities (more on this in chapter 7).

Instead, Michael sought to prove that removing Terri's feeding tube would be consistent with her wishes. To meet the standards under Florida law, he would have to prove this by "clear and convincing evidence." "Clear and convincing" is a legal term: it is the standard of evidence between our heaviest burden of proof, *beyond a reasonable doubt*, which we use in criminal cases, and *a preponderance of evidence*, a "more likely than not" standard, which we use in most civil cases. This requirement of clear and convincing evidence of the person's wishes appears to be the majority approach among states, although there is considerable variation regarding what kind of evidence will suffice, as well as numerous other differences in end-of-life law among the states.

Following the 2000 hearing, Judge George Greer concluded that Michael had met this burden. He wrote, "The court specifically finds that these statements [related by Michael Schiavo, his brother, and his sister-in-law] are Terri Schiavo's oral declarations concerning her intention as to what she would want done under the present circumstances and the testimony regarding such oral declarations is reliable, is creditable and rises to the level of clear and convincing evidence."[15] Later, the Florida appellate court would affirm the order to remove Terri's feeding tube, concluding that Judge Greer had sufficient evidence to make the decision that he did. It acknowledged and approved of Judge Greer's assessment of Terri's "values, personality, and her own decision-making process" in determining what she would have wished.[16]

As I'll explain in coming chapters, although Michael Schiavo met the required burden of proof about Terri's wishes, this high evidentiary standard is nevertheless problematic when applied to cases of permanent vegetative state. I'm not even sure we need *any* evidence that someone in a permanent vegetative state would want artificial nutrition and hydration continued, and I'll explain that in coming chapters, too. Alarmingly, however, media and political attention on Terri Schiavo's case suggested that we need to move in the opposite direction—toward insisting on even more drastic burdens of proof, some so high that they can't reasonably be met.

Requiring Absolute Proof

There's an instinctive appeal to wanting absolute proof when making life and death decisions. Supporters of the Schindlers argued that proof of the patient's wishes should be "beyond a reasonable doubt" (the standard in criminal cases) or determined by a jury. The court's order to remove Terri's feeding tube was called a "death sentence" and the governor's order to reinsert the feeding tube in 2003 a "stay of execution." Along the same lines, the argument was made that Terri should be given at least as much protection against erroneous decisions at trial as an inmate on death row. This was effective language in the media and in political offices, although not in the courts.

On the other hand, the idea of requiring a written declaration from a patient before withdrawing nutrition and hydration did gain some traction among lawmakers. Conservative commentator Wesley Smith expressed this view: "Most of us have undoubtedly made similar casual statements in response to the death of a relative or the emotions generated by a movie. But shouldn't much more be required to justify the intentional ending of a human life? At the very least, shouldn't we demand a well thought out, informed, and preferably written statement that not only indicates what is desired, but also shows that reasonable alternatives have been fully considered?"[17]

Many lawmakers agreed. During and in the few years following the Schiavo controversy, bills were introduced in at least twenty-four state legislatures to alter end-of-life legal standards.[18] Most of the bills insisted on stronger evidence of a patient's wishes before nutrition and hydration can be withdrawn. These proposals either required a written declaration of the patient's wishes or severely restricted the kind of oral evidence that would satisfy the clear and convincing standard. Many of the bills that were introduced were based directly on a "model act" drafted by the National Right to Life Committee (NRLC)—the same version of legislation that the Florida legislature considered, but failed to pass, in its second bid to reinsert Terri's feeding tube in early 2005.[19]

The NRLC's model act applies to all individuals who are legally incapable of making health care decisions and prohibits, in the absence of a specific written declaration, any "guardian, surrogate, public or private agency, court, or any other person" from authorizing the withholding of nutrition and hydration except in certain narrowly defined circumstances: when it would not be medically possible to provide it, or it would hasten death, or it could not be ingested or absorbed by the patient. Additionally, nutrition and hydration could be withheld on the basis of oral statements when "there is clear and convincing evidence that the person, when legally capable of making health care decisions, gave *express and informed consent* to withdrawing or withholding hydration or nutrition *in the applicable circumstances*" (emphasis added). The definition of "express and informed consent" requires that the patient have an understanding of the procedure to provide artificial nutrition and hydration, the risks and hazards of the procedure, and alternatives.

To withdraw artificial nutrition and hydration on the basis of the patient's oral statements, then, a surrogate would have to show that a person like Terri Schiavo understood what a permanent vegetative state was and how artificial nutrition and hydration was medically provided and what the body would experience without it. This is a level of understanding that we would certainly expect from a surrogate before making a present decision to continue or refuse artificial nutrition and hydration for such a patient, but it is not the sort of understanding we can reasonably insist that patients have prior to their incapacity.

Wesley Smith's commentary on the Terri Schiavo case reveals just how rigid this kind of requirement could be: "[I]f Terri did say she didn't want tubes, did she know that it would include a feeding tube and that it could mean a dying process that involved seizures, heaving, nose bleeding, cracked lips, parched tongue, and the extremities becoming cold and mottled? If she did, would that have made a difference to her?"[20] The NRLC, in its "Frequently Asked Questions" section of its Web site pertaining to the model act, explained that the evidence regarding Terri Schiavo's wishes to have her feeding tube removed would not have met the standard of "express and informed consent."[21]

The kind of oral evidence that would be acceptable under the NRLC's proposal is so restrictive that it would require a remarkably detailed living will in every instance. Oral expressions would rarely be sufficient. In fact, after its initial distribution of the proposal, the NRLC modified its model act to eliminate the option of oral informed consent altogether—under the new version, only a written living will is sufficient to withdraw treatment.

Were the criticisms leveled by right-to-life groups regarding evidence of Terri's wishes justified? As later chapters will consider in depth, there is reason to be skeptical about whether the evidence of Terri's wishes met the "clear and convincing" standard. At the same time, as we'll see, such a high evidentiary standard is not justified for these kinds of cases; it causes us to err too far on the side of biological life and allows too little respect for the individual. The NRLC proposal to require a written directive compounds that error many times over, erecting a mechanical apparatus for decision making where human perception is needed instead.

Who Speaks for the Patient Who Has Lost Decision-Making Capacity?

What we've seen in the previous section is that certain proposed legal changes would make having a "proxy," or surrogate entrusted to determine what a person would want when that person can no longer decide for himself or herself, almost pointless. If, as the NRLC proposes, life support should be discontinued only with such detailed, express consent by the incompetent patient beforehand, then there really is no decision left to make—people in a permanent vegetative state who failed to sign such a document must continue to have their bodies kept biologically alive indefinitely. If they can't speak and haven't filled out the right forms ahead of time, then even if we have compelling evidence that they would have refused the treatment, it doesn't matter: they must be treated.

This flies in the face of a lot of law. In the past, in a wide variety of health situations, a surrogate has been allowed to speak for another. And there are good reasons for this: people can't know exactly what's going to happen to them. They might not take the time to consider every possible health condition they might face—much less write out detailed directives for each of those possibilities—and even if they did, after living that way for a while, they might change their minds.

We have surrogates to make decisions not only because people can't foresee everything that might happen to them but because our laws have long recognized that when it comes to the most intimate, personal, and critical decisions, people generally want those who know them best to speak for them when they cannot. All states allow individuals to choose and appoint their own health care agent or proxy. But when the patient hasn't done so, states generally look to the patient's spouse to perform this function—the person he or she has chosen to share the most intimate, personal, and critical decisions with. This doesn't mean that every spouse is the perfect choice or makes the perfect decisions or that everyone loves and trusts their spouses without reservation. It does acknowledge, though, that marriage confers special benefits and special rights and is primary among our relationships.

This also doesn't mean that it's the only relationship that matters: states also look to adult children, siblings, and parents to act as surrogates, understanding that these relationships too are often marked by very high degrees of trust, familiarity, and care. For minor children, single adults, and those whose spouses have been found unfit to act as surrogates, these other family members are generally favored by our laws and courts to act on their behalf. And even when they are not designated surrogates, courts have shown a willingness, as they did with Terri Schiavo, to consider the opinions and concerns of these other family members. And courts do, as did the court with Terri Schiavo, appoint outside guardians ad litem to provide a more objective perspective on the medical evidence, illuminate potential conflicts of interest on the part of surrogates or witnesses, and so forth.

The decisions a surrogate might make can be minor, of course—would the patient prefer the television on?—but they are often major and can determine life and death. And, as we've already seen, there are certain standards—legal and ethical—that a surrogate is asked to follow. Chief among these is that a surrogate does what he or she believes the *patient* would want, not what the surrogate would want.

Anyone who has ever been involved in a marriage or other close relationship knows that this must be an inexact science, this *what would he or she want*, and that it would be easy to argue against just about anything. I do not like television, for instance; just having it on in the room usually annoys me. Still, my husband keeps it on sometimes, even when I'm there, and he's not really paying attention to it. He turns it off if I say something; we live with it just fine. But what if I couldn't speak for myself—what if he were there in the room with me, hour after hour, with nothing to do? He knows I wouldn't want the television on. But he knows too that I wouldn't mind him watching it some, and he might even venture to guess that if I couldn't hear or see anything, it would probably be okay if it were always on. But that's really what *he* would want, isn't it? The truth is that if I couldn't hear or see the TV—and sometimes even if I could—it would be fine with me if he had it on, because I care about his comfort, too; because often, I want him to have what he wants more than I want to have what I want. This is not unusual. And what it comes down to, and not just for the little things, is that I would trust him to decide.

Surrogate decision making is slippery and inexact and personal. But we generally trust surrogates to make health care decisions for patients, and on the whole the system appears to work fairly well. End-of-life treatment decisions are generally made within a community—the designated surrogate not only communicating with other family members but also engaging in wider conversation and receiving input from doctors, nurses, social workers, and ethics committees. We also have legal safeguards, ways of checking in when it really matters, ways of ensuring that people in surrogate roles are doing the right thing.

Terri's case is in fact an extreme example of the operation of such safeguards. Michael Schiavo brought the petition to the court, acting on Terri's behalf as he believed (even if imperfectly, as is always the case) she would have wanted. It *did* matter what the Schindlers thought; their story, their side, was heard. Others—doctors, court appointed guardians, other members of her family, friends—were heard as well. The court, in effect, took guardianship of Terri to see that the laws were followed and that her wishes were respected.

We might see the complexity of making such decisions and demand even clearer laws and processes and statements of rights. But our nation is now, as it has been since it was formed, in a process of ever-understanding and not in an immutable state of all-knowing. Nancy Cruzan's case didn't settle the issues here—we have witnessed how people concerned with the sanctity of life and protection of vulnerable people clearly have questions that haven't been answered; likewise, those desiring a stalwart right to refuse treatment (and to have loved ones speak for them when they cannot) have weaker protections than they may have realized. In the suffering of Terri Schiavo's family and in her tragic situation, we see that work needs to be done—but *carefully*.

Responsibility

This chapter—like the Schiavo case itself and the attention it generated—has dealt with rights: trying to define them, identifying their sources, considering how they might be properly exercised, and so on. But if we focus only on rights, we leave out an equally important consideration—our responsibility. In that space outside constitutions, court decisions, statutes, and other law, there lies responsibility—for ourselves and for others.

I propose that we ask, of everyone and ourselves: Is the decision I am making one that isn't just right for me (or my loved one) but that is responsible in terms of everyone it might affect? What if Michael Schiavo had assumed responsibility to fully and honestly consider the Schindlers' concerns? What if they had considered the same with respect to their responsibilities to Michael? And their lawyers—how much posturing might have been avoided and replaced with information-sharing and attempted resolution? What if Governor Jeb Bush had considered, as publicly and passionately as he considered Terri's plight, his responsibility as Florida's chief executive, charged with enforcing the law and respecting it and the judicial process, even when he disagreed with the results? What if Senator Bill Frist, before he delivered his suspect diagnosis based on snippets of television, had considered his responsibility as a doctor to not only Terri but all patients who might fear such a hasty, ill-considered, and publicly delivered diagnosis? And the other doctors who gave the Schindlers false hope—again, based on videotape diagnoses rather than clinical examinations—what if they had considered their responsibility? What if the pope had spoken not as though he had been given the answer but as though he were responsible in his answer not only for his own faith but for how his faith implicated those outside it, or even those within the Catholic faith who might be in need of fewer rules and more listening?

It is not laws, though, that would lead us to this kind of consideration—it is an attitude, an orientation, that reaches beyond laws to our humanity.

The dead, for example, have no rights. That is the legal truth: our rights end with our last breath, and what happens after that has to do with notions of respect, the rights of others, and custom. And we sense deeply this need for respect for the body and respect for the rights of the survivors—a matter, to many, of religious importance. Even though the dead can claim no right to this treatment under law, we act out of a sense of responsibility that we owe one another—even those who cannot in any way demand it—the consideration of respectful treatment. It is a mark of our civilization that even with our most dreaded enemies, even with those we defeat in war, we treat their corpses with respect. Our laws don't preclude our media from broadcasting the pruriently gruesome; it is their sense of responsibility—not only to their viewers but to their own ethical standards—that limit it. We as a nation can measure, in many ways, our humanity by the depth of our sense of responsibility even to those who cannot demand it or who least deserve it.

Contrast this with the images of Terri Schiavo that were broadcast repeatedly to the nation with the permission (even urging) of her parents (for what they considered a good cause)—of a person who only barely resembled the Terri Schiavo who once thought, felt, and participated in the world. Neither the news nor her parents would likely have displayed those photographs and that footage with such lack of respect for the life she once lived if she *were* dead. What happened was that the Schindlers, their supporters, the media, and the politicians were so blinded by what they believed to be the rightness of their cause that they lost sight of the full measure of responsibility that they owed, not only to Terri, but to others in her family, to others unknown to them who have loved ones living in a vegetative state, to all of us, who would like to trust that our own images would not end up someday on television like that.

We are faced every year with more difficult, complex decisions to make in our health care system. We have to decide who pays and for which conditions; whether certain experiments are appropriate; what kinds of medical testing we ought to allow or encourage; who should be born; and when they should die. These questions defy simple answers because we have to consider the full context, not only the angles we choose, and because good decisions must be responsible to everyone involved.

Terri Schiavo was as defenseless as a human being can be, completely dependent on others for everything. And yet she was so readily *used* by the very people who claimed to care for her. Her privacy was disregarded, her family destroyed, her name caught up in base speculation and frenzied opinion because *they thought they were right*. Almost every person or group with an interest in the Schiavo case, including the pope, put great value on being *right*. How much more humane, respectful, and caring our responses to Terri might have been if instead everyone put greater value on being responsible.

Many of those who supported the removal of Terri Schiavo's feeding tube have pointed out how much "process" her case received. They have noted, for example, that Terri's parents had exhausted every legal avenue of relief, that many different courts again and again had confirmed that the law was correctly applied, and that the case was in the courts for seven years. This is all true. But what is often not appreciated is the fact that the essential question about Terri's wishes was resolved by one judge in one hearing that lasted a few days in 2000. The determination made on the basis of that hearing—that Terri would want to discontinue feeding—was never revisited in any fundamental way.

Nor should we have expected it to be. Litigants usually only get one shot at presenting the facts. And appellate courts generally don't upset the conclusions of the trial court on the facts, unless they are clearly erroneous. And since no new, compelling evidence emerged about Terri's wishes, later courts did not rehear the issue.

Supporters of the decision to remove her feeding tube have generally overstated the amount of attention placed on determining Terri's wishes, as if that issue had been exhaustively investigated, parsed through, debated, and reviewed. But just because the case saw seven years of litigation doesn't mean this issue was pored over for seven years; it had been resolved in a few days back in 2000. Supporters of the removal of Terri's feeding tube were also able to emphasize that the evidence satisfied Florida's requirement that her wishes were proved by "clear and convincing evidence." This sounds like quite definitive evidence. The clear message was: We know the truth about her wishes.

But the evidence was actually fairly sparse and nonspecific. It consisted mostly of recollections of conversations that Michael, his brother Scott, and his sister-in-law Joan had with Terri at different times regarding the medical treatment received by family members or other people they knew or in which they were discussing the story of someone from a television show or movie. Clearly, there was no sense of a formal instruction from Terri ("If I'm ever in a permanent vegetative state, do not let them keep me alive") or even a less formal but specific preference ("I would rather not be kept alive like that"). In fact, the kind of evidence that was offered in the case of Terri Schiavo is similar to the kind of evidence initially offered in the Nancy Cruzan case—which the Missouri Supreme Court found insufficient to justify removal of Nancy Cruzan's feeding tube (later, additional evidence in the Cruzan case did emerge). But while the Missouri Supreme Court found the Cruzan evidence to be insufficient proof of Nancy's wishes, the Florida court was satisfied with the evidence of Terri's wishes.

So which court got it right and which got it wrong?

I believe our laws and our courts frame the question incorrectly. Our laws demand standards of evidence that are unrealistic in these cases, and our courts (or at least some of them), because the standards are unrealistic, reach. That is why neither the supporters nor the opponents to the removal of Terri's feeding tube could base their positions on really solid ground. Supporters, as I've already indicated, basically said, "The standard is high, and the standard was met—end of discussion." Opponents said the standard was too low, it permitted unreliable "hearsay" evidence, and it required trust in Michael Schiavo (who they urged had a conflict of interest) and his family to truthfully represent their conversations with Terri.

These tactics, on both sides, were understandable and even to be expected in the arenas of politics and the media—where issues are often radically simplified. But the current legal standards for removing life support also clearly caused the debate to be framed in this way—making figuring out what Terri Schiavo might have said the most important issue to be resolved—meaning people take whatever evidence they find and work with it. The court took the evidence presented to it and expressed a certainty about it that should surprise us.

The truth is much messier than the law allows a court to recognize. And the values implicated in these decisions are much richer. In this chapter, I will review in depth the evidence presented about Terri's wishes. In the next chapter, I will argue that our insistence on high burdens of proof in these kinds of cases actually contributes to more error rather than more accuracy in honoring patient wishes.

Witnesses Offered by Michael Schiavo

Scott Schiavo, Michael's brother, testified that at a reception following the death of his and Michael's grandmother, the general conversation around the table, among Scott and his brothers and sisters-in-law, was about how they were upset about the treatment their grandmother had received at the hospital. Their grandmother had a Do-Not-Resuscitate Order, but the doctor did not have it when she took a turn for the worse; the hospital staff performed CPR and placed her on a ventilator. According to Scott, Terri said, "If I ever go like that, just let me go. Don't leave me there. I don't want to be kept alive on a machine."[1] He said that "pretty much everybody at that table had made the same comment."

Scott Schiavo explained that to him, being kept alive by a machine meant being kept alive "artificially," including by a feeding tube. He was asked whether it was his understanding that Terri shared his opinion about artificial life support—that is, that it should not be continued in the circumstances he described as when somebody is "gone" or "not really living." He replied that Terri appeared to share that opinion by agreeing with others at the table that his grandmother's life was wrongly prolonged. He said that Terri "made a statement that if I was in this predicament, let me go. If it is my time, it is my time."

The cross-examination revealed that Michael and Scott's grandmother's condition was far different from Terri's, and so was the form of treatment (a ventilator compared to a feeding tube). Their grandmother was kept alive on the ventilator only for several hours, not even a full day, before she died. The ventilator was highly intrusive (Scott testified that it was upsetting to go into her room to say good-bye to her and see that "the machine ha[d] her lifting off the bed for air"). Her life could not have been saved or extended by any means; she expired even with the ventilator. There was never a question about feeding her.

Terri's comments, as related to the court by Scott, do not really answer the question of whether she would want a feeding tube sustaining her in a permanent vegetative state. "If it is my time, it is my time" sounds more like a statement about treatment during a terminal illness. And a feeding tube is not quite the "machine" that a ventilator is (as in her comment, "I don't want to be kept alive on a machine"). Scott gave his own opinion (not Terri's) about what a machine is and, under the clever questioning of Michael Schiavo's attorney (unchallenged by the Schindlers' attorney), equated a machine to anything artificial.

Importantly, Scott also testified that he would not want a feeding tube if he were in Terri's condition, which raises the possibility that he was projecting his views onto her. He also testified that it was upsetting to see Terri in her current condition ("It was very uneasy for me to see her arms and legs, which were curled up, twisted. It was—it was just like it was not Terri. It was like an old beat up car. Just mangled up. It was sickening"). On the one hand, this testimony might reveal that Scott thought Terri would not want to be left in this situation; on the other hand, it also suggests that he himself found her situation grotesque, one in which people generally should not continue to exist.

Joan Schiavo was Terri's sister-in-law, the wife of Michael's older brother, Bill. She described Terri as "my best friend and like a sister that I never had." During the time that both couples lived in Philadelphia, right after Terri's marriage to Michael, Joan saw or talked on the phone with Terri nearly every day. In the 2000 hearing before Judge George Greer, she related two events around which she and Terri had conversations about life support.

The first event concerned a husband and wife couple who were good friends with Joan. Their newborn baby was very sick and had been placed on a ventilator. The parents decided after about a month to take the infant off the ventilator because, as Joan put it, "there was not anything they could ever really do for the baby." Joan testified that she and Terri talked about the situation of Joan's friends many times during the month the baby was on the ventilator. According to Joan, Terri "said that if her and Michael were ever put in that kind of a situation that that would be a situation she really would not want to have to deal with, but she knows that her and Michael would make the best decision and that would be to do the same thing my girlfriend and her husband did because she would not want to put the baby through anything like that." Joan testified that this was not an isolated comment but a repeated sentiment.

The second event, a movie Terri and Joan watched together about a man who had an accident that left him in a coma, resulted in more discussion about life support. Joan couldn't remember much about the movie, but she said that both she and Terri said "we would want it stated in our will we would want the tubes and everything taken out." When asked what kind of life support the person in the movie was on, Joan was vague: "No. I don't know all the different—I just know there was some tubes in him. Like what you call the breathing machine. The feeding machine. I don't know all the different names of the machines." Joan further offered that Terri said that she "did not want to live like that [like the guy in the movie]. She didn't want to go through that. Have people come and see her like that. Do that to her family and friends." And then she repeated that she and Terri agreed that they wanted it stated in a will that "if it came down to something like that, we would not want any kind of life support."

On cross-examination, the Schindlers' attorney pointed out that Terri's comments about the baby were more from the position of what she would do as a parent rather than what she would want for herself. Ultimately, Judge Greer also found that these statements did not carry much weight, since they were "more reflective of what Terri Schiavo would do in a similar situation for someone else."

The evidence about the movie spoke more to what Terri would want done for herself. It related to a state of unconsciousness, presumably permanent unconsciousness, and about all forms of life support. One thing that is particularly informative was Terri's focus on the kind of condition in which continued life would be intolerable rather than on the kind of treatment that would be intolerable—in *that condition* (again, presumably permanent unconsciousness, the condition that Terri was in), all forms of life support were essentially the same and equally rejected.

At the same time, Joan couldn't name the movie or really offer much information about it. And these are exactly the kinds of conversations that Wesley Smith and other conservative commentators charge are inadequate to serve as a basis for removing life support. They are casual, made in reference to fictional characters in a movie that is likely calculated to produce this kind of response from viewers—the response that continued life in the condition of the character is intolerable. In addition, as with Terri, such conversations typically take place during or right after the movie, when the emotional response is still high.

Michael Schiavo had less to offer than either Scott or Joan in terms of distinct memories of conversations with Terri about life support or life in certain conditions that she might find intolerable. He recalled that she once said she would never want to be a burden to someone, the way her uncle had become dependent on Terri's grandmother following a car accident. (Mary Schindler would later testify that the uncle, Fred Schindler, drove a car, ran his own business, and lived on his own after the grandmother's death, which took place not long after the conversation Michael said he had with Terri.)

He also recalled speaking with Terri two or three times in a general way while watching television shows about people on life support.

> Terri and I would be home. We would be watching TV. You know, a documentary would come on. It would depict, you know, adults, children that are being sustained and kept alive by parents at

home. People that had to be on ventilators. People getting tube feedings. Medications through IVs.

She made the comment to me that she would never want to be like that. Don't ever keep her alive on anything artificial. She did not want to live like that. I looked at her and I said do the same for me.

His testimony also included a few references to the effect that Michael was pursuing this course of action because he thought it was what Terri would want.

One other witness testified that Terri would wish to refuse further artificial nutrition and hydration—an expert named Beverly Tyler, the executive director of Georgia Health Decisions, an organization that, among other things, conducts research into people's values and opinions regarding health care decisions, including decisions to discontinue life-sustaining treatment. Tyler testified about a number of issues regarding American values in end-of-life decision making and typical ways of communicating about those values. She explained that people avoid filling out living wills because "[t]hey have a whole problem with the legal business of putting it in writing, but they trust their family members to do what they want done for them." People's conversations are usually very short, begun by some kind of external stimulus (like a television program), and generally involve a "spontaneous observation about something they do not want to happen to them." Usually the comments are general and vague rather than detailed conversations about which specific treatments a person would want or would not want. Metaphors are used, like "being hooked up" or "pull the plug."

Judge Greer, in his initial order reporting his findings as to Terri's wishes, referred to Tyler's testimony. He wrote that it "clearly establishes that the expressions made by Terri Schiavo to these witnesses are those type of expressions made in those types of situations as would be expected by people in this country in that age group at that time. They (statements) reflect underlying values of independence, quality of life, not to be a burden and so forth. 'Hooked to a machine' means they do not want life artificially extended when there is not hope of improvement." On appeal, the Schindlers would argue that the trial court should not have heard Tyler's testimony. The appellate court appeared to agree that this testimony was problematic. Survey evidence of people's values generally does not answer the question as to what Terri's values were. Its introduction might cause a trial judge to make a decision for the patient not on the basis of his or her wishes but on the basis of what is in that patient's "best interest" (an option apparently not available in Florida unless there is no indication of what the patient would have chosen). Nevertheless, the appellate court found that Judge Greer "did not give undue weight to this evidence" and had instead properly considered only Terri's wishes.[2] On the other hand, Judge Greer's opinion actually ends with a reference to Tyler's testimony. After identifying those statements he found that Terri Schiavo did make that were reliable with regard to her wishes (the statements recounted by Scott, Joan, and Michael Schiavo), he concluded: "Those statements above noted contain no limitations or conditions. However, as Ms. Tyler noted when she testified as to quality of life being the primary criteria in artificial life support matters, Americans want to 'try it for awhile' but they do not wish to live on it with no hope of improvement. That implicit condition has long since been satisfied in this case."

The Credibility of the Schiavo Witnesses

Judge Greer found the witnesses offered by Michael Schiavo to be credible. He wrote: "The court has had the opportunity to hear the witnesses, observe their demeanor, hear inflections, note pregnant pauses, and in all manners assess credibility above and beyond the spoken or typed word. Interestingly enough, there is little discrepancy in the testimony the court must rely upon in order to arrive at its decision in this case." With respect to Joan Schiavo and Scott Schiavo, Judge Greer found that "neither of these witnesses appeared to have shaded his or her testimony or even attempt to exclude unfavorable comments or points regarding those discussions. They were not impeached on cross-examination. Argument is made as to why they waited so long to step forward but their explanations are worthy of belief."

The 2000 hearing was attended by only a few people; the rest of us clearly do not have the benefit of seeing and hearing the witnesses in order to judge for ourselves their credibility. Nevertheless, one commonly heard objection was their delay in coming forward with these stories of long-past conversations with Terri.

During the years following Terri's collapse, Scott Schiavo never did tell his brother Michael about the conversation at the reception following their grandmother's funeral. According to Scott, he did not share this story until George Felos, Michael Schiavo's attorney, was canvassing family members and friends to see if any of them remembered conversations that might be helpful in proving that Terri would wish to discontinue treatment. This was about nine years after Terri Schiavo's collapse.

A number of commentators have implied that this delay might signal fabrication—that the conversation did not really take place, or did not take place as later testified to. For example, O. Carter Snead, a law professor from Notre Dame, has written, "Curiously, Scott Schiavo failed to mention this one instance to anyone until nine years after Ms. Schiavo became severely cognitively disabled and profoundly dependent."[3]

But the delay is not as bothersome as Snead suggests. In fact, it seems perfectly understandable. For many years, Michael Schiavo held on to hope that Terri would recover. Even Mary Schindler, in her own family's book, reports of Michael's devoted attention to Terri's recovery in the years immediately following her collapse. Is it reasonable to expect Scott during that time to have challenged Michael's decision to continue artificial nutrition and hydration because of the earlier conversation he remembers having with Terri? How would he have brought this information forward, and to whom? To nursing home administrators? Just to Michael? Would we expect him to say, "I had a conversation with Terri after grandmother's funeral, and on that basis I think what you're doing is wrong and against her wishes"? Such an action would seem intrusive and insensitive, especially since Scott lived in the Northeast and Michael in Florida and they were rarely able to visit. It would certainly seem reasonable on Scott's part to withhold judgment about Michael's decision to continue life support for Terri and instead to offer support and encouragement.

In fact, Joan Schiavo explained her nine-year delay in coming forward with evidence of her conversations with Terri in a similar way. She explained at the hearing that in the early period following Terri's collapse, "He [Michael] was going through too much at the time. I didn't mention it." When asked by the Schindlers' attorney whether it wasn't odd not to tell him during this nine-year period, she answered, "I think if he questioned me, I would have told him. He never questioned me. It never came up in a conversation between him and I. If he would have said something to me, I would have."

A similar explanation, it seems, can be reasonably accepted for Michael Schiavo's own delay in coming forward with information about his prior conversations with Terri about life support. This delay is consistent with his conviction that she would recover, a conviction that was eventually and reasonably abandoned in the face of mounting evidence to the contrary. In his book, Michael himself explains his change of heart as occurring around 1994, when Terri's internist, Dr. Patrick Mulroy, confronted him in brutally clear language about the hopelessness of Terri's condition: "[T]his is the way Terri is going to be the rest of her life." Mulroy questioned why he didn't "let Terri go" and suggested that Michael decline to consent to treatment for Terri's next urinary tract infection. Such infections are common in patients in a permanent vegetative state and, according to expert Dr. Bryan Jennett, are a common cause of death among such patients if left untreated.[4] Michael followed Mulroy's suggestion and ordered that the next infection go untreated, but in the face of protests by her parents and the nursing home caring for Terri, he relented.

According to Michael, Mulroy went even further in that 1994 conversation, suggesting that Michael stop artificial nutrition and hydration. Later in the year, a neurologist, Dr. Thomas Harrison, who examined Terri and studied her EEG results, told Michael that "[s]he died three years ago."[5] He also suggested that Michael consider discontinuing artificial nutrition and hydration. But according to Michael, it was not until his mother died in 1997 that he "was ready to let Terri go," that he realized that he was keeping Terri alive for himself.

This, of course, is Michael's story. The issue here is not whether these events occurred as Michael relates them in his book and, to some extent, in his sworn testimony in depositions and in court. Again, we were not there in the courtroom to listen to testimony and determine whom to believe. But the delay in coming forward is not in and of itself evidence of any deception or dishonesty on Michael's part. Judge Greer would later conclude in his opinion, "It has been suggested that Michael Schiavo has not acted in good faith by waiting eight plus years to file the Petition which is under consideration. That assertion hardly seems worthy of comment other than to say that he should not be faulted for having done what those opposed to him want to be continued."

But there is another fact that relates to Michael's credibility that has troubled a number of people. In 1992, during the medical malpractice suit he had filed against Terri's doctors, he testified that he wanted to bring Terri home and take care of her for the rest of his life. This appears inconsistent with his later testimony in front of Judge Greer that Terri would not want to continue living in her present condition. If Michael Schiavo believed that Terri would not want to continue living, and that belief was based on conversations he had had with her, then why would he insist that he planned to take care of her for the rest of his life? The Schindlers emphasized this point again and again in their media and courtroom attacks on Michael Schiavo's credibility. They recount his testimony from the malpractice suit in their recent book:

Q (GLENN WOODWORTH) [Michael Schiavo's attorney]: Why did you learn to become a nurse?

A (MICHAEL SCHIAVO): Because I enjoy it and want to learn more how to take care of Terri.

Q: You're a young man. Your life is ahead of you. When you look up the road, what do you see for yourself?

A: I see myself hopefully finishing school and taking care of my wife.

Q: Where do you want to take care of your wife?

A: I want to bring her home.

Q: If you had the resources available to you, if you had the equipment and the people, would you do that?

A: Yes, I would, in a heartbeat.

Q: How do you feel about being married to Terri now?

A: I feel wonderful. She's my life and I wouldn't trade her for the world. I believe in my wedding vows.

Q: You believe in your wedding vows. What do you mean by that?

A: I believe in the vows I took with my wife, through sickness, in health, for richer or poor. I married my wife because I love her and I want to spend the rest of my life with her. I'm going to do that.[6]

The Schindlers' book also points out that only three years later, Michael was engaged in conversations with lawyers to explore the possibility that Terri's feeding tube might be removed.[7] Why, they ask, did he swear under oath that he wanted to spend the rest of his life with Terri and then a few short years later seek to remove her feeding tube? It seems that Michael was saying one thing in the courtroom one day (during the medical malpractice trial) and the opposite another day (in the hearing about removing Terri's feeding tube), and, to raise suspicions further, these statements were always in accord with his own interests.

But what might have been reasonably expected of Michael under the circumstances? Consider the following. First, even if Michael had, during the medical malpractice suit, contemplated seeking the withdrawal of Terri's feeding tube, he did not know whether that effort would be successful. And if it weren't successful, then money would be needed to take care of Terri's needs. Second, one can be certain that the attorneys in the medical malpractice suit assiduously avoided the question of whether Terri's feeding tube would ever be removed. They saw their clients' interest as achieving the highest monetary award possible—that was their focus. It is important to remember that Terri Schiavo was their client as much as Michael Schiavo. In addition to bringing his own claim of loss of consortium, Michael brought suit on behalf of Terri and for Terri's benefit. Her attorneys would need to focus on her interest in having sufficient funds for proper care.

The goals for Terri, Michael, the attorneys, and the court in the malpractice suit were so different, and that trial took place relatively soon after her collapse, that what was argued at that time could be reasonably viewed in a very different light when the question became not who was to blame for Terri's condition but whether to allow her to die.

Witnesses Offered by the Schindlers

Diane Meyer knew Terri as a young girl; their families were close and spent a lot of time together as the two girls grew up. Diane and Terri became especially good friends the summer after high school graduation. At the 2000 trial, Diane related a conversation that took place between the two women in 1982 in which Terri had become very angry with Diane when she told a joke about Karen Ann Quinlan. With apologies to others in the courtroom, Diane repeated the joke: "What is the state vegetable of New Jersey? Karen Ann Quinlan." According to Diane, her telling of the joke had made Terri lose her temper and say things like, "How did they know she wouldn't want to go on?" It was not a lengthy conversation, according to Diane, more like a "soliloquy" on Terri's part. Diane summarized Terri's remarks: "She did not approve of what was going on or what happened in the Karen Ann Quinlan case." In her testimony, Diane appeared to remember the conversation not so much for the content of Terri's comments about what should or should not have been done in Karen's situation but because Terri had reacted so strongly to the joke.

The attorneys for Michael Schiavo had earlier questioned Diane on the timing of the conversation, which she had said took place in 1982. Wouldn't the conversation more likely have taken place when the Quinlan case was in the headlines and in the courts, around 1976? This would have meant that Terri would have been only twelve at the time, hardly an age at which a court would give much credibility to her statements concerning life-support decisions. At the trial, though, Diane repeated that it was 1982 and explained that the topic came up because she had seen a movie about Karen Ann Quinlan on television. But Felos, attorney for Michael, pressed Diane further to admit that Terri had talked about what Karen's parents *were doing*, not what they *had done*. Still, Diane maintained that the 1982 date was accurate—she had even looked it up, after the question was raised in the deposition, because she thought Felos would make an issue of it.

Finally, Felos focused on the fact that Terri's statement to Diane expressed concern that Karen Ann Quinlan's parents did not know what she wanted. In this way, Felos tried to emphasize that Terri was concerned about a lack of respect for Karen's wishes—while in Terri's own case, her wishes could be known and respected. He also suggested that Diane's credibility was weak because her friendship with Terri broke off painfully in 1986, and Diane seemed to place at least some of the blame for that on Michael. Diane also acknowledged during her testimony that she was a practicing Catholic who believed that the Catholic faith was opposed to withdrawing life support at any time.

Mary Schindler also testified about a conversation with Terri about Karen Ann Quinlan. According to Mary, Terri said, "Just leave her alone. Leave her, if they take her off, she might die. Just leave her alone and she will die whenever." But Felos was able to get Mary to say that that conversation must have taken place when Terri was eleven or twelve years old, because that would match up with the time when Quinlan's ventilator was removed. Mary Schindler also acknowledged that even if Terri *had* said that she didn't want to be kept artificially alive, Mary would not change her position. She would still want Terri maintained on a feeding tube because "I don't want her to die."

Credibility of the Schindler Witnesses

Judge Greer did not find either Diane Meyer's or Mary Schindler's testimony very convincing. He took the testimony about Karen Ann Quinlan as reflecting more how Terri would have handled the situation of loved ones rather than what she would want herself. In addition, he concluded that since the conversation between Terri and her mother about Quinlan took place when Terri was eleven or twelve, it did not really represent her opinions as an adult.

Diane insisted, however, that her conversation with Terri took place when Terri was seventeen or eighteen. But Judge Greer's opinion noted that Diane's recounting of the conversation had Terri using "present tense verbs" in describing Karen Ann Quinlan. He expressed doubts about the timing of the conversation for other reasons as well—including discrepancies between Diane's deposition and her trial testimony. "While the court certainly does not conclude the the [sic] bad joke and comment did not occur, the court is drawn to the conclusion that this discussion most likely occurred in the same time frame as the similar comments to Mrs. Schindler [when Terri was eleven or twelve years old]."

Evidence of Terri's Personality and Values

A court in Florida, as in some other states, is allowed to take into account a patient's personality and values, in addition to statements that the patient has made relating to treatment refusal issues. The appellate court reviewing Judge Greer's order specifically approved of his consideration of Terri's personality and values, although his opinion does not actually indicate that he did so.

Evidence of personality and values is not likely to be either surprising or helpful, though, in cases of this sort, and it wasn't in Terri's case. Terri was, according to various witnesses, vivacious and active.

In other cases of this sort, this kind of evidence is referred to as if it indicates a personality that might oppose continued life in a permanent vegetative state.

But what kind of descriptions would we expect to elicit from the relatives and friends of a generally healthy woman in her twenties? And what kind of personality would be aligned with a preference for being kept alive in a vegetative state? I am reminded of a *New Yorker* piece in which the author humorously rendered a living will. One of the instructions was, "If I should remain in a persistent vegetative state for more than fifteen years, I would like someone to turn off the TV."[8] As law professor Sandra Johnson once quipped, if "vivacious" and "active" equates with wanting to discontinue life in a permanent vegetative state, is being a "couch potato" the kind of personality we should equate with a desire to continue life in a vegetative state? And would we expect a relative to emphasize the sedentary tendencies in a loved one's life? Evidence of personality seems to add little to the inquiry of what a person would want regarding life support in a permanent vegetative state. Or at least it seems hard to pin down what it should mean.

One value that was attributed to Terri in the hearing was that she would not want to be a burden to others, and this appeared to carry some weight with Judge Greer. Noting that one can be a "burden" not solely because of financial cost but because of emotional or physical toil, Judge Greer wrote, "Statements which Terri Schiavo made which do support the relief sought by her surrogate (Petitioner/Guardian) include statements to him prompted by her grandmother being in intensive care that if she was ever a burden she would not want to live like that."

Certainly, Terri's views about being a burden did not determine the outcome of this case, as there was other testimony about her wishes, but we should still be wary of putting much weight at all on such sentiments. First, Terri was not a burden to Michael or her parents either financially or in terms of the provision of nursing care; she was continuously cared for in a nursing home, hospital, or hospice.

She could remain alive without their physical tending. And couldn't we impute this value to almost everyone—would anyone *want* to be a burden? Just because people don't want to be a burden doesn't mean that they wish their lives to be ended rather than be that burden. People with severe mental or physical disabilities do rely on others for daily care, and we should not relieve our burdens of their care (whether the burdens are physical or only emotional) by eliminating their lives. We should especially not do this in the name of respecting their autonomy, by saying that this is what they would want. It can be a roundabout way of satisfying the wishes of the speaker (often the surrogate decision-maker), who is essentially saying, "The patient would want what is best for me."

Consider, however, the values that Mary Schindler ascribed to Terri. While not a part of her testimony in court, in the Schindlers' book Mary writes, "In Terri's case, we *know* that she would have wanted to live, because she would have found her life surrounded by the people who loved her, and because she would know how much we wanted her with us."[9] This statement is quite revealing as to why she believed that Terri's own wish would be to keep the feeding tube in place. She is essentially saying that Terri would want to live for Mary's sake, in the same way that Michael's statements about Terri not wanting to be a burden essentially mean that Terri would want to die for Michael's sake.

These kinds of statements about values don't really shed much light on what the individual patient would want if he or she were suddenly competent for a few moments and could tell us.[10] They seem to tell us more about what the *speaker's* interests are than what the patient would decide. That doesn't necessarily mean we should have a process, like that of the state of Missouri, that *excludes* consideration of a patient's values and personality. But it does mean that simply recounting casual conversations and describing people as vivacious or sedentary is often going to be fairly weak evidence of their wishes. And as I'll discuss in the next chapter, even written instructions can be less helpful than we might imagine.

Terri's Wishes: Reasonable Doubts and More

The evidence about Terri's wishes is weak. Her statements were generally made in connection with someone else's health and treatment decisions, and she made only abstract comments about what she would want in vaguely similar conditions. Michael's grandmother, for example, was elderly, on the brink of death, and being supported by a ventilator. The diagnoses of the characters in the movies or TV shows were never clearly testified to. In discussing the baby of Joan Schiavo's friends, Terri and Joan were putting themselves in the position of parents making a decision about their baby, not making statements about when they might discontinue their own treatment.

Not one of the statements expressly related to a permanent vegetative state or to feeding tubes. The Missouri Supreme Court had rejected even stronger statements than these about Nancy Cruzan's wishes, saying they constituted insufficient evidence, and they at least referred to a vegetative state.

We did have *some* evidence that Terri would not have wanted to continue living in a permanent vegetative state. Her conversations with others do indicate that she was not morally opposed to making quality-of-life valuations when determining whether treatment should be continued or discontinued for herself or loved ones. She did not take an absolute pro-life position, concerning her own life or that of others. In certain instances, she would wish treatment to be forgone, even if death resulted. We can also reasonably conclude that the doctrines of her religious faith (Catholicism) did not direct her thinking about these issues, because Catholic teaching did not enter into any of these conversations. Nor did she have a general disposition to hold out for miracles or harbor unusually high hopes for recovery due to scientific advances.

Did she have any views on artificial nutrition and hydration in particular? We don't know. Under current Florida law, such particularized evidence is not necessary. What the court focused on instead was whether Terri would wish to continue living in a permanent vegetative state.

Does the evidence rise to the level of *clear and convincing evidence*—

the standard in Florida and most other jurisdictions? This is the standard that has been described as evidence that "produces in the mind of the trier of fact a firm belief or conviction as to the truth of the allegations sought to be established, evidence so clear, direct and weighty and convincing as to enable [the fact finder] to come to a clear conviction, without hesitancy, of the truth of the precise facts in issue."[11] We certainly have reason to question whether this standard was met. There was *some* evidence that Terri would wish to end life support, but I think to reach "clear and convincing," that evidence had to be stretched pretty thin. I question whether Judge Greer was convinced that the evidence met this high standard at least partly because of his own views, or in deference to the views of the majority of Americans, about the intolerability of continued life in a permanent vegetative state. And he might have deferred to Michael's views on the matter because he was Terri's spouse.

But even if we might reasonably have doubts about whether the evidence of Terri Schiavo's wishes met the clear and convincing standard, such doubts do not settle the larger question of whether Terri's feeding tube should have been removed. Instead, they open up another set of questions, questions that are essential for us as a society to begin addressing, namely: How certain *should* the evidence be about a patient's wishes? Is the standard of "clear and convincing evidence" the appropriate one to apply in these cases? And, more important, is autonomy the only value to consider in cases like these— in other words, are Terri's wishes the only thing that matters?

5

THE LIMITS OF EVIDENCE

As discussed in the previous chapter, we might reasonably ask if the evidence of what Terri Schiavo would have wanted was really all that strong. But the equally important question to ask is why we should presume, in the absence of very strong evidence that she would want to die, that she would want to continue living? Because Terri's life experience at the time was so profoundly without meaning to her, because she had no hope—not even slight—of recovery, and because the means of keeping her alive were intrusive and endlessly so, why should the burden be on proving, to such a high standard, that she would have wanted to die? Why might not the burden, in these extreme situations, be equally on showing that she would have wanted to continue living in such circumstances? Might we not at least equally assume that she, like a majority of us, would want to die? In fact, to many people, showing the deepest respect for life and protecting what makes life worth living is taking care to avoid suspending someone between life and death indefinitely for purposes that do not enrich that life.

For people in a permanent vegetative state, the common legal standard requiring proof of their wishes to end life support by clear and convincing evidence means that instead of trying to respect their wishes, we are already assuming an answer—that they will stay "hooked up"—instead of seeking to weigh their wishes in a more balanced way.

The touted solution to avoid this legal assumption and regain control over treatment decisions is the living will. But when policymakers, the media, and others direct everyone toward living will forms, they are making a lot of unfounded assumptions about the way people see these decisions and the role of their loved ones, and they're vastly discounting the amount of uncertainty that comes along with these medically, legally, and morally complex situations when they actually do arise.

I'll be proposing a more modest answer in some ways—one that allows us to consider evidence of what someone would want in a more evenhanded way. We should allow the evidence to be weighed fairly—a preponderance of evidence for one answer or another is preferable to a more onerous standard when determining the course of action with respect to permanently vegetative patients. We should not be required to produce overwhelming evidence of a wish to refuse treatment before allowing it to be withdrawn. Second, I'll urge much more caution about living wills, especially those that are poorly written, and argue that for many, if not most, of us, a good discussion with loved ones and appointment of a health care proxy are better than even a well-written living will.

Clear and Convincing Is Unconvincing

It is hard to argue against a "high standard" of evidence when life and death decisions are at stake. We want to believe that a higher standard of evidence means a decision will be more accurate.

But does it? If my husband asks me what I'd like to do for dinner and I say that sushi sounds good, he might reasonably, without further discussion, drive us to a Japanese restaurant. But what if he wanted Italian and instead just drove us to an Italian restaurant? What if, in this situation, he were to demand a higher level of commitment on my part—that I *demand* we eat sushi, that I say something like, "We have to go to the Japanese restaurant or I'm not going out to eat." Then my wishes would have been much clearer and we'd be much more likely to go where I want for dinner (though the meal might not be much fun). But expecting such forceful language from me would have been an unreasonable requirement. My original request was not, of course, set in stone—but it wasn't like I didn't have an opinion, either.

Our discussions of how we might wish to be treated if we're incapacitated are often just this informal. Some of us, for certain, have very definite, completely thought-out, unchangeable beliefs on this. These people might indeed speak about (and even write out) exactly what they want. And we should do what we can to honor those requests.

But others of us — even those of us who spend years studying these kinds of cases — might find ourselves questioning what we would want, expressing concerns that are less ideological and more emotional, less demanding and more "wishful." We might have certain indications that we've expressed to loved ones — but we don't think of these in terms of "evidence."

Clear and convincing — the legal standard applied for evidence in cases like deportation, denaturalization, termination of parental rights, an oral promise to make a bequest — is generally meant to *favor* one side: to err on the side of constitutional rights over some other interest, or the written over the oral promise. One side has a very heavy burden of proof. In cases like Terri's, where this is the standard, a judge cannot allow the removal of a feeding tube, even if he or she believes, on the basis of the evidence, that the patient would want it removed, unless there is such a great wealth of evidence "so clear, direct and weighty" that the judge is convinced, "without hesitancy, of the truth of the precise facts in issue."[1] This means that the judge could not allow the removal of the feeding tube even if the evidence favored it. So accuracy in reflecting Terri's (and similar patients') wishes is not what the law currently aims for when, as in many states, the standard is clear and convincing evidence.

The point here is one made by Justice William J. Brennan in his dissent in the case of Nancy Cruzan, that the Missouri court, by demanding clear and convincing evidence of a patient's wishes before ending life support, clearly favored life — but at the cost of accurately determining the wishes of the patient.

When the standard is *preponderance*, though, both sides bear similar burdens and opportunities with respect to proof. When applied to withdrawal of life support, this means that we are asking, "Which way would the patient want this to be handled?" and accepting that we are doing our best to determine the wishes of the patient.

A preponderance standard would mean that we would give *greater* respect to patients' wishes. This is not the same as favoring life, however. What we gain, though, is a keener appreciation for the wishes of the patient—in other words, while we may not continue to favor artificially feeding a person who has been properly diagnosed as in a permanently vegetative state, we will more likely do what this person has indicated (by a preponderance of evidence) that he or she would have wanted. We would no longer err on the side of life, and we need to acknowledge that. I don't suggest that we should change the evidence standard across all end-of-life choices and for patients in all conditions. But for this unique condition, for which there is no cure and in which the person has only the barest of biological signs of life—with no consciousness, no emotional capacity, and no ability to enjoy spiritual or any other meaning—it is reasonable to do so. I want to acknowledge that for some, still, this is life that must be protected and prolonged; for those, I would say as well, if a preponderance of evidence indicates that this is what that person would want, we ought to respect that, too.

It might seem that if I propose that people in a permanent vegetative state should be allowed to die without the protections that a higher evidentiary standard provides, I begin down a slippery slope toward the severely disabled. In fact, I think the opposite is true: there's a bright line separating the two—the complete and irrevocable loss of any conscious capacity. And acknowledging that the permanent vegetative state calls for more attentiveness to a person's wishes and fewer barriers to removal of life support because it is such a unique condition can cause us not to slide toward less protection for the severely disabled but to climb up toward more protection for them (a point I'll discuss more fully in chapter 7).

Moreover, we have to acknowledge that preponderance of the evidence—or, even more likely, much less evidence about the wishes of the patient—guides the vast majority of these decisions, which are made outside the courtroom and the public eye. We may expect or hope that hospital administrators and doctors would not approve of withdrawal of treatment unless the situations match those listed in state laws. But in these cases, we don't know if evidence of patients' wishes is clear and convincing, a preponderance, or barely considered. We have no comprehensive studies reviewing what hospitals and doctors actually insist upon in these circumstances regarding the quality of evidence of the patient's wishes—but if we think they are routinely going by clear and convincing standards before removing life support, we are likely mistaken.

I recently reviewed a form that one Florida hospital asks surrogates to sign when they've chosen to request an end to life support for their relatives. This form should give us all pause. It states: "This decision is made on the basis of clear and convincing evidence of the patient's wishes." I can imagine the family member signing this form having no idea what it means or what its purpose is.

Forms like these are the product of hospital risk management, with an eye on legal liability rather than care of the patient or patient's family. The idea here, like the idea behind many "informed consent" forms produced by hospitals, is to reduce the hospital's risk of legal liability, not to ensure dialogue about what the surrogate might be basing his decision on. There is no place on the form, for example, where a member of the hospital staff might document conversations with the surrogate or describe the evidence the surrogate has provided to explain his decision. This does not mean, necessarily, that a hospital that uses forms such as this one is failing to engage in dialogue about the patient's wishes, although we might reasonably suspect this to be the case. There are significant studies showing that doctors as a group typically perform poorly in this regard, both in seeking information from patients about their wishes and in understanding what those wishes are.[2] Until we have studies showing otherwise, there is no reason to believe that doctors and hospital and nursing home administrators are using these forms to better ensure that a patient's wishes are honored.

In Writing: The Living Will Solution

The great hoped-for answer offered for these dilemmas is to have everyone fill out a living will. Then there won't be any dispute over a patient's wishes; they'll be in writing, on a legal document. If a person is incapacitated, his or her surrogate needn't worry over decisions on the patient's behalf—all the surrogate needs to do is follow the patient's instructions. I have to admit that some of these forms seem quite thoughtful about the experience of dying patients, encouraging people to think about such things as whether they'd want a television on in the room or to have prayers said.

Countless times during the unfolding of the Schiavo controversy, the public was told that the way to avoid this sort of prolonged battle was to sign a living will. Typical among news outlets were expressions like that found in the "Health and Family" section of the *Florida Sun-Sentinel*: "Terri Schiavo had not made out a living will, a document also called an advance health-care directive that would have specified what life-prolonging measures, if any, she wanted. She had not chosen a health-care proxy, a person authorized to make those medical decisions for her. Those documents would have avoided years of bitter legal and family disputes. They would have allowed everyone, including her doctors, to know for sure what Schiavo would have wanted."[3]

In fact, the living will seems like such an attractive solution that in the aftermath of the Schiavo case, many state legislatures considered (although did not pass) laws that would have gone beyond demanding clear and convincing evidence that a person in a permanently vegetative state would want nutrition and hydration ended. The proposed laws would instead have insisted on a living will before life support could be ended. On the surface, this approach might seem reasonable—a means of protecting both life and liberty rather than preferring one over the other.

Why, then, if living wills are the answer, have so few of us taken the time to fill them out?

Consider studies that show only 15 to 20 percent of adults in this country have executed an advance directive of some kind.[4] (The term "advance directive" can cover two kinds of documents: the living will, which provides instructions, and the appointment of a health care proxy.) This number has remained relatively constant despite efforts to educate the public about living wills, despite legal requirements that hospitals inform patients about the availability of living wills, and despite programs to increase the facility of doctors and other health care providers in talking to patients about living wills. The number does not appear to have significantly increased since the publicity surrounding the Schiavo case and all the accompanying exhortations to fill one out, although some organizations that distribute living will forms reported an increase in requests.

And yet, although approximately 80 percent of the public do not have living wills, about that same percentage do not want to be kept alive if ever in a permanent vegetative state. Justice Brennan's dissent in the 1990 *Cruzan* case cites a Colorado Graduate School of Public Affairs study in which 85 percent of those people surveyed answered that they would not want a feeding tube if they became permanently unconscious. Surveys taken during the unfolding of the Schiavo controversy in 2005 were consistent with this earlier survey data. They also revealed that a high percentage of Americans (78–82 percent) would not want to be kept alive if they were in a permanent vegetative state. When asked specifically about disconnecting a feeding tube in such a condition, the numbers dropped some but were still high—between 61 percent and 69 percent.[5] Put together, these data reveal that although a clear majority of the public do not wish to be maintained by artificial nutrition and hydration in a permanent vegetative state, they have not executed a living will that expresses that preference.

Given, then, that most people do not have living wills, how can lawmakers hope that requiring one will improve the accuracy of surrogate decision making? In fact, requiring a living will would make it *more* likely that patient wishes (for the majority who do not have a living will and who do not want to be kept alive artificially) will be disregarded. As with the common standard of clear and convincing evidence, a stronger presumption in favor of life is purchased at the expense of honoring the rights and interests of patients concerning when to withdraw treatment.

Constitutional Limitations

The requirement of a living will before withdrawing treatment may even be unconstitutional, according to Justice Sandra Day O'Connor in the *Cruzan* case. She explained that a state may be constitutionally required to follow the directive of a proxy duly appointed by an individual to make decisions on his or her behalf, even in the absence of a more specific, written directive. If there is a right to refuse treatment, as the Supreme Court has indicated, it is hard to see how that right is not violated by requiring a living will in order to exercise it. When procedural hurdles to exercise a right are too high, the right might as well not exist.

State courts, interpreting state constitutions and state law, might take an even stronger position. Florida's constitution explicitly includes a right to privacy, which has been interpreted to include the right to refuse medical treatment.[6] This right would be severely burdened by the requirement of a living will, without any countervailing governmental interest to justify that burden. As we have seen, the government's interest in ensuring the *accuracy* of the surrogate's choice is not furthered by the requirement of a living will. A state might try to justify a living will requirement because of the government's general interest in preserving human life. As discussed further in chapter 9, however, courts have generally found that this abstract interest in preserving life is, in the words of the Florida Supreme Court, "insufficient to override the decision of a guardian or close family members carrying out the wishes of an incompetent patient."[7]

Even the Supreme Court majority in *Cruzan* emphasized the state's interest in protecting the "personal element" of an individual's choice rather than the state's more generalized interest in the preservation of life. The Court's opinion acknowledged that Missouri's requirement of clear and convincing evidence meant that errors in surrogate decision making would be skewed more toward life than death but stated that such skewing was permissible because erroneous decisions in favor of life could be corrected (for example, by a patient's unexpected death or the discovery of new evidence about the patient's wishes), whereas erroneous decisions in favor of death were irrevocable. In discussing the preservation of life interest, then, the Court still focused on protecting individual choice.

Problems with Living Wills

Requiring a living will is problematic for other reasons as well. Not only does it burden patient self-determination for those who do not have one and thus must be maintained in a permanent vegetative state or other undesired condition even when they would not wish so, it also burdens patient self-determination when it forces people to put what they want into writing *when they do not want to*. In a 2004 *Hastings Center Report* article, "Enough: The Failure of the Living Will," Angela Fagerlin and Carl Schneider reviewed existing studies of patients' attitudes and experiences with living wills. Debunking conventional wisdom that living wills would enhance people's autonomy if we could just educate more people to sign them, these authors conclude that "people have reasons, often substantial and estimable reasons, for eschewing living wills, reasons unlikely to be overcome by persuasion." Moreover, there is strong evidence that people cannot make predictions about their future preferences that are stable "over time and across contexts." And they do not "reliably know enough about illnesses and treatments to make prospective life-or-death decisions about them." Even if people could accurately predict what they would want regarding medical treatment in the event they became terminally ill or permanently vegetative or otherwise extremely incapacitated, there are additional problems of accurately articulating those preferences in ways that are not too general or too specific or otherwise difficult to apply in an actual clinical setting. Fagerlin and Schneider convincingly argue that living will forms are a poor tool for expressing patient wishes and that it is a mistake to believe that better forms are the answer.[8]

I can speak of my own recent difficulties in putting my wishes into writing. While the Schiavo case was pending, I became concerned that Florida hospitals and doctors might react to the case by insisting on a living will or a court order before they would allow the withdrawal of life support from a person in a permanent vegetative state. I am quite confident that I would want life support removed in that situation and wanted to make things easier for my family members to see my wishes carried out. But in filling out a form, I began to contemplate whether I should also say the same (no life support) if I were in a minimally conscious state. I kept thinking of one of the videotapes continually replayed on national television of Terri Schiavo. The recording appeared to show Terri's eyes following the path of a balloon in the room. We knew then that the videotape was misleading. We know even more certainly, after the autopsy, that Terri was in fact blind. But if Terri had been able to consistently follow the path of the balloon with her eyes when requested to do so, then she would have been in a minimally conscious state rather than a permanent vegetative state. That looked to me like a condition I would not want to linger in for years. So in the living will I drafted, I wrote a special section about discontinuation of life support in a minimally conscious state (people can write in whatever they want, although that doesn't necessarily mean their instructions carry legal weight).

Now I have second thoughts. As discussed in chapter 1, we're learning about the potential for late recovery from severe disorders of consciousness that fall short of permanent vegetative state. We're also learning that there may be more "going on" with respect to the consciousness of some of these people than appears obvious. Do I want to lock myself into a decision in the midst of such new discoveries?

It seems reasonable that an individual would rather trust a family member to make these decisions at the time they need to be made, in light of the circumstances and the state of medical science at the time. Joanne Lynn, a physician and expert in end-of-life decision making, has written, "I, and surely some other patients, prefer family choice over the opportunity to make our own choices in advance. The patient himself or herself may well judge the family's efforts less harshly than he or she would judge his or her own decisions made in advance or by the professional caregivers."[9] In explaining why she herself does not have a living will, Lynn cites concerns that living wills can be overgeneralized by health care providers and therefore sometimes contribute to decisions to undertreat rather than overtreat the patient. She further explains that designating a health care proxy, as opposed to giving specific instructions regarding treatment, appears to be a more desirable mechanism for giving patients some comfort about how these decisions will be made for them in the event of their later incompetence. Lynn continues: "I have had a number of seriously ill patients say that their next of kin will attend to some choice if it comes up. When challenged with the possibility that the next of kin might decide in a way that was not what the patient would have chosen, the patient would kindly calm my concern with the observation that such an error would not be very important." Fagerlin and Schneider generally agree that the appointment of a trusted health care agent to make such decisions — rather than detailed written instructions that attempt to predict and resolve all possible contingencies — appears to be a better means of giving patients a choice in their treatment.

The law should continue to allow individuals, if they wish, to refuse to precommit to some medical treatment plan in the event of their future incapacity. Neglect or refusal to execute a living will should not mean that an individual risks a complete loss of his or her right to refuse treatment.

What If Terri Schiavo Had Had a Living Will?

During the Schiavo controversy, there were occasional lone voices that said a living will would not have avoided the battle between the Schindlers and Michael Schiavo, but saying so went against the popular grain. Those voices were right, for a number of reasons.

First, a living will can be challenged as out of date or too vague or coerced or executed in ignorance of its meaning. In fact, in 2004, the Schindlers made an argument that Terri's present views would be different from those she might have had four years earlier, at the time of the 2000 hearing. The argument was that Terri would have chosen to continue her feeding tube after Pope John Paul II's declaration in 2004 that artificial nutrition and hydration was a form of basic care. This same argument could have been made even if Terri had had a living will.

Another reason that a living will would not have solved the Schiavo controversy—or at least a living will that was drafted in accordance with the state of Florida's model form—is because the poor drafting of that form and many others makes them vulnerable to attack by someone opposing treatment withdrawal. It also makes them open to alternative interpretations that leave neutral parties unsure how to proceed. The Florida model form, provided in the Florida statutes, is printed in figure 1.

The most glaring deficiency of this form is that it is supposed to be applicable to someone in a permanent vegetative state, but it states a desire "that my dying not be artificially prolonged" and directs "that life-prolonging procedures be withheld or withdrawn when the application of such procedures would serve only to prolong artificially the process of dying." People in a permanent vegetative state, however, are not in the condition that we normally think of as "dying." They can often live, with artificial nutrition and hydration, for twenty or thirty years, perhaps longer.

Moreover, the form refers to "life-prolonging procedures" but does not state that that includes artificial nutrition and hydration. While the Florida statutes now clearly define "life-prolonging procedures" as including artificial nutrition and hydration, a family member opposing the removal of a feeding tube could probably argue with some degree of credibility that the signer of the document did not realize that that phrase includes artificial nutrition and hydration. This argument is bolstered by the fact that under an earlier version of the Florida statutes, artificial nutrition and hydration was specifically *excluded* from the definition of life-prolonging procedures that could be withdrawn through operation of a living will.[10] While the legal distinction between different types of treatment (for example, ordinary versus extraordinary; artificial nutrition and hydration versus a

LIVING WILL

Declaration made this _____ day of _____, (year) , I, _____, willfully and voluntarily make known my desire that my dying not be artificially prolonged under the circumstances set forth below, and I do hereby declare that, if at any time I am incapacitated and

(initial) I have a terminal condition

or (initial) I have an end-stage condition

or (initial) I am in a persistent vegetative state

and if my attending or treating physician and another consulting physician have determined that there is no reasonable medical probability of my recovery from such condition, I direct that life-prolonging procedures be withheld or withdrawn when the application of such procedures would serve only to prolong artificially the process of dying, and that I be permitted to die naturally with only the administration of medication or the performance of any medical procedure deemed necessary to provide me with comfort care or to alleviate pain.

It is my intention that this declaration be honored by my family and physician as the final expression of my legal right to refuse medical or surgical treatment and to accept the consequences for such refusal.

In the event that I have been determined to be unable to provide express and informed consent regarding the withholding, withdrawal, or continuation of life-prolonging procedures, I wish to designate, as my surrogate to carry out the provisions of this declaration:

Name: _____

Address: _____

Zip Code: _____ Phone: _____

I understand the full import of this declaration, and I am emotionally and mentally competent to make this declaration.

Additional Instructions (optional):

_____

_____

_____

_____ (Signed) _____

_____ Witness _____

_____ Address _____

_____ Phone _____

_____ Witness _____

_____ Address _____

_____ Phone _____

Figure 1. Suggested Living Will Form Contained in Fla. Stat. §765.303.

ventilator) has largely disappeared—and the majority of courts never bought into these distinctions in the first place—the patient may not have realized that. At least a credible argument could be made that the patient was unaware that nowadays, a term like "life-prolonging procedures" is typically thought to embrace artificial nutrition and hydration.

Someone might also argue that artificial nutrition and hydration is encompassed in the term "comfort care," which the form directs should be continued. Again, this would not be a convincing argument to someone well versed in the law and ethics of the field—who would understand that "comfort care" is referring to other things, like pain relief and warmth, and who would be aware of studies showing that in many instances, the provision of artificial nutrition and hydration can cause discomfort rather than relief. But the argument would be that Terri would have understood that the direction to provide comfort care included nutrition and hydration, and again, earlier Florida statutes would have provided some basis for this belief because these two forms of treatment were lumped together confusingly in an explicit exception to life-prolonging procedures.

Finally, if Terri Schiavo had not been in a permanent vegetative state—as her parents argued—then a living will such as this one would not even have been operative, since none of the three conditions to be "checked" would have existed. In any event, as in the Schiavo case, family members opposed to the removal of a patient's feeding tube could delay its removal by challenging the diagnosis in protracted lawsuits.

In Favor of Hard Decisions

Simple solutions rarely exist for complex problems. And the problem of removing life support from patients—and in particular the problem of removing artificial nutrition and hydration from patients in a permanent vegetative state—can be exceedingly complex.

If we truly do value patient self-determination, then the standard of evidence for determining his or her wishes should be lowered (to preponderance of the evidence) rather than ratcheted up (such as by requiring a living will). But even that would be just a partial solution. In some instances (perhaps many), patient wishes may simply be indeterminate. While the law assumes that there is an objective answer to the question "What would the patient want?," there is good reason to believe that in many cases, we cannot determine what the patient would want with any confidence. As one judge has explained, "[T]he inquiry at issue is not factual. It is an attempt to predict a choice that cannot be made."[11] End-of-life choices are hard, involving valuations of continued life and the tolerability of various degrees of disease, pain, disability, and dependence, further complicated by possibilities (though remote) of some degree of recovery. Hard choices for the patient make for even harder choices for the surrogate—or the court—years after competency has been lost.

We want to cling to the idea, though, that everybody gets to decide for himself or herself what will be done. The image of attorney Barbara Weller on television reporting that Terri had told her she wanted to live, the "Aaaaah waaaa" impersonation, captures this insistent desire. Even at the time she was relating her story, Weller was not credible. As a nation, we had already been educated about Terri's condition and the overwhelming evidence of a lack of consciousness. Even if some people might have been persuaded that Terri had some small degree of consciousness, Weller's description of sudden, purposeful activity and speech on the part of Terri was simply not believable.

But the image is compelling and memorable because of what Weller was doing. She was *putting words into someone else's mouth.* She understood that the law puts great weight on the words of the patient—even if she failed to understand that the law also requires those words to be truthfully reported.

It is naive to believe that we can be certain what a now-incompetent patient would want, even if he or she is one of the minority who signs a living will. Gaps in evidence, in time, in knowledge require that we look to additional sources to determine what should be done in the individual case. And for that, we have traditionally looked to the family. But the family is more than a source of information; as I'll discuss in the next chapter, these decisions affect them, deeply. What the families need and want and believe do matter—just as they do in life generally, where our decisions and responsibilities, no matter how personal they may seem, and whether we wish it or not, matter to others.

6

THE IMPLICATIONS OF SURROGACY

While it was Michael Schiavo's preference, and request, that Terri's feeding tube be removed, it was never his *decision*. As we've already seen, under the law, the surrogate speaks for the patient, but it is the patient's wishes that must direct the surrogate's expression. Law professor Norman L. Cantor describes the question we should ask as follows: If the patient could become competent for a moment, what would this person tell us he or she would want done? Unless the patient has left a written directive, the surrogate must speak for the patient on this question. Even when the patient has left written instructions, these instructions often do not address the exact situation encountered, or they give ambiguous or sometimes even contradictory directions. In those situations, too, someone has to speak for the patient, explaining what that person must have really meant when he or she provided the written instructions. As the Florida Supreme Court wrote in the 1990 case of *In re Browning*, "One does not exercise another's right of self-determination . . . by making a decision which the state, the family, or public opinion would prefer. The surrogate must be confident that he or she can and is voicing the *patient's* decision."[1] In one of the appellate court opinions reviewing the order to remove Terri Schiavo's feeding tube, the court wrote that the case "is about Theresa Schiavo's right to make her own decision, independent of her parents and independent of her husband."[2] In other words, the surrogate is supposed to be a mere conduit and should refrain from injecting personal wishes into his or her statement of the patient's wishes.

But, of course, this method is fraught with problems. In the vast majority of cases, no court ever assesses the surrogate's actions. And who does the law look to as surrogates? Spouses, parents, adult children, siblings—people who have their own interests tied up in the decision of whether to extend life or hasten death. Sometimes we may sympathize with their interests, like the difficulty parents face in letting their child die, but sometimes their interests may be less than honorable, like selfish desires for a patient's estate. So we have to wonder, when surrogates speak for the patient, are they putting their *own* words into the patient's mouth and placing their own interests first? Realizing that this is a risk with our system of surrogate decision making, how do we account for it? Why do we even look to families to speak for patients? What is their proper role?

The Schiavo case is an excellent one for considering these questions because the guardianship of Terri (and therefore the authority to speak for her) was bitterly contested.

Powers and Limits to Family Surrogacy

While the Schiavo case provides a rich context for considering the role of the family—parents and husband at odds, accusations of falsehood, neglect, and self-interest—it was not a typical case for reasons other than extreme acrimony. Something happened in the Schiavo case that does not happen in most end-of-life decision-making cases: a court got involved. And when a court gets involved, the surrogate decision-making process changes. When Michael Schiavo sought a court order to withdraw Terri's feeding tube, the *court essentially became Terri's surrogate*, because it now had to determine and express what Terri would want done. To do this, Judge George Greer listened to evidence about Terri's wishes from a number of different witnesses, including family and friends. It is true that he believed Michael's testimony about his conversations with Terri and the corroborating testimony of his brother and sister-in-law. He found their testimony to be more credible than that of Mary Schindler and Terri's childhood friend. He may even—though we do not know—have been more willing to listen to Michael's point of view because Michael was Terri's husband and the spouse usually does, under law, get to act as surrogate and speak for the patient.

But Michael had nothing like the kind of power that is granted to most family members in these kinds of situations, who make these decisions outside of court. He especially had nothing like the kind of power that the Schindlers would have had if either of them had been designated Terri's surrogate. If one of her parents had been her surrogate, Robert and Mary could have easily kept her feeding tube in place until she died of other causes, twenty or thirty or more years later. They would not have had to produce evidence that this is what Terri would have wished. This extraordinary power would not have stemmed from the fact that they were Terri's parents instead of her husband but because the decision they would prefer—keeping Terri's feeding tube in place—is the decision current law also prefers.

The power of family surrogates to continue to treat patients *even when the patient would not want it* is one of the most underappreciated aspects of the Schiavo case. Interestingly, the most vocal calls for reform generated by the Schiavo controversy have been aimed at a problem that likely does not exist—family members deciding to withhold artificial nutrition and hydration from patients who want it or might benefit from it. Instead, the real problem that the Schiavo case revealed is that family members can easily continue artificial nutrition and hydration for patients who wouldn't want it—and for people in a permanent vegetative state, this can mean decades of unwanted existence sometimes for no reason other than that a family member wishes to avoid a difficult decision.

I am sympathetic to how traumatic it must be to make such a decision. At the same time, as we've already seen, avoiding an explicit decision about whether to continue or discontinue feeding means nonetheless that a decision is made (to continue feeding) and lived with. In the last chapter, I urged that we move to a preponderance of the evidence test to more accurately honor patient wishes about life support when the patient is in a permanent vegetative state. In addition, we should consider changing the legal presumption from continuing tube-feeding to discontinuing tube-feeding for these patients after some reasonable (and conservatively lengthy) period of time, such as one or two years. This change would mean that an explicit decision to continue feeding would have to be made and would have to be supported by evidence that it is what the patient would want.

Currently, the combination of two aspects of the law in Florida—found in many other states as well—makes it likely that someone would have to live those unwanted years. First, we have no easy mechanism for judicial review for decisions to *continue* treatment. Second, as we've seen, the proof we require to *discontinue* treatment is lopsided, favoring indefinite feeding and hydration. If a surrogate seeks withdrawal, he or she generally must do so on the basis of clear and convincing evidence that this is what the patient would have wanted. But if the surrogate seeks to continue treatment, he or she does not usually have to give *any* evidence that this is what the patient would have wanted. In fact, the Schindlers as surrogates would likely not even have had to request that feeding be continued, because it would be assumed. A doctor after several years might have suggested that they consider withdrawing artificial nutrition and hydration—just as Michael Schiavo reports in his book that Terri's doctors suggested to him—but few doctors would have pushed the idea. The Schindlers probably would not have been challenged by physicians or nursing home administrators to provide any evidence of Terri's wishes to continue feeding. They could even have continued treatment if other family or friends, someone like Michael Schiavo, produced strong evidence—even a preponderance of the evidence—that Terri would have wanted feeding discontinued, because a preponderance of evidence in favor of discontinuing treatment is not enough (in Florida and many states) to legally justify its withdrawal. Since Terri wasn't burdened by feeding, in terms of pain or suffering, it would be difficult for anyone to successfully challenge the Schindlers' treatment decision in court.

This means that even though courts and legislators and ethicists identify self-determination as the guiding principle of end-of-life law, actually, in the vast majority of cases—outside of courtrooms and public view—surrogates have considerable discretion to do what they want, as long as it is not clearly against the patient's interests.

They can, instead, satisfy their own interests or their own values and principles.

The Schindlers' Failure to
Understand the Role of the Surrogate

The Schindlers' arguments for removing Michael Schiavo as guardian and replacing him with one of the two of them did not emphasize their superior ability or inclination to respect Terri's wishes. In fact, Jay Wolfson's comprehensive guardian ad litem report revealed the Schindlers' willingness to push for continued feeding of Terri Schiavo even if they believed she would have wanted to die. The report discloses that at one point in the proceedings to determine what should be done about Terri's continued feeding, members of the Schindler family were questioned about their commitment to do everything medically possible to keep Terri alive. According to Wolfson's report, they were asked about a number of "gruesome examples." For example, they were asked whether they would agree to Terri's forgoing a highly invasive heart surgery if Terri at that point also had had all four limbs amputated because of gangrene. They replied that the surgery should be done. The report continues, "Within the testimony, as part of the hypotheticals presented, Schindler family members stated that even if Theresa had told them of her intentions to have artificial nutrition withdrawn, they would not do it."[3]

The various positions that the Schindlers took throughout the litigation and media war on the issue of continuing feeding emphasized either that there was hope for Terri's recovery or that feeding was a form of basic care that should not be withdrawn but never that they would have respected Terri's wishes better than Michael Schiavo.

This exercise of considering what would have happened if the Schindlers had been higher up on the list of family members who could serve as a surrogate (currently in Florida, a spouse is favored over parents) is not meant to suggest that surrogates' decisions to continue treatment contrary to the wishes of the patient can never be successfully challenged in court. In fact, a case decided in Florida in the fall of 2004—during the last, heated months of the Schiavo controversy—involved a successful challenge to a surrogate's decision. Unfortunately, however, the case of Hanford Pinette is not a model for how these issues should be handled.

Considerations of the Needs of Others

Hanford Pinette, a seventy-three-year-old man suffering from chronic failures of the respiratory, circulatory, and renal systems, was being sustained by invasive life-support systems. Doctors certified that he was in a terminal condition and unresponsive. Carol Paris, director of risk management for Orlando Regional Healthcare Systems, which operated the hospital in which Pinette was being cared for, sought a court order allowing the hospital to remove life-sustaining treatment. To support this petition, the hospital relied upon Pinette's living will, executed in 1998 and presented to the hospital by his wife upon admission to the hospital. The living will, in language suggested by the Florida statutes, stated that life-prolonging procedures should be withheld or withdrawn when their application would serve only to prolong the process of dying.

Pinette's wife of fifty-three years, Alice Pinette, disagreed that life support should be removed. She was Pinette's surrogate, appointed through a durable power of attorney that he had also executed. Mrs. Pinette believed that her husband still enjoyed watching sports on television with other family members and that he was responsive. She insisted that he would not yet want to die.

The Circuit Court for Orange County determined that the living will dictated that treatment be discontinued and authorized the hospital to withdraw it. The short opinion of the court stated, "The argument should not center on the 'surrogate's' wishes or desires, but whether the 'patient' meets the medical requirements for the Living Will to be enforced in order to carry out the wishes of the 'patient.'"[4]

While immediate responses to the Pinette case varied, they were on the whole generally positive. The living will had triumphed. After years of reports that people do not execute living wills in high percentages, that they are difficult to apply, that they are routinely ignored—here was a case in which a living will had been written, it seemed fairly straightforward to apply, and hospital officials and health care providers, rather than ignoring the living will, were insisting that it be followed. For those who have championed the living will as an instrument for choice and control in the dying process, the case was a success and the judge was to be applauded for his courage to uphold a person's living will in the face of disagreement from his health care surrogate. A president of a local hospice urged that the lesson to be learned from the controversy was that family members may not make the best health care proxies because of their emotional involvement.[5]

My view of the case is more guarded. Are we certain this legal outcome is what Hanford Pinette wanted? We have to ask whether he really would have minded so much if his wife insisted on a little more time with him. If he were in pain during this extra time, then that would weigh heavily toward discontinuing life support, but if he were not in pain (and the court order and newspaper accounts said nothing of any pain or suffering), then it does not seem too far a stretch to say that he might have wanted the hospital to defer to his wife's wishes. The evidence of his long-standing relationship with his wife, the evidence of her continuing devotion to him, and the fact that he named her as health care surrogate may suggest as much, perhaps even more, about what he would have wanted as the clumsy legal mechanism of a form document that he executed in a state of relative health. In fact, it's not hard to imagine that some people, if given the option, would even write into their living will that if their spouse or children needed a little extra time, that would be okay with them.

Law professor Rebecca Dresser cautions us against assuming that patients like Hanford Pinette want their living wills honored to the letter. In addition to pointing out other flaws of living wills (such as their failure to provide meaningful information and the difficulty people have in understanding what they are deciding when they fill them out), she tells about a study that tests the idea that people want their living wills to be strictly followed:

Investigators asked competent people dependent on dialysis to complete advance directives indicating whether they wanted dialysis to continue if they developed advanced Alzheimer's disease. After the directives were completed, investigators asked the study participants whether they wanted their directives to be followed. About one third of the participants said their directives should be strictly followed, about one third said their families and physicians should have some "leeway" to override their directives, and the remainder said their families and physicians should have "complete leeway" to override their directives.[6]

Dresser concludes that the concept of "precommitting" to certain treatment decisions in the event of later incapacity is a seductive but ultimately misguided and morally troubling concept: "Although a person's statements about future care can be relevant, they are just one element of a complex situation."

In Hanford Pinette's case, the fact that he executed both a living will and a health care power of attorney adds to that complexity. He may in fact have executed the living will as *further protection* of his wife's decision-making power rather than as a *limitation* upon it. We have all heard stories of families not being permitted to end life support when they thought best, stories as prominent as Nancy Cruzan's and others that are known to us through friends and family. It seems reasonable that Pinette may have wished through the living will to provide his wife with the documentation needed to support her decisions. If she determined that it was "best" that life support be withdrawn, then she would have had less difficulty doing so with a properly executed living will. Ironically, then, he may have executed the living will to allow his wife to avoid a controversial legal battle if she determined that it was appropriate to withdraw life support. Instead, she became embroiled in a legal battle because of it. It's not hard to imagine that he would have rather lived a few more weeks than to see her dragged through court.

Moreover, it is not uncommon to hear of a living will described as a gift that people can give to their loved ones. Instead of leaving it to family members to agonize over these life and death decisions, the living will theoretically relieves family members of difficult choices because the patient has taken responsibility for them. If we saw Pinette as less of a staunch individualist trying to control the detailed circumstances of his death and more of a protective husband who wished to relieve his wife of burdensome tasks, then we might see the living will in a different light and be less inclined to pit it against his wife in litigation that almost looks like *Mr. Pinette v. Mrs. Pinette*.

Finally, putting aside the question of what Hanford Pinette *really* meant to accomplish in executing these legal documents, shouldn't we have some sympathy for his wife of over fifty years, a woman who was having severe difficulty accepting the inevitable death of her husband? Is *no* accommodation of her interests permitted?

Some delay should be acceptable. I am not too bothered by the fact that a now-incompetent, terminally ill individual may live a few days, maybe even a few weeks or months, longer than we think he would have preferred if that extra time is of value to family members and he is not suffering. This position may be quite scandalous in the current heyday of patient autonomy, but I think it is both realistic and mindful of our responsibilities to other people in addition to the patient.

The Reaches of Responsibility

The law, however, rarely seems to acknowledge that family members have a role in these decisions, that our society has responsibilities to them as well as to the patient. The assumption in the law has been and continues to be that family involvement in end-of-life decision making is merely *part of the process*—a means of determining the incompetent patient's wishes or, in some cases, his or her best interests. What may be surprising, though, is that family members often have little to contribute with respect to knowledge of the patient's wishes. Studies have shown that they usually cannot predict any more accurately than a stranger what a close relative might choose in terms of treating or not treating in various disease and disability scenarios. Law professor and medical doctor David Orentlicher has written:

Surrogate decisionmaking is premised on the belief that surrogates will make medical decisions that reflect patients' preferences. The empirical data indicate, however, that surrogates do a poor job of carrying out patients' wishes. Several studies have examined the accuracy of surrogate decisionmakers by presenting individuals with hypothetical scenarios and asking them to indicate their treatment preferences for each scenario. Potential surrogates are simultaneously asked to predict the preferences of the individuals. These studies consistently demonstrate that the potential surrogates' predictions do not reach a statistically significant degree of agreement with the choices of the individuals. This holds true even when individuals chose people that they would feel most comfortable with as surrogate decisionmakers.[7]

The risk that a family surrogate might get it wrong appears heightened by the fact that often only one family member is chosen for this purpose (at least by law, although in practice family members do often consult together about these decisions and health care providers often look to them as a group). Further, in the absence of an appointment of a proxy by a patient, this choice is based on a standardized list prioritizing potential surrogates by their legal relationship to the patient (for example, spouse comes before parents; lesbian/gay partners are generally not included) rather than on an individualized assessment of who would most likely know about the patient's wishes. And while different family members may have important information to contribute to the surrogate's knowledge about a patient's wishes, there is no systematic mechanism or requirement for gathering such information prior to the surrogate expressing a decision about treatment.

But family involvement is probably justified even though family members may not be particularly knowledgeable of the patient's wishes. Most people want family members to make these decisions, and family members will usually have a lot at stake that should be valued and protected in these decisions. In many instances, the suffering of the patient is exceeded by that of family members, who, with all their faculties intact, experience fully the loss of a spouse's companionship, the grief of a parent's decline, and the uncertainty about the morality of the choices they are asked to make. While as a general rule the wishes of family members should not override the wishes of the patient, they should not be entirely ignored, either. How to navigate that further involvement, how to recognize and respect family members' own interests in a patient's continued life or hastened death, and yet limit the effect of those interests so that they do not overcome the patient's own interests and wishes, is a challenge we have yet to address adequately. My hope is that as we begin to understand the full reach of our decisions—how each participant in the decision has responsibility to the others—we will stop seeking a gold standard (patient's wishes! protecting life! living wills!) and instead will begin seeking more complete understanding and appreciation of the complex web of values implicated.

Some reasonable accommodation of family interests can be justified as satisfying, in many cases, a broad understanding of patient self-determination (understanding that often, this would be what the patient would want). For example, we can allow some amount of delay in order to allow family members to understand the patient's condition and to accept it. We can show some deference to the surrogate in interpreting a living will, understanding such a document as a signal of someone's intent rather than as a complete and precise legal directive. Instead of having family members "sign off" on surrogate decision forms (like the risk management form that asked a surrogate to confirm that his or her decision was backed by "clear and convincing evidence"), we can implement hospital processes and practices that require more listening to families about their needs and observations and require clearer descriptions about the patient's condition and prognosis. This latter point deserves some emphasis. Family members generally do not appear to be unhappy with the decisions reached about treatment of their relative—what *does* distress them is lack of timely and effective communication about their loved one's condition and prognosis.[8]

These considerations of the responsibilities of everyone involved mean that we can see more easily how issues like patient self-determination and concern for family members fit together. On the one hand, I've expressed concern about family members acting on their own interests and continuing treatment despite what the patient would want. In the Schiavo case, this likely would have been the result if the Schindlers had been Terri's surrogate, because they would have been granted the discretion to continue to tube-feed Terri on the basis of their own personal interest and ideas about sanctity of life.

On the other hand, I have said that what was done in the Pinette case may also have been wrong—that perhaps more discretion should have been given to Alice Pinette to continue life-support systems for her husband, even if that appeared to be contrary to the letter of his instructions in his living will.

Two cases—Schiavo and Pinette—and two different answers, answers that depend on conditions, prognoses, and balancing different kinds of interests. A one-size-fits-all answer doesn't fit. And yet, interest groups, legislators, and many ordinary citizens want just that—the one right answer—and fail to see that reducing all end-of-life questions to the one answer they each want is not only unnecessary but can be harmful.

Surrogacy Factors Unique to Permanent Vegetative State

For a patient who is likely to die shortly from the natural progression of his or her disease, deference to a family member's decision to continue treatment for at least some period of time may be warranted as long as treatment does not cause the patient to suffer significantly and is not clearly contrary to his or her known preferences. But we also have to understand that this deference (which is built into much current law) comes with some risk—that there may be instances in which a surrogate's decision to continue treatment *does* result in the patient's experiencing significant suffering or goes against the patient's wishes. This risk is probably acceptable because, on the whole, family member surrogates do put the patient first, ahead of their own considerations, and we have some confidence that health care providers can generally provide a check against the provision of treatment that would actually burden rather than benefit the patient. Moreover, a system that didn't permit this deference but instead imposed judicial or similar scrutiny on every family's decisions to continue treatment would be both administratively and emotionally burdensome to families and health care providers alike. For these reasons, for the now-incapacitated, terminally ill patient, this seems like a reasonable and appropriate method of making treatment decisions. In such cases, the primary effect of "overtreatment" will be to cause a delay in the inevitable death of the patient. If the surrogate has allowed his or her own interests (or the interests of others) to dictate the continued treatment of the patient, then at least for the dying patient, this will be short-lived.

But this is true for the terminally ill patient in ways that are not true for the person in a permanent vegetative state. For the person in a permanent vegetative state, the ease with which a surrogate can continue tube-feeding, even if that is not what the patient would want, more clearly fails to respect the patient's self-determination. Instead of a few unwanted days or weeks of life in a diminished condition, the result could be a few unwanted decades of life.

Much end-of-life law, however, authorizes the same sort of decision-making process for permanently vegetative patients and terminally ill patients (that is, typically no required judicial review and a presumption in favor of continued treatment unless the patient's wishes or best interests clearly indicate otherwise). What we need instead are different rules for decisions to continue or discontinue life support when the patient has entered a permanent vegetative state because the rules appropriate for the terminally ill patient don't work well here. We should consider judicial or quasi-judicial review of decisions to indefinitely feed patients in a permanent vegetative state; indefinite feeding of someone in that condition should not be the default position. That review would allow surrogates to bring forward evidence about whether the patient would want to continue living in that condition. To provide some check against the surrogate merely expressly his or her own judgment about whether the feeding tube should remain in place, a guardian ad litem should be appointed, as was done for Terri Schiavo. The guardian ad litem would inquire into the patient's wishes by speaking with family, friends, and others who might have information to share on this issue and also report any conflicts of interest he or she uncovered on the part of the patient's surrogate or others providing information about the patient's wishes.

This leaves the issue of what should be done with this evidence once gathered. While the high "clear and convincing" standard of proof and the inaccuracies it allows may be acceptable for terminally ill patients, the consequences for the permanently vegetative patient are too great. I've said earlier that I think the standard of clear and convincing evidence misguidedly thwarts the right of these patients to refuse treatment and that a preponderance of evidence, a "balancing" rather than a favoring of one side, is more appropriate. But the burden of proof (even with this lower evidentiary standard) is going to have to lie on one side or the other. There are good reasons to believe that for the unique condition of permanent vegetative state, the burden should be on the party favoring continued life support. The law should in fact favor *discontinuing* feeding after a certain period of time (such as one or two years) following a firmly established diagnosis. And this is because otherwise, and as explained more fully in the following chapter, the person in a permanent vegetative state is especially vulnerable to being treated as an object rather than as a person.

Interestingly, the Florida statutes do contain a unique provision that is somewhat, but not entirely, along these lines (in favor of discontinuing tube-feeding persons in a permanent vegetative state, and only persons in that condition), although we certainly never heard about it during the Schiavo controversy.[9] This provision permits the withdrawal of artificial nutrition and hydration from patients who do not have a living will, "for whom there is no evidence indicating what the person would have wanted under such conditions," and *who do not have a family member or other personal surrogate to speak for them*. In these cases, a judicially appointed guardian can, in conference with a hospital or nursing home ethics committee, authorize the withdrawal of artificial nutrition and hydration if they agree that doing so would be in the patient's best interests.

This is a remarkable exception to the general biases about end-of-life decision making. It allows a judicially appointed guardian, who may not even know the patient, to make a decision to withdraw life support even though the guardian lacks "clear and convincing evidence" or even *any evidence* that it is what the patient would desire. What a contrast from the demands for evidence about Terri's wishes!

Now, it is true that there are general rules in Florida that allow surrogates to withdraw life support when there is no evidence of the patient's desires—for instance, if withdrawal would be in the patient's best interests. But, courts are reluctant to apply this standard to people in a permanent vegetative state, because generally the "burden" of treatment would need to outweigh the "benefit," and since people in a permanent vegetative state can't experience *any* burdens, and life itself may be seen, at least by some, as a benefit, ending treatment doesn't seem to fit our usual understanding of best interests. Certainly Michael Schiavo didn't attempt this tack; when others have done so, they've generally been told that the best interests test is inapplicable or that because the burdens of treatment will not outweigh the benefits, continued provision of artificial nutrition and hydration is necessary.

The Florida statute relating specifically to permanently vegetative patients goes against this grain. It allows the judicially appointed guardian to determine that withdrawing life support is in the best interests of the patient. One way to make sense of the statute would be to understand it as adopting a different best interests standard— one that requires benefits to exceed burdens in order to *continue* treatment rather than the way most law defines the test, as requiring burdens to exceed benefits before *discontinuing* treatment. There's some intuitive appeal to this understanding for the person in a permanent vegetative state. It fits the commonsense notion that if the patient has *no* interests in continued life, then it can't be in his or her *best* interests to continue it.

But even with this sympathetic reading, there's a huge problem with this provision: it allows guardians to make this best interest decision on a case-by-case basis. Yet all permanently vegetative patients share in common their complete lack of experience of benefits and burdens. A best interests calculation, no matter how delineated, should come out exactly the same for these patients across the board. Giving appointed guardians the authority to make this decision only opens the door for the decision to vary not by the qualities inherent in the patient but by the qualities inherent in the decision-makers.

Nevertheless, a lesson can be taken from this unusual provision in Florida law. The statute has, correctly I think, chosen to treat the permanently vegetative patient differently from other types of patients, such as the terminally ill or patients with advanced Alzheimer's or even minimally conscious patients. In particular, the statute recognizes that patients in a permanent vegetative state are not like dying patients: an early decision to treat, left unchecked, may lead to perpetual feeding of patients in a permanent vegetative state when it does not benefit them and it is not what they would want. The provision seems to take into account the limbo that people in a permanent vegetative state could become lost in—years of life without any meaning to the individuals themselves—and to allow a humane end to those lives.

7

QUALITIES
OF LIFE

At the end of the last chapter, I argued that someone who is in a permanent vegetative state should be treated differently from someone who is terminally ill or someone who is minimally conscious. In doing so, I have opened myself to the charge that I endorse "quality-of-life" distinctions—a perspective that disability rights groups decry and a number of courts have cautioned us against.

Why are quality-of-life assessments disturbing? Because when a life or death decision is made based on quality of life, it seems that the decision-maker is saying that the life has no value or too little value. And therefore others should not undergo the cost, the pain, and the trouble associated with keeping the individual alive.

Quality-of-life assessments are not as much of a problem when patients are competent to make decisions for themselves, because if they choose to refuse treatment based on quality of life, it is their own assessment of that quality that is controlling. Of course, the issue is not entirely absent with competent patients, either, because if they are refusing treatment when their prognosis for a healthy life is good, then doctors and others will question their competency— or perhaps merely insist upon a delay in order for them to be talked around to a different point of view. If the prognosis for a healthy life is poor, however, then doctors and others may confirm the wisdom of a patient's decision.

But when patients are incompetent and others are making the decision about life-sustaining treatment, then families, doctors, and courts (in individual cases) and legislators (in setting general legal parameters) are, to some extent, unavoidably, judging the quality of people's lives to determine whether that quality is high enough to be worth the burdens of continued treatment.

With some conditions — such as terminal illness — these are much more complicated issues that I am now suggesting, because the doctor and surrogate also must take into account the chance that treatment will be successful in extending life for some period of time, the risk that the quality of the patient's remaining time will actually be diminished rather than improved by the treatment, and other such factors. But with a condition like the permanent vegetative state or the minimally conscious state or other severe conditions of disability where life might be sustained without much burden to the patient, and yet family members or physicians suggest that treatment be withheld, then what is factored into that decision-making process is much more clearly an assessment of quality of life — whether it is a life worth continuing.

Concerns of this sort spurred disability rights groups to join the side of the Schindlers to prevent removal of Terri Schiavo's feeding tube. In October 2003, twenty-three disability organizations signed onto a joint statement that compared her condition to autism, Down syndrome, and cerebral palsy and argued that the fate of Terri Schiavo was "entwined with all disabled people who rely on surrogates."[1] It denounced the removal of her feeding tube as "death by starvation." In a brief filed in support of "Terri's Law," they claimed that because quality-of-life considerations drove the decision to remove her feeding tube, she could not be "distinguish[ed] from anyone else who is 'incompetent,' including thousands who cannot speak due to developmental or physical disabilities."[2]

Disability rights groups joined the "right to life" interests in the Schiavo case out of what appear to be two primary concerns. First, people with disabilities are often misjudged, their capabilities go unnoticed, and, as a result, they are not adequately appreciated or appropriately treated. The Schindlers' challenge of Terri's diagnosis (their argument that she did respond to those around her) fit with this long-standing disability rights issue. Second, disability rights groups are protective of life support for people with disabilities against those who argue that these lives lack sufficient quality. As they wrote in their brief in support of Terri's Law, "It is naïve to believe such attitudes would not be used to justify the death of people with severe disabilities if the opportunity arose."[3]

To some extent, disability rights groups are correct to be concerned on both these grounds. Studies show that "more abled" people repeatedly express their belief that life with certain kinds of disabilities are not worth living. And these are common disabilities—such as incontinence—that we're talking about, not unconsciousness. In one study, when people were asked whether they would want life-support systems, including artificial nutrition and hydration, withdrawn if they had "an illness that made [them] totally dependent on a family member or other person for all of [their] care," 51 percent said they would want treatment stopped. When asked about the withdrawal of life-support systems in the event they "had a disease with no hope of improvement that made it hard for [them] to function in [their] day-to-day activities," 44 percent said they wanted treatment stopped.[4] These are the everyday conditions of the profoundly mentally disabled—conditions under which many of them embrace life.

Other studies underscore the vast difference in opinion between competent people without disabilities and competent people with severe physical disabilities. One study of health professionals' attitudes revealed that of a group of 153 emergency care providers, only 18 percent imagined they would be glad to be alive with a severe spinal cord injury. A comparison group of 128 persons with high-level spinal cord injuries provided very different results: 92 percent of that group said they were glad to be alive.[5]

Disability rights groups are also concerned about concepts like "dignity" that have become associated with the "right to die" movement. It is not uncommon for courts, in analyzing the claims of competent disabled individuals to a "right to die," to place substantial emphasis on the "indignities" of depending on others for intimate care. For example, the appellate court that declared Washington's ban on physician-assisted suicide unconstitutional suggested that dignity is incompatible with existence in "a childlike state of helplessness, diapered, sedated, incontinent."[6] Similarly, a California appeals court in another case, *Bouvia v. Superior Court*, in recognizing a right to refuse life-sustaining treatment, suggested that the plain-tiff—a competent individual—lacked dignity because she had "to be fed, cleaned, turned, bedded, [and] toileted by others" and to "lie physically helpless subject to the ignominy, embarrassment, humiliation and dehumanizing aspects created by her helplessness."[7] Even the opinion of the Florida Supreme Court in *Bush v. Schiavo* mentions that the nursing home "changes her [Terri's] diapers regularly"—a gratuitous detail that had no bearing on the court's appraisal of the separation-of-powers' infirmities of Terri's Law.[8]

These objective-seeming criteria for dignity are actually quite sub-jective—coming from the subjective view of the competent individual who does not have these characteristics. These are the kinds of characterizations that offend disability groups, and with good reason. The concept of dignity is virtually useless in this context and is probably harmful. It is used indiscriminately to refer to conditions like a permanent vegetative state and conditions that individuals with disabilities live with every day as they lead successful and meaningful lives.

Our instinct is—and should be—to safeguard any advances in the protection of the lives and well-being of all people with disabilities. History is too heavy with the horrors of forced sterilizations, eugenics experiments, and medical neglect and abuse for us not to think very carefully about making quality-of-life decisions for those we judge to lack decision-making capacity. Even today, in every society and in virtually every realm of life, the discrimination against people with disabilities in employment, access, education, and health care is so pervasive that it is tempting to see the struggle for rights as one straightforward push in one invariable direction: more rights protecting life and equal treatment and inclusion. The idea that distinctions might be made between different disabilities adds complications that are simpler to avoid.

Protecting the Profoundly Disabled

On the other hand, can we—should we—equate Terri's condition to that of someone who is profoundly mentally disabled but still interacts with the world? Is it really convincing to say that there is no difference between unconsciousness and some consciousness, however small? Doesn't saying so fail to appreciate the interests that even the profoundly mentally disabled person does have—interests in experiencing care, human relationships, sensory stimulation of some kind or degree? Professor Kenneth Goodman of Miami has coined the term "not abled" to distinguish permanently vegetative patients from those who have some abilities and lack others and are therefore "disabled." To equate the conditions of permanent unconsciousness and profound mental disability not only appears false but seems fundamentally disrespectful to people who are profoundly disabled because it ignores and discounts their abilities to interact meaningfully with other people and their environment.

Sometimes a simple remark from the wrong person at the wrong time can bring things into focus. I found this to be true of a televised statement made in October 2003 by Johnnie Byrd, then the Speaker of the Florida House of Representatives and a supporter of the Florida legislation that allowed Governor Bush to reinsert Terri's feeding tube. In a broadcast of the *NewsHour with Jim Lehrer*, Byrd said that the legislature and citizens of Florida had lost confidence in the legal process because of the "conflicts of interest between the husband and the best interest of this beautiful lady." Clips of videotaped footage of Terri had already been shown and would continue until her death to be repeatedly broadcast on television and widely available on the Internet. In those clips, her face is puffy, her mouth slack, her limbs contorted.[9] When I heard Johnnie Byrd refer to Terri Schiavo as a beautiful lady, the description seemed patronizing and insulting. But why? Was he merely saying that all people are beautiful? And if so, what could be offensive about that?

But Terri Schiavo *had* been a beautiful woman in the way we normally talk about beauty—a vivacious young woman struck down in her prime. And a politician calling her that now, clearly to advance his own political agenda, seemed to deny everything she had lost.

And this, I think, is the key point. People who enter a permanent vegetative state have lost everything. They are not merely profoundly disabled. In fact, if someone profoundly disabled from birth suffered an injury that caused him or her to enter a permanent vegetative state, that person would have lost as much as any competent person who entered a permanent vegetative state has lost. They each would have lost all they had: all cognition and all meaningful sensation they otherwise had. It would be just as tragic for a person with a profound developmental disability to enter a permanent vegetative state as it would be for any single one of us. For each individual, sentient humanity is lost—it is as if the person has for all purposes died but simply failed to take the body along.

In Respect of Living Persons

This does not mean that people in a permanent vegetative state are dead, because they are clearly not. It is true that arguments have been made for a number of decades, by philosopher Robert M. Veatch and others, that they should be considered dead because they have no higher brain function. Under such theories, to be a living person, consciousness or the possibility of future consciousness must be present. An obvious benefit of this proposed redefining of death would be the availability of the bodies of such individuals for organ harvesting.

The argument to redefine death to include people in a permanent vegetative state or others who are permanently unconscious has generally fallen on deaf ears, and for good reason. The biological fact is that those people are breathing on their own, without any ventilator support, and therefore fit just about everybody's idea of what constitutes "living." Moreover, removing the vital organs of such people would clearly cause them to pass into another state—the state we universally understand as death, where respiratory and cardiac function are irreversibly lost. Clearly, efforts to change the legal definition of death to encompass individuals who have no higher brain function are less about defining biological life and death and more about saying that we should exclude certain individuals from the community that matters.

The reality, however, is that for most people, including myself, people in a permanent vegetative state, people like Terri Schiavo, do matter. There may have been wide disagreement among us about what should be done for Terri, but she clearly counted as a person—deserving of our respect—while living in a permanent vegetative state.

Drawing Distinctions

The tougher question is whether we can and should draw a distinction between the permanent vegetative state and other conditions of severe disability in determining what should be done. Disability rights groups say we can't. The law currently says we can, and we do, because we routinely allow the removal of life support, including artificial nutrition and hydration, from patients in a permanent vegetative state but not from people who are profoundly disabled.

The legal rhetoric about this issue is often different from the legal reality; it also varies considerably. Much of the rhetoric in court opinions adopts the disability rights groups' position that distinctions are treacherous. For instance, the Missouri Supreme Court in the *Cruzan* case rejected the idea of a "sliding-scale" approach to the state's interest in protecting life; in other words, they would not put up fewer obstacles to life-support removal when the patient's prognosis was poor. In affirming the Missouri court's decision, the U.S. Supreme Court would describe the state's position with some approval: "We think a State may properly decline to make judgments about the 'quality' of life that a particular individual may enjoy, and simply assert an unqualified interest in the preservation of human life to be weighed against the constitutionally protected interests of the individual."[10] And when the U.S. Supreme Court reversed the Ninth Circuit Court of Appeals' ruling in *Washington v. Glucksberg* on a constitutional right for the terminally ill to physician-assisted suicide, the Court reiterated its approval of states' refusal to grant greater or lesser protection to the lives of those in better or worse conditions of health. The state of Washington "has rejected this sliding-scale approach and, through its assisted-suicide ban, insists that all persons' lives, from beginning to end, regardless of physical or mental condition, are under the full protection of the law."[11]

In contrast, some courts appear more comfortable with the idea that the law should make it easier to withdraw life support when the patient's quality of life appears poor. In the *Quinlan* case, the New Jersey Supreme Court held that the state's interest in continuing an individual's life "weakens and the individual's right to privacy grows as the degree of bodily invasion increases and the prognosis dims."[12] The Ninth Circuit Court of Appeals took a similar position when it recognized a constitutional right to physician-assisted suicide in *Glucksberg* (later reversed by the U.S. Supreme Court). In holding that a ban on physician-assisted suicide was unconstitutional, the Ninth Circuit recognized that the state of Washington did have an interest in protecting life but held that the weight of the state's interest in protecting life depends on the "medical condition and the wishes of the person whose life is at stake."[13]

State statutes, however, are generally less equivocal. There, different treatment for different conditions is often embedded within the very structure of end-of-life procedures. Many of these laws (like Florida's) specify that the patient must be in a specific condition—usually terminal illness or permanent vegetative state—for life support to be withdrawn without fear of liability. In addition, living will forms recommended by state statutes often contain a checklist of the conditions in which the individual wants life-sustaining treatment refused, such as a terminal condition, or "when death is imminent," or a permanent vegetative state. The Florida form would not cover a person in a minimally conscious state or a person who was profoundly disabled.

Courts also treat people who are severely disabled differently than they treat people in a permanent vegetative state or the terminally ill. In the 2001 California case *In re Wendland*, the court found that the conservator (Robert Wendland's wife, acting under California law as a surrogate) failed to prove by clear and convincing evidence that the patient—who was severely brain damaged but not permanently vegetative—wished to refuse life-sustaining treatment or that to withhold such treatment would have been in his best interest. In that case, the court noted that "[i]t is . . . worth mentioning that no decision of which we are aware has approved a conservator's or guardian's proposal to withdraw artificial nutrition and hydration from a conscious conservatee or ward."[14]

In sum, the law does treat withdrawal of life support from someone in a permanent vegetative state differently than it does for someone with a profound mental disability. It is generally permitted in the case of the permanently vegetative patient and is not, unless the treatment is burdensome, in the case of a person with a profound mental disability. The "slippery slope" fears of disability rights groups do not appear to be justified, at least at this time. The law does not sanction the withholding or withdrawal of artificial nutrition and hydration from individuals with severe mental disabilities simply because they lack certain abilities.

Being Used

As I stated in chapter 6, I think an even sharper distinction should be drawn between the permanent vegetative state and profound disability, terminal illness, or any other condition. My concern is that continued tube-feeding of people in a permanent vegetative state, unless they have indicated their wish to be fed in these circumstances, cannot be justified as an action taken in their interest. Rather, such feeding is done in the interests of others—whether for politicians, or loved ones, or certain members of the medical profession who believe feeding is morally required, or society in general.

The result is that the person in a permanent vegetative state becomes an object or instrument. In the Schiavo controversy, this was taken to an extreme—to patent exploitation. Photographs and videotapes of Terri's slack mouth and vacant expression were broadcast repeatedly on television and could be seen at any time, by anyone, over the Internet. These images look nothing like the woman she used to be. While they were offered by her parents in their fight to keep her alive, the broadcast of these images demonstrates quite tragically that Terri was being used for others' purposes rather than being treated as a person deserving of respect and privacy. The congressional attempt in March 2005 to issue a subpoena for Terri's "testimony" before a congressional committee and the sensational offers by private individuals of millions of dollars to Terri's husband to relinquish guardianship to her parents are of the same ilk. Could it really have been supposed that her public display in a congressional carnival would have counted as testimony? Could her life or death have been auctioned to the highest bidder?

These actions were justified as being for Terri's benefit. But there was no benefit to her in continued living. She could not feel, see, hear, taste, smell, perceive, think, or experience life in any way, nor had she been able to for fifteen years, nor was there any realistic hope that she would ever again. Nor had she made it clear, prior to entering her state of permanent unconsciousness, that she would want to continue living in such condition—perhaps to hold out hope of a cure, however slim, or because she believed a good afterlife required it, or for any other personally held hopes, beliefs, or principles. Our society was neither being benevolent nor respecting her right to self-determination when we continued to tube-feed her. Instead, she was kept alive for others' benefit and on the basis of their hopes, beliefs, or principles.

Terri's case was unusual in its level of public exploitation. But other cases, quiet cases, cases we've never heard of, also involve a use of patients in a permanent vegetative state for others' purposes—because they are not realistically being kept alive for their own benefit. Removing the presumption in favor of perpetual tube-feeding would in those cases treat the person in a permanent vegetative state *as a person* as opposed to a mere object to be kept alive solely for others' benefit.

Treating people as ends in themselves and never as mere means to others' ends has both ancient (Aristotle) and modern (Kant) philosophical exponents and is a foundational assumption of American jurisprudence. In fact, the reason a number of scholars who advocate taking the organs of people in a permanent vegetative state argue that such individuals are dead is to work around this fundamental prohibition against using a person solely as an instrument for others.

People like Terri Schiavo, who are permanently unconscious, should be treated as the living persons they are. In respecting them, we should honor their prior capacity for self-determination and follow their wishes regarding continued medical treatment (including artificial sustenance), if they can be determined. But if there is not sufficient evidence that the individual would want to continue living in a permanent vegetative state, the assumption should be that after a certain period of time, tube-feeding would be discontinued.

Experience as an Interest in Life

The argument that people in a permanent vegetative state have no significant interest in continued living is not new. A number of commentators have recognized this point because of the severely diminished ability to process experience to the point that any perceptive responses they might have are without appreciable cognitive value. They have lost what some call "experiential interests." This lack of experiential interests is what makes the condition of the permanent vegetative state unique and calls for appropriately unique ethical and legal consideration.

Sometimes, in the more theoretical of discussions about patients' interests at the end of life, a distinction is made between experiential interests, which people in a permanent vegetative state do not have, and other interests that a patient, even a patient in a permanent vegetative state, may have. Arguments have been made that these other sorts of interests should be factored into a decision of whether or not to continue life-prolonging treatment. For example, in his book *Life's Dominion*, philosopher Ronald Dworkin agrees that people in a permanent vegetative state have no "experiential" interests, but he argues that they may nevertheless have "critical" interests — interests that their lives as a whole be successful according to certain critical judgments that they as individuals once possessed. For example, a person may believe that a successful life includes being remembered as an independent, alert, dignified person. Forgoing life-prolonging treatments in a state of dependency may be in keeping with that earlier judgment. Another person may believe that a successful life would entail staying alive with "the virtue of defiance in the face of inevitable death."[15] The critical interests of the latter person may be respected by continuing, rather than forgoing, life-prolonging treatment.

Philosophers Allen E. Buchanan and Dan W. Brock have identified a similar way of looking at the interests of people in a permanent vegetative state that are not limited to experiential interests. They say that some people, prior to entering a vegetative state, may have "had certain future-oriented interests which will be satisfied or thwarted depending on what happens to him or her after becoming permanently unconscious."[16] For example, according to Buchanan and Brock, a person may have an interest in being sustained in a permanent vegetative state for some time because of religious values.

In my view, non-experiential interests of the "critical" or "future-oriented" sort are important but are better understood as patient wishes rather than interests per se. Evidence of the views the patient may have had about life in a permanent vegetative state should be brought to bear on a surrogate's decision about whether continued feeding is in accordance with or contrary to the wishes of the patient.

But I would caution against making generalizations about what people's critical or future-oriented interests may be. There may be a temptation to consider interests in dignity, for example, or interests in being remembered in a pre-disability state as so common and universally possessed that we should consider existence in a permanent vegetative state itself as a burden in respect to these interests. In other words, some scholars, like Norman L. Cantor, would argue that there are burdens associated with the continued life of a person in a permanent vegetative state—burdens of humiliation, dependence, and indignity.[17] The patient has an interest, under this argument, in avoiding these burdens by dying.

Admittedly, there is something compelling to this line of argument, and (again) if we are trying to figure out what patients would want if they could now tell us, these might be some of the things they would say. But the absence of beneficial experience alone should be enough to discontinue life-prolonging treatment for people in a permanent vegetative state unless there is sufficient evidence of their contrary wishes. It is enough because if tube-feeding is not done to benefit the patients who are fed, then it is done to benefit others, and that is an unacceptable instrumental use of those individuals. Understanding people in a permanent vegetative state as being burdened by an artificially extended life is, by contrast, an approach that could apply just as well to those who are severely disabled but conscious and opens the door to a set of objections that we don't have to face in treatment questions about the permanently vegetative.

Two very difficult issues are embedded in end-of-life decision making about the severely disabled that support a more cautious approach to discontinuing treatment for such individuals than for patients in a permanent vegetative state. First, a decision to terminate life-sustaining treatment for a severely disabled individual may involve, or may be perceived as involving, unacceptable judgments about the quality and value of the person's life vis-à-vis his or her abilities. Concerns expressed about a life without dignity in a permanent vegetative state also suggest an inhospitableness toward dependency in general, with potentially negative consequences toward those who are dependent, even in less burdensome ways.

Second, if a decision to terminate treatment is made on the basis of the individual's living will or other pre-disability statements about the undesirability of continued life in a certain condition, then the individual's pre-disability *autonomy* might be given preferential weight over the individual's post-disability *interests*, and it is not at all clear that this should be so.[18] With the terminally ill, this trumping of "critical interests" (like autonomy) over "experiential interests" (like pain and pleasure) has become fairly accepted, as long as present interests in comfort are maintained. In other words, life-sustaining treatment might be removed from a patient with only a few weeks to live on the basis of his formerly expressed wishes, even though he still retains some level of consciousness and might be said to benefit from continued life. But we do not generally allow withdrawal of life-sustaining treatment from the severely disabled who are not terminally ill, unless the treatment itself causes suffering. There is more at stake in these cases—more life would be forgone. In such cases, a surrogate's decision to forgo treatment is much more problematic, even when based upon the patient's expressed wishes when competent, because the individual can experience some benefits in living and is not going to die soon anyway.

Protecting People with Profound Disabilities

Disability rights groups in the Schiavo case chose not to acknowledge any distinction between the permanent vegetative state and profound mental disability. My disagreement with that position on the merits is clear. But I also worry that it may have been a poor move strategically, if the aim—as it surely must have been—was to protect people with profound disabilities. My worry is that by blurring the line between the permanently vegetative and the profoundly disabled, disability groups may be jeopardizing existing legal protection for the profoundly disabled. If the American public is confused about the difference between these conditions, it is not clear to me that the ultimate outcome would be more life support for the permanently vegetative: it may be instead *less* life support for the profoundly disabled. Firm in their belief that the permanent vegetative state is intolerable and told that the permanent vegetative state is not very different from profound disability, the American public might, for example, wish to *add* to the categories of conditions receiving legal sanction for treatment refusals. One possibility would be to add "minimal consciousness" to the types of conditions identified by state statutes as those in which treatment withdrawal may occur by surrogate decision making. This, of course, was the condition that the Schindlers, in the later years of the Schiavo controversy, claimed that Terri was in. The evidence presented in court was clearly otherwise, but for some Americans, the specificity of the diagnosis may not have mattered much—what they saw was a condition for which they approved removal of the feeding tube.

In my view, if disability groups wish to protect the profoundly disabled from the withdrawal or withholding of life support, then they should seek to preserve and emphasize the distinction between a loss of conscious capacity to experience life and some conscious experiences. They should highlight the fact that for people with profound disabilities who are not permanently unconscious, there are benefits to continued living—rich and meaningful benefits.

Moreover, the capacity of the profoundly disabled, in the main, to experience and benefit from human relationships means that disability groups should educate the public about the importance of and value in establishing relationships with people with profound disabilities. Despite the campaign of misinformation feeding the media about her condition—such as the few seconds of videotape that appeared to show Terri Schiavo responding to her mother's presence—Terri no longer experienced a conscious relationship with her mother. (This does not mean that visiting with those in a permanently vegetative state is useless—we should acknowledge the real and important benefit that visiting provides for the visitor.) But for people with profound disabilities, the care and concern that others show for them is experienced in conscious ways and should be encouraged.

In all cases, respect and care are due to those who cannot speak for themselves in the same measure, or more, than it is given to everyone else. All people are due privacy, and all have a right to be considered for their own value as human beings, not for their value to others. I believe that we should continue to steer away from judging the quality of any other person's life by his or her abilities in ways that reduce the rights of the most vulnerable among us. In seeking fairer application of the right of those in a permanently vegetative state to refuse treatment (through surrogate decision-makers too), I am not saying that these individuals have nothing of value to contribute to the world; I'm saying instead that there is no value to *themselves* in continuing to live. I don't question whether Mary Schindler ought to have held Terri's hand; I only question whether Terri should have been kept alive once it became clear that Mary was the only one who could enjoy the benefits of it.

8 FEEDING

Throughout this book, artificial nutrition and hydration has been referred to as "life support" or "life-sustaining treatment" or a "life-prolonging procedure" that might be refused under the same rules as other forms of medical treatment. This reflects an ethical and legal consensus that has existed for at least two decades or more. But for many people, artificial nutrition and hydration is different. Some of those who protested the removal of Terri Schiavo's feeding tube did so not because they believed that Michael Schiavo was misrepresenting her wishes or that Terri had some degree of consciousness but because they believed that food or water should never be withheld from anyone. To fail to feed is to fail to care, in this view, and is an unacceptable way for human beings to treat one another.

Pope John Paul II made a statement on this issue in the spring of 2004 that substantially elevated attention to the ethical questions involved and challenged the consensus view. The pope's address to participants in the International Congress on Life-Sustaining Treatments and Vegetative State included the following:

> The sick person in a vegetative state, awaiting recovery or a natural end, still has the right to basic health care (nutrition, hydration, cleanliness, warmth, etc.), and to the prevention of complications related to his confinement to bed. He also has the right to appropriate rehabilitative care and to be monitored for clinical signs of eventual recovery.
>
> I should like particularly to underline how the administration of water and food, even when provided by artificial means, always represents a *natural means* of preserving life, not a *medical act*. Its

use, furthermore, should be considered, in principle, *ordinary* and *proportionate*, and as such morally obligatory.[1]

At the time, the policy of many Catholic hospitals in the United States had been to allow family members more discretion than this statement suggested with respect to the withdrawal of artificial nutrition and hydration—both for patients in a permanent vegetative state and for other patients. Withdrawal was permitted under the general church policy that artificial nutrition and hydration, like other forms of life support, can be withdrawn from incompetent patients when continued treatment is disproportionately burdensome to the patient or—in contrast to most U.S. law, which does not allow explicit consideration of the interests of the family—disproportionately burdensome to the patient's family. The pope's statement called these prevailing practices into question, and U.S. Catholic organizations scrambled to understand what it should mean for them.

Because of this uncertainty—and the claim of some scholars and theologians that the pope's statement was a departure from past church doctrine—the U.S. Conference of Bishops asked for clarification from the Vatican. The response, approved in August 2007 by Pope Benedict XVI (the successor to Pope John Paul II, who died in 2005), confirmed the earlier pope's 2004 statement. "Question: Was the administration of artificial nutrition and hydration to a patient in a 'vegetative state' morally obligatory? Answer: Yes. . . . Question: May it be discontinued when competent physicians determine that the patient will never recover consciousness? Answer: No."[2]

These sentiments, expressed at the height of national debate over Terri Schiavo's fate and then confirmed one and a half years later, have had more of an influence in framing the discussions about artificial nutrition and hydration than we might expect in a pluralistic society that, as a constitutional matter, honors the principle of separation of church and state. There are a number of reasons for this unusual influence. For one, the Catholic Church—more so than other dominant religious organizations—has for years been at the forefront of and deeply involved in sophisticated discussion and writing about end-of-life treatment decisions and bioethics generally. Second, the Schindlers are Catholic and so was Terri Schiavo, even if she was not a regular churchgoer. Finally, the pope seemed to say, at just the right time during the Schiavo controversy, from a position of some moral authority and in accessible and unambiguous terms, what a lot of the American public found troubling about the Schiavo case. The statement that artificial nutrition and hydration was "basic care" had a simple emotional and moral appeal.

What are we to make of the argument that feeding is basic care and should be subject to different rules in end-of-life decision making? On the whole, I think the introduction of notions of care into debates about end-of-life treatment is very positive. The traditional framing of these issues as the preservation of life versus the patient's self-determination has left out emphasis on care as an essential duty we owe to all patients. Certainly, care has not been absent in the treatment of patients in a permanent vegetative state or patients in a terminal condition. But it has been conspicuously absent, or present only at the margins, in *legal discussions* of what should be done in particular cases or of what rules should govern those decisions.

But going from a duty of care to a perpetual obligation to provide artificial nutrition and hydration is a leap. There's an assumption here that "basic care" means something that we all know and understand. Merely labeling something as "basic care" does not make it so, nor does it explain what the label is intended to mean. What are the impetus, motivations, and ultimate goals of the provision of basic care? And how do these relate to the patient in a permanent vegetative state?

In deciding whether something is required as "care," we should look not only at the ends it achieves (such as prolongation of life) but at how the individual receives or perceives the treatment that is given—*whether it is taken in as care or not*. For severely disabled yet conscious patients, an awareness of the feeding, even if done through a tube, may still be care, if they can positively experience the satiation or the attention, or if, in its absence, they can experience the want of food and water. But when feeding cannot be experienced as care, either because it is burdensome because the body cannot absorb it or because the patient has permanently lost consciousness, then it is no different from other forms of treatment that might be rejected. For Terri Schiavo, feeding was not experienced as care, for she was consciously unaware that she was being fed or that she had been fed, nor could she experience a want of these.

Even if we might consider feeding to be basic care, not because of the *experience* of feeding in and of itself but because of the *end* it produces—continuation of life—there are difficulties with this that are unique to the permanently vegetative patient. We may well think that feeding is required for someone in a coma even though they cannot experience such feeding as care because for that person, there may be some possibility of recovery. Feeding perpetuates the life of the comatose person with the possibility that life may once again be experienced. But in the case of the permanently vegetative patient, there is virtually no possibility of a life that will ever be experienced again.

Lack of the ability to experience care does not mean, however, that we are relieved of other duties for *appropriate* care. Permanently vegetative patients should be kept clean and presentable and free of bedsores, even though they would not know the difference, even though they would not benefit in terms of any experience. We owe people living in a permanently vegetative state respect for their appearance and for their bodily integrity.

The Meanings of Medical Treatment

While I don't think tube-feeding someone in a permanent vegetative state is required care, I also question the insistence in much legal argument that feeding by tube is an "artificial" means of prolonging life that must be understood as "medical treatment" if we are to allow its withdrawal. In court opinions and state end-of-life statutes, however, these are the kinds of characterizations that rule the day: emphasis is placed on the medical intrusiveness of the apparatus that delivers the nutrition and hydration; the fact that what is delivered is essential sustenance is de-emphasized. For example, in her concurring opinion in the *Cruzan* case, Justice Sandra Day O'Connor took pains to explain the medical aspects of Nancy Cruzan's feeding tube:

> The artificial delivery of nutrition and hydration is undoubtedly medical treatment. The technique to which Nancy Cruzan is subject—artificial feeding through a gastrostomy tube—involves a tube implanted surgically into her stomach through incisions in her abdominal wall. It may obstruct the intestinal tract, erode and pierce the stomach wall, or cause leakage of the stomach's contents into the abdominal cavity. The tube can cause pneumonia from reflux of the stomach's contents into the lung. Typically, and in this case, commercially prepared formulas are used, rather than fresh food. The type of formula and method of administration must be experimented with to avoid gastrointestinal problems. The patient must be monitored daily by medical personnel as to weight, fluid intake, and fluid output; blood tests must be done weekly. Artificial delivery of food and water is regarded as medical treatment by the medical profession and the Federal Government. . . . The Federal Government permits the cost of the medical devices and formulas used in enteral feeding to be reimbursed under Medicare. The formulas are regulated by the federal Food and Drug Administration as "medical foods" and the feeding tubes are regulated as medical devices.[3]

Other legal opinions that have explained why tube-feeding is properly understood as medical treatment have focused, like Justice O'Connor's concurrence, on the following characteristics of such feeding: the invasiveness of the procedure to insert the tubes; the inherent risks and side effects; the need for special personnel and training and special nutritional formulations; and coverage by insurance.

Those advocating the removal of Terri Schiavo's feeding tube likewise emphasized that it was a form of medical treatment. Kenneth Goodman of the University of Miami Ethics Programs has written that using the term "feeding tube" instead of PEG tube to describe the device whose removal was the subject of the Schiavo dispute is a mistake. According to him, "[T]oo many of us [bioethicists] called them 'feeding tubes,' making it sound as if removing one were like snatching a spoon out of your mouth."[4]

While I agree with much of what Goodman has said about the Schiavo case, on this point I disagree. The tube whose removal Michael Schiavo sought and the Schindlers protested was delivering nutrition and hydration—the equivalent of food and water—because Terri could not take in these necessities of life any other way. We don't need to deny or avoid what was at issue. We can't simply think that what this case involved was removing *any* sort of unwanted, intrusive medical device. That medical device was keeping Terri Schiavo alive by delivering her the equivalent of food and water.

In any event, does it matter so much anyway whether it is medical treatment or not? Isn't what's important—for purposes of honoring a patient's bodily integrity—whether it is wanted or not?

Hand-Feeding

Some of the cases that have upheld the right to withhold or withdraw artificial nutrition and hydration have defined it at least in part by reference to what it is presumably *not*, which is feeding by hand. For example, in the case of In re Estate of Longeway, the Illinois Supreme Court said that there was agreement among the states that allow the withholding of artificial nutrition and hydration that such feeding is "medical treatment and therefore analytically distinguishable from spoon-feeding or bottle-feeding." Similarly, some state laws clearly define artificial nutrition and hydration as that provided through means other than by mouth, such as through tubes, catheters, or needles.[5]

The assumption of the court in the case of In re Estate of Longeway, and the message of these state statutes, is that while patients have a right to refuse medical treatment (and therefore tube-feeding because it is medical treatment), they do not have a right to refuse feeding by hand. Yet it is not at all clear that this is a valid assumption, and further examination of the issue of hand-feeding as it arose in the Schiavo case reveals certain insights into how we should view tube-feeding as well.

To be clear about the Schiavo situation, it is extremely doubtful that Terri could have been sustained through hand-feeding, although her parents sought—and were denied—this option when her feeding tube was removed. In the early years following Terri's collapse, when Michael Schiavo aggressively pursued various therapies for her, Terri underwent several rounds of swallowing tests and swallowing therapy. She was also annually evaluated with respect to any capacity to take food by mouth. All of the tests and attempted therapies proved unsuccessful. We do not know definitively, however, whether she might have been able to take some amount of food orally. The late Dr. Ronald Cranford, a renowned expert on the vegetative state and one of the physicians who examined Terri and testified about her condition, explained that patients in a vegetative state "usually retain an intact swallowing reflex and thus can swallow to some degree in an involuntary, reflex fashion." This explains why Terri could handle her own secretions, which some of the affidavits filed by physicians on behalf of the Schindlers erroneously identified as incompatible with the vegetative state. Cranford concluded that "[i]t is possible (but highly unlikely) that, with a great deal of attention and care, and an understanding of how to optimize swallowing by using the involuntary swallowing reflex, Terri's nutritional and hydration needs could be maintained by the oral route. . . . But such an undertaking is medically inadvisable, as it would greatly increase the risk of aspiration pneumonia and death."[6]

In 2003, Jay Wolfson, in an attempt to help resolve the dispute between Michael Schiavo and the Schindlers (and, at this point, Governor Jeb Bush as well), recommended that Terri Schiavo once again be given swallowing tests and swallowing therapy. One implication of this recommendation—although Wolfson did not explicitly state this—seemed to be that if Terri could swallow and therefore take food by mouth, the feeding tube's removal would be less of an issue. The feeding tube could then be removed, in accordance with Terri's proven wishes to withhold medical treatment in such circumstances (as Florida law provides and as Michael Schiavo requested), *and* Terri could have continued living (as her parents wished). Wolfson, in fact, attempted to mediate this solution between Michael Schiavo and the Schindlers, but according to his report, those efforts were ultimately unsuccessful. Judge George Greer also declined to follow Wolfson's recommendation to order swallowing tests and therapy and later denied a separate similar motion by the Schindlers. The judge's refusal was based on the unsuccessful tests in the past and on the risk to Terri that such tests and therapy would cause her to aspirate into the lungs with the accompanying complications of pneumonia. Judge Greer also viewed these motions as further attempts at delay.

Yet even if Terri Schiavo could have been fed by mouth, the controversy would have been no closer to resolution; instead, we would have before us another set of difficult questions to confront—namely, does a person have a right to refuse food by mouth? If so, does that right exist for people who have become incompetent, as we normally do not think that incompetency warrants a forfeiture of rights? How could the right be exercised? Would there be any limitations on the right?

Some may argue that, in some cases, hand-feeding is "artificial" and "medical treatment" for the same reasons that tube-feeding is so. For example, in a case such as Terri's, hand-feeding would basically have required the careful forcing of food down her throat, if her body could be made to reflexively swallow. It would have been invasive, carried the inherent risk of aspiration pneumonia, required either special personnel or special training of caregivers, required special nutritional formulations, and likely been covered by insurance. It would not resemble the more typical image of hand-feeding, a bowl of chicken soup spoon-fed to an ailing patient who is able to open his or her mouth to receive it.

The answer to the question of how to consider feeding by hand is not to be found, however, in likening it to or distinguishing it from medical treatment or tube-feeding. The underlying basis for the constitutional, common law, and moral right to refuse tube-feeding is not dependent upon whether it is medical treatment but on the fact that tube-feeding against the patient's will is an intrusion into the bodily integrity of the individual. Unconsented-to medical treatment is a battery, in common law terms, and a violation of one's liberty interests in constitutional terms. The critical issue is not whether a particular "touching" or "intrusion" is "medical treatment," although describing something as medical treatment has become shorthand for explaining why these intrusions can be refused. The primary issue instead is whether the touching is unwanted. This conclusion is borne out by the precedents that the Supreme Court relied upon in the Cruzan case when it assumed that people had a constitutional right to refuse life-sustaining treatment. The focus of these precedent cases was not medical treatment but unwanted intrusions upon the body, including cases concerning government-imposed vaccinations and searches and seizures of a person. In fact, the Court even began its discussion of the constitutional right to avoid unwanted medical treatment with the statement, "At common law, even the touching of one person by another without consent and without legal justification was a battery."[7] The Court quoted an 1891 case that stated, "No right is held more sacred, or is more carefully guarded, by the common law, than the right of every individual to the possession and control of his own person, free from all restraint or interference of others, unless by clear and unquestionable authority of law."[8] It is this "notion of bodily integrity" that, the Cruzan court told us, "has been embodied in the requirement that informed consent is generally required for medical treatment."[9] The court further quoted Justice Benjamin Cardozo's famous line from a 1914 New York case: "Every human being of adult years and sound mind has a right to determine what shall be done with his own body."[10]

But if the issue is not one of medical treatment versus other kinds of treatment and is instead about unwanted intrusions on a person's body, then unwanted hand-feeding can also be a violation of one's right to bodily integrity and should be just as easily rejected by a competent patient. In fact, noted philosopher Bernard Gert together with medical doctors James L. Bernat and R. Peter Mogielnicki argued over a decade ago that a medically, morally, and legally superior alternative to physician-assisted suicide for competent patients was simply to refuse feeding. These coauthors wrote, "[E]ducating chronically and terminally ill patients about the feasibility of patient refusal of hydration and nutrition (PRHN) can empower them to control their own destiny without requiring physicians to reject the taboos on PAS [physician-assisted suicide] and VAE [voluntary active euthanasia] that have existed for millennia."[11] A group today, called Caring Advocates, urges those who wish to do so to take advantage of their right to voluntarily refuse food and fluid as a means of hastening death.[12]

But what about patients who have lost the capacity to decide for themselves anymore? We usually assume that if a form of treatment can be rejected by a competent patient, then an incompetent patient can also reject it, through his or her surrogate or through a living will, as long as the patient's wishes are clear. Yet there may be reasons to treat hand-feeding differently from tube-feeding when patients are no longer competent even though our current legal standards for refusing unwanted treatment don't appear to delineate any. The thought of not attempting to hand-feed an elderly patient with dementia is more disturbing than not placing a feeding tube in his or her stomach—even if both forms of treatment were clearly rejected in a duly executed living will and the surrogate confirms this as the patient's wishes. Why is this so?

First, well-meaning caregivers ought to be given some latitude to care for patients according to the specific situation they encounter—just as we might insist that caregivers be allowed to preserve the hygiene of the patient (although not to a burdensome degree), we might insist that caregivers be allowed to offer food in the form of hand-feeding to a person who experiences hunger. Second, hand-feeding might be experienced as comfort care by the patient in ways that tube-feeding is not, either in the social relationship established through the process of hand-feeding or through the pleasurable sensation of taking in food. Finally, and perhaps most important, patients may indicate that they desire hand-feeding by appearing interested in food, by opening their mouths, and so on, so that we might say that these present actions trump their earlier declarations, or we might say that they are not presently incapable of making the decision to consume food, and so their living wills or the surrogates' instructions are not operative on that point.

Of these three concerns, only the first might have been relevant in Terri Schiavo's case, because even if she had been a candidate for hand-feeding, she could neither experience the intake of food nor indicate a desire for it. That would leave only concern for her caregivers to weigh against her desire (as expressed by her surrogate and accepted as proven by the court) not to continue living in her present condition. As between the two, law and ethics clearly direct us to respect her self-determination over the interests of her caregivers.

I would say, then, that even if Terri Schiavo could have been fed by mouth, that she should not have been. If her wish would be to not continue living in a permanent vegetative state, and thus to reject treatment that prolonged her life in that state, then her wish should not be overridden by society's and her caregivers' feelings about their duties to feed her.

An important part of this analysis, though, depends upon the fact that Terri was in a permanent vegetative state. The question addressed in this chapter is simply whether feeding should be considered different from other forms of treatment. When other forms of life support (like a ventilator or antibiotics) can be removed, can feeding also be removed? With the permanent vegetative state, the law allows the removal of these other life-support mechanisms; there is no reason to treat tube-feeding (or hand-feeding, for that matter) differently. As Cranford wrote about Terri, "The overwhelming fact is that, whether Terri is fed via a PEG tube or fed orally, she is still in a permanent vegetative state, and the manner of feeding her will not result in any change in her clinical condition."[13]

Refusing Feeding versus Avoiding Certain Conditions

The possibility that a person might have a right to refuse hand-feeding reveals some uncertainty in the foundation of the legal right to refuse treatment. That foundation so far has been built primarily upon notions of bodily integrity rather than on a broader principle of protecting important, uniquely personal decisions or "self-determination." And a right to reject hand-feeding, as we've seen, might also be justified on this basis, if we see hand-feeding as an unwanted forcing or coaxing of food through the lips. But what would a living will that rejected hand-feeding realistically be saying? It would not be saying, "I reject the intrusion on my body imposed by caregivers offering to spoon-feed me." Instead, its real intention would be more accurately expressed as, "If I end up in condition x, I want to die."

If, as this example illustrates, the right to refuse treatment should actually be seen as based on making important personal decisions rather than on merely making decisions about intrusions of one's bodily integrity, then the right looks more like a broad "right to die"—which the Supreme Court, at least, has resisted. When the Court rejected a constitutional right to physician-assisted suicide in *Washington v. Glucksberg*, it explained that the *Cruzan* decision, at most, stood for the proposition that there was a right to refuse bodily intrusions, not a right to determine the circumstances of one's death.

Consideration of the issue of hand-feeding, however, renders this reasoning questionable, because the method of death is revealed as less important than the avoidance of life in certain conditions. Rejecting a constitutional right to physician-assisted suicide may still be appropriate, but a new explanation for that rejection would be needed. (Some commentators, for example, argue against physician-assisted suicide because they fear it would erode patient trust in the physician's role as healer or because of concerns that vulnerable populations, like the elderly or people with severe disabilities, would be coerced into hastening their deaths.)

Understanding the right to refuse treatment as grounded in a broader right to make important personal decisions (rather than as simply growing out of our right to bodily integrity) could have substantial implications as a matter of constitutional law. This shift would also mean that it would be less important to know *what kind of treatment* a patient would wish to refuse and more important to know *what kinds of conditions* they would wish to avoid, even if avoiding them meant death.

Unfounded Fears

But this is exactly the opposite direction that policy-makers seem interested in going. As discussed earlier, the legislation proposed in many states in the wake of the Schiavo case focused on *kinds of treatment* — artificial nutrition and hydration, in particular, proposing stricter rules for refusing this kind of treatment.

Ironically, though, while the legislative proposals seemed to spring from concern that artificial nutrition and hydration is basic care that should always be provided (as evidenced by politicians decrying the "starvation" of vulnerable patients), the justification for them has usually been stated not in terms of care but in terms of respecting choice. Supporters of these proposals express concern that artificial nutrition and hydration not be removed from a patient unless we are certain that that is what the patient would want. But to impose a stricter standard on this basis — on the basis of protecting patient *choice* — we would have to have reason to believe that surrogates are more likely to be mistaken about individuals' decisions regarding nutrition and hydration than they are about decisions regarding other life-sustaining treatments. In fact, since the bias of these proposals is toward providing nutrition and hydration, the concern must be that nutrition and hydration will be withdrawn contrary to the wishes of the patient.

Legislative proposals imposing stricter requirements for withholding or withdrawing tube-feeding have it backwards, however. Surrogates are more likely to insert or continue a feeding tube for a patient when that is *not* what he or she would want.

Recent studies back this up. They show that feeding tubes are often used when they do not benefit the patients who receive them. For example, for patients with advanced dementia, survival rates do not appear to increase with the use of artificial nutrition and hydration.[14] And in some circumstances, feeding tubes increase rather than decrease the discomfort of dying patients because of the body's physical inability to tolerate the nutrition provided. Patients with advanced dementia receiving nutrition and hydration through a PEG tube face "an increased risk of aspiration pneumonia, diarrhea, gastrointestinal discomfort, and problems associated with feeding-tube removal by the patient."[15] Patients with advanced dementia may also have to be physically restrained so that they will not pull out their feeding tubes, adding to the discomfort and disorientation of these patients.

It is not surprising, then, that while family members of patients with advanced dementia tend to authorize a feeding tube, they later regret that decision as it becomes burdensome to the patient. These same family members say they would not want a feeding tube if they found themselves in similar circumstances.[16]

Family members may agree to a feeding tube in part because physicians are more likely to suggest feeding tubes for patients than other forms of life-sustaining treatment. Family members often report feeling left out of the decision-making process, as though they have no alternative but to consent to tube-feeding. Many surrogates are also initially biased toward providing nutrition and hydration because of their own perceived role in caring for their relative or loved one or because of their religious beliefs that sustenance should never be withheld. As we witnessed with the Schindlers, family members often state that they cannot let a relative "starve to death." As mentioned above, of course, these attitudes commonly change over time as the ramifications of the feeding tube become clearer.[17]

There does not appear to be any solid basis for believing that most surrogates will seek to withdraw or withhold a feeding tube when the patient for whom they speak would wish otherwise. A number of studies reveal that a very high percentage of people, about 70 to 85 percent, would wish to refuse a feeding tube if they were in a permanent vegetative state or an end-stage condition or suffered severe brain damage. In a study of randomly selected, competent nursing home residents, only one-third said they would want a feeding tube if they became unable to eat because of permanent brain damage. This number of positive responses was reduced by a fourth when the participants learned that they might need to be physically restrained to accommodate the feeding tube and would likely have been reduced even more if they had been informed about growing evidence of the lack of efficacy of such tubes for patients with advanced dementia.[18]

Pain and Suffering

What about the charge that dying of dehydration is painful? (A person who dies after the withdrawal of a feeding tube typically dies of dehydration rather than malnutrition.)

Of course, dying in this way would not be painful to someone in a permanent vegetative state like Terri Schiavo, who could not feel pain or even experience thirst or hunger. This truth did not stop congressional leaders, like former representative Tom DeLay, from admonishing his fellow legislators to act quickly and pass federal legislation to save Terri because, "[f]or 58 long hours, her mouth has been parched, and her—and her hunger pains have been throbbing. If we do not act, she will die of thirst. However helpless, Mr. Speaker, she is alive."[19]

But even for someone who is terminally ill or in the advanced stages of dementia, dying by dehydration does not appear to be experienced negatively. There are numerous reports that such patients do not experience much, if any, discomfort.[20] Hospice nurses report that patients who stop eating or drinking experience a comfortable and peaceful death. Any thirst the patients might experience is relieved by the use of ice chips and mouth swabs.[21]

In any event, in order to justify closer scrutiny of decisions to withdraw nutrition and hydration on this basis, we would need evidence (which we do not have) that dying of dehydration is more painful than dying from the withdrawal of other life-prolonging treatments—more painful, for example, than dying of untreated pneumonia or respiratory, cardiac, or renal failure. When we remove a ventilator from a patient, we understand that the patient may die, but we do not say that we are causing him or her to suffocate to death; when we remove dialysis, we do not say we are poisoning the patient. Statements that Terri Schiavo was starved to death, or even "dehydrated to death," are likewise inflammatory, suggesting a lack of care that was not true.

For most people who enter a permanent vegetative state, being kept alive under such circumstances would be against their wishes. As with other forms of life support, tighter restrictions on surrogate decision making for nutrition and hydration would mean that such wishes would be less likely, rather than more likely, to be honored. And, of course, the greater likelihood of error in reflecting patient preferences would have especially profound consequences for someone in a permanent vegetative state, whose life may be extended for decades against his or her wishes.

But, as we've seen, concern for patient preferences does not really appear to lie at the heart of proposals to make it more difficult for surrogates to withhold or withdraw feeding from their loved ones. Instead, the concern is for the preservation of all life. More clearly perhaps than other types of treatment, the removal of artificial nutrition and hydration results in certain death. When a ventilator or other medical device or treatment is withdrawn, there is always the possibility, even if remote, that the body will spontaneously recover or perform the function that the device was performing artificially. But that is not the case for a patient who cannot take food orally; when artificial nutrition and hydration are withdrawn, the body will inevitably, after some period of time—one to two weeks—expire. This goal—of preserving life at all costs—requires further examination and will be addressed in the following chapter.

When Feeding Causes Suffering

One final point, however, should be made about proposals to require a feeding tube unless the patient has executed a living will. While feeding tubes can sometimes satisfy the goal of prolonging life, at times the bit of extra life achieved is purchased at significantly increased pain and suffering. And people who cannot execute a living will, such as people who have been profoundly disabled since birth or childhood, would be at particular risk of this outcome.

Consider again the case of Sheila Pouliot, the terminally ill, profoundly disabled woman whose life was inappropriately extended by the provision of artificial nutrition and hydration because New York law appeared at the time to require it (or so the attorney general's office insisted). As an infant, Pouliot had contracted a severe case of mumps that left her profoundly retarded as well as physically disabled; she could not walk or even eat. When she was forty-two years old, she was admitted to the hospital because of gastrointestinal bleeding and abdominal pain. Physicians advised Pouliot's sister, her closest competent family member, that this was likely Pouliot's final illness. She could no longer tolerate feeding through her gastronomy tube.

Upon the advice of her physicians that further treatment would only prolong her suffering, family members requested a discontinuation of all life-support measures, including artificial nutrition and hydration. The physicians and ethics committee of the hospital agreed. But hospital administrators, in consultation with the state agency protective of persons with mental retardation and developmental disabilities, stepped in to seek judicial guidance on the matter. They were concerned that the withdrawal of life support from Pouliot was illegal because New York law did not explicitly permit a surrogate to make these decisions for an incompetent individual. It is not necessary here to review all the legal intricacies of the case. The end result was two months of legally enforced half-measures of artificial nutrition and hydration. Because Pouliot's body was unable to tolerate a gastronomy tube that might provide adequate nutrition, she was instead intravenously fed a glucose-only formula that did not prevent her body from being starved of protein. One of her physicians wrote in her chart two months after her admission to the hospital, "The patient is kept alive for her own body to consume/eat itself. . . . [T]his current plan of IV hydration promotes an increase in patient suffering, does not promote life quality, and maintains her heart/lung capacity only—and, indeed, therefore this current tact [sic] is outside of acceptable medical bounds, in effect worsening her condition, since she is *consuming herself calorically.* It is thus, not medically indicated."[22] Despite substantial pain relief medications, Pouliot clearly suffered in the last two months of her life—as evidenced by her crying, moaning, and grimacing—from the forced administration of half-measures of nutrition and hydration.

The National Right to Life Committee's proposed model act (see appendix) would prohibit the withholding or withdrawal of artificial nutrition and hydration from individuals without a written directive or a very precise oral directive, which Sheila Pouliot did not and could not have. There is an exception for medically inappropriate treatment, but it is too narrow to have likely applied in Pouliot's case. The exception applies only when artificial nutrition and hydration could not be absorbed and therefore would not contribute to sustaining the person's life. In Pouliot's case, the intravenous feeding did sustain and extend her life, although at the cost of great suffering.

Some disability rights groups appear to support legislation like the NRLC's model act. According to the National Council on Independent Living, artificial nutrition and hydration should not be removed from those who have never been competent unless their bodies are unable to digest or absorb the nutrition and hydration.[23] Other disability rights groups have adopted different statements that may or may not have approved the use of intravenous feeding to sustain Pouliot's life.[24]

Yet Sheila Pouliot's suffering was real. It was not the projected or imagined suffering that is sometimes used to justify the avoidance of the births of people with developmental disabilities. Nor was it the suffering imagined or at least rhetorically recognized by Nazi doctors who euthanized children with disabilities and the elderly. Concerned with protecting the disabled as a group from such prejudices, disability groups have sometimes advocated policies that fail to adequately protect individuals from actual suffering. They appeared to follow that course during the Schiavo controversy by lending support for proposed changes to state end-of-life laws, which would not allow artificial nutrition and hydration to be withheld even when the burdens of its provision far outweigh the benefits. This must be an oversight or a misunderstanding of how the proposed legislation would actually work rather than an actual indifference to the potential harm that such policies and practices could have. But even if well-intentioned, these groups' position on artificial nutrition and hydration needs to be clarified or corrected to protect the interests of the profoundly disabled.

Providing food and water to someone who hungers or thirsts is a most basic and recognizable sign of human compassion and responsibility. When we think of a person dying of thirst in a desert and crawling up to someone who has the water he needs, we recoil to think that someone might be so cruel as to refuse. This is right, and with the millions of people who do die, every year, because they lack clean water or proper nutrition, we ought to view with sincere shame our inadequate efforts to provide them what they so desperately need.

But when a person cannot experience hunger or thirst, when a person's life has become only a biological effort, and when we recognize that nutrition and hydration are likely to be provided only to satisfy our own sense of caring rather than to respond to what the person can feel or would want, we are a far cry from helping. Our fear of letting another die when we might extend that life must be balanced by our understanding that we cannot use—or demand—another human being's existence to improve our own. How much better if we were to spend our efforts on feeding and providing water to those who we know deeply desire it rather than misplacing our good intentions on those who cannot say no.

9 THE PRESERVATION OF LIFE

When decisions are made to continue or discontinue life support for people who have lost the capacity to make their own decisions, current law generally places greater value on the preservation of life than on the patient's self-determination. This has been accomplished through the requirement that the patient be in certain specified physical conditions (terminal illness, permanent vegetative state) and the requirement that a surrogate's determination that life support be removed be demonstrated by clear and convincing evidence that it is what the patient would have wished (or, in some states, evidence that it is in the patient's best interests to end life support). In some states, there are additional barriers to withholding or withdrawing artificial nutrition and hydration, which more directly and certainly results in the death of the patient. Patient self-determination, however, has clearly also been important—Karen Ann Quinlan, Nancy Cruzan, and Terri Schiavo, as well as many other formerly competent individuals who have entered a permanent vegetative state or become terminally ill, have had life support removed and have died on the basis of our understanding of what they would have wanted.

Those who opposed the removal of Terri Schiavo's feeding tube sought, and still seek, changes in law, ethics, and culture that will place greater emphasis on preserving life. This chapter examines how the debate over the preservation of life and its relationship to patient self-determination appeared to change during the Schiavo controversy and the potential consequences of that shift. It attempts to answer a question law professor Charity Scott posed following Terri's death: How in the world did the right to die turn into a right to life?

Changing Terms

For the past thirty years, since the *Quinlan* case in 1976, the protection of the patient's life in legal cases of this sort has typically been described as a *state interest*, meaning that our government sees that it has a unique role to play in protecting the lives of vulnerable citizens from harm. This means that the typical dispute about removal of life support has been whether an *individual* has rights (to exercise self-determination by choosing to have life support removed) that are greater than the *state's* interest in protecting human life (by maintaining life support). As the law governing end-of-life decisions has evolved, the states, through court decisions and legislation, show their interest in the protection of life through the procedures and evidentiary burdens placed on those who seek removal of a patient's life support. They have shown little interest in protecting human life against the proven wishes of the patient. While many appellate opinions still note that the state has an interest in protecting human life, they rarely elevate this interest over the patient's interest in self-determination. As we saw in the dispute over the removal of Terri Schiavo's feeding tube, Florida law also has this focus. It has adopted the clear and convincing standard of evidence for life-support removal, and this, in and of itself, is indicative of the state's interest in protecting life. Outside of this standard, the state's interest in protecting life is not separately weighed and balanced in every case against the patient's right of self-determination.

The advocates who opposed the removal of Terri Schiavo's feeding tube presumed a different formulation of the dispute, and this newer way of framing the issue permeated discussions of the case. The shift was subtle but important for practical and cultural reasons. It was this: rather than understand the competing concerns as the individual's right to self-determination versus *the state's interest* in protecting human life, we should understand the dispute as between the individual's right to self-determination versus *her own right to life*.

The counterweight to Terri's self-determination right—her life—gained political and cultural weight when it was reclaimed for herself, no longer to be characterized as something that the state was interested in but that she was not. The importance of this shift cannot be overstated. The "right to die" could in advocacy terms now be placed on par with a "right to life."

The shift was most powerful in its political and cultural implications, but it also opened up novel legal claims as well (although these legal claims were ultimately unsuccessful). For if the case could be characterized as being primarily about Terri's rights generally, and especially her rights to protection of her life, then it made sense to also think about her rights under the Americans with Disabilities Act, her rights as a nursing home patient, her status as a vulnerable individual under the protective watch of the Florida Department of Children and Families, and so on—arguments that the Schindlers' attorneys raised at various points during the controversy.

Ironically, at the same time that the opponents to the removal of Terri's feeding tube advanced her "right to life," Terri Schiavo as an individual became lost. Religious groups, right-to-life groups, and some disability rights groups, as well as individual supporters who spoke out on behalf of the Schindlers' cause, seemed to be championing an abstract conception of life much more than Terri's life or Terri's interest in her own life.

This, too, was a subtle shift and therefore merits careful explanation. In the earlier *Cruzan* case, Justice William J. Brennan, in his dissent, argued that there is no state interest in preserving life in any abstract sense. The interest is instead particular to the individual involved. And if the individual involved would not wish to continue living in his or her present condition, then the state has no interest in forcing that person to live. According to Justice Brennan, the state of Missouri was in effect doing just that through its adoption of its quite onerous "clear and convincing" standard of proof regarding what Nancy Cruzan wished, which required prior express statements about life support.

And the *Cruzan* majority, in upholding Missouri's high evidentiary requirement, did not try to justify its result under an abstract interest in the preservation of life. Instead, it took some pains to explain that *the state's interest in protecting life helped to preserve the patient's interest* in *self-determination*. It did this by arguing that Missouri's decision to err on the side of life was acceptable because the continued life of a patient meant that the decision could be changed—for example, with the discovery of new evidence about the patient's wishes or new medical advances. But if an error was made in the opposite direction—if Nancy's feeding tube was removed when she would have wanted it continued—then that error would be irrevocable because death is irrevocable. Justice Brennan did counter that either error is irrevocable to the patient—just as death is irrevocable, so are the years spent in a condition that one wished to avoid.

The *Cruzan* majority tried to link the state's interest in protecting life to the preservation of the patient's interest in self-determination. The attempt of the majority to link these two concepts is significant in their focus on the individual patient. It was the individual patient—not government promotion of respect for all life—that was most important.

Using Terri Schiavo

The Schiavo controversy had a different tenor. It attracted certain religious groups and right-to-life groups who folded the Schiavo case into their already existing advocacy for the protection of human embryos and fetuses. To be sure, similar groups also camped out in 1990 at the facility where Nancy Cruzan was cared for in order to protest the removal of her feeding tube. But with the Schiavo case, continuous media coverage resulted in a wider and more politicized dissemination of these viewpoints. Moreover, the political strategies of protecting "innocent human life" had advanced significantly between 1990 and 2005. Right-to-life groups had enjoyed substantial success in getting states to adopt laws either reducing access to abortion services or raising the status of the fetus toward being understood as a person (examples include fetal homicide statutes, fetal pain statutes, partial-birth abortion bans, and parental consent or notification laws). In fact, we have even seen unprecedented federal abortion legislation in the form of the Partial-Birth Abortion Ban Act, which the U.S. Supreme Court recently upheld as constitutional.[1]

With respect to the protection of human embryos, President George W. Bush had in 2001 limited federal funding on embryonic stem cell lines to those that had already been created, so no additional embryos would be destroyed in federally funded research. In the summer of 2006, he would exercise his first veto on legislation passed by Congress to expand that funding to cover research on leftover embryos from in vitro fertilization. At the ceremony in which he signed the veto, he surrounded himself with children who had been born following their "adoption" as embryos, clearly embracing an alternative to the use of leftover frozen embryos in stem cell research.

But as law professor Janet Dolgin has explained in a recent article, the conservative political base had been split on the issue of federal funding for human embryonic research.[2] Some conservatives had come out in favor of such research because of the potential for improving and extending the lives of people who are already clearly people rather than merely potential people. Focusing at this critical time on Terri Schiavo allowed conservative politicians to reinforce their "culture of life" credentials in a manner that did not involve some of the divisive issues of human embryonic stem cell research.

For a number of advocacy groups, the Schiavo case was less about Terri Schiavo and her interest in either self-determination or her interest in living. It was about fetuses and embryos or, more generally, about the "culture of life." The Schiavo case was embraced by right-to-life groups for its symbolic value as a case in which vulnerable, "innocent" human life was threatened. Terri was used by these groups as an easily recognizable example of the idea that all life must be valued and zealously protected. We should not, according to this view, make any judgments about the quality of an individual's life, just as we should not disregard human life in the form of fetuses and embryos. In particular, we should not allow those with interests in ending that life (and here, the finger was pointed at Michael Schiavo) to be in a position to make decisions regarding it.

Certainly, these groups often used the language of "erring on the side of life" during the Schiavo controversy and afterward to promote

changes in state laws. But "erring on the side of life" is not enough—
rather, the goal of these groups has been more substantially to "preserve life." This is evident in their efforts to change state laws to prevent the removal of artificial nutrition and hydration unless there is a
written document by the patient that specifies its removal. It is even
more evident in the promotion by right-to-life groups of a new living
will form called the "Will to Live."

The Will to Live

The Will to Live is a document drafted and distributed by the National Right to Life Committee and like-minded groups for individuals to sign to express their wishes in favor of continued life support,
particularly nutrition and hydration. It is aimed at accomplishing at
least two very important changes in the perspectives of the American people. The first is to unsettle the confidence that individuals
may currently feel regarding the intentions and ability of their close
family members to make appropriate medical decisions on their behalf in the event of their incompetence. Making people feel insecure
about their own situation—that the "plug" will be "pulled" before
they are ready—reinforces the belief that changes in the current law
are needed. The Will to Live can therefore bolster support for legislative proposals to further restrict the removal of feeding tubes.

In addition, the Will to Live is aimed at changing people's minds
about their *own* decisions regarding nutrition and hydration so that
they are more likely to favor feeding tubes and other forms of life
support. While the main instruction in the Will to Live is for continued
treatment of all kinds, up until death, the form does contain a space
for the individual to reject certain kinds of medical treatment in two
specified circumstances (and one for circumstances the individual
might describe for himself or herself—an "other" category, for which
no suggestions are given). The two conditions are imminent death and
terminal illness with less than three months to live. There is no mention of the permanent vegetative state. For the blanks following these
two conditions, people signing the form are offered suggestions for
the kinds of treatment that they might wish to have withheld—cardio-

pulmonary resuscitation, nonbeneficial surgery, and "treatment that will itself cause me severe, intractable, and long-lasting pain but will not cure me." With respect to the rejection of nonbeneficial surgery, the form suggests specific language about the kind of surgery that a person might want to reject and discourages ever using the term "benefit" or "burden," describing these terms as unreasonably vague. Therefore the suggested language to reject surgery when death is imminent or the person is terminally ill is: "Surgery that would not cure me, would not improve either my mental or my physical condition, would not make me more comfortable, and would not help me to have less pain, but would only keep me alive longer."[3]

There is no suggestion that the individual might wish to refuse nutrition and hydration and, in fact, every suggestion, or rather, instruction, otherwise. The form itself states: "Food and water are not medical treatment, but basic necessities. I direct my health care provider(s) and health care surrogate to provide me with food and fluids orally, intravenously, by tube, or by other means to the full extent necessary both to preserve my life and to assure me the optimal health possible."

This form presumes that people will want all forms of treatment in all circumstances except those in which it would be considered pointless to provide it. The form does not encourage people to exercise choice about the kinds of treatment that might be desired or refused but instead to follow the instruction of right-to-life groups to preserve the continued functioning of their bodies at virtually all cost. Even the rhetorical slant of the title of the Will to Live is directive—directive to the people filling out the forms to dig deep within themselves and find that will to live that courageous and right-thinking people have.

The Will to Live form is deeply disturbing, in part because it might appear quite reasonable to people unfamiliar with the effect of various medical interventions. For example, one life-sustaining treatment that people commonly express a desire to avoid (when they are in terminal or vegetative conditions) is the ventilator. But this is not one of the kinds of treatments suggested for people to list as one they would refuse. One has to wonder, though, whether people filling out the form will be confused by the reference to CPR (applicable to emergency situations) and think they have rejected a ventilator for all purposes by listing CPR as a treatment that they wish to avoid, when this is not the case. The form also directs that artificial nutrition and hydration always be provided. Yet we have consistent reports that feeding tubes are currently overused—meaning that they are used even when they are unlikely to extend life or improve the quality of life. Misleadingly, the form suggests that artificial nutrition and hydration will *both* extend life and lead to optimal health, when in fact these are sometimes opposing objectives.

We know that a significant majority of American adults would not want to continue living in a permanent vegetative state, yet people signing the Will to Live form will have, perhaps unknowingly, provided written consent to the provision of artificial nutrition and hydration *without an end*. And some will have had their minds changed about the propriety of refusing nutrition and hydration within a campaign of misinformation about Terri Schiavo's condition and the eagerness of others to similarly deprive them of their own lives.

Proponents of both the Will to Live and legislative proposals to restrict the removal of artificial nutrition and hydration argue that they only seek to protect patient choice. This strategy has the potential to garner more public support than a blanket prohibition against removal of nutrition and hydration. In thinking about their own situation, people will be assured that they can protect their own desires to have nutrition and hydration removed in certain circumstances as long as they take the step to execute a living will. We've already seen, however, that patient choice is not furthered by legislative proposals to require more specific evidence of patient preferences. Nor is the Will to Live an instrument that furthers patient choice. It is only disguised as one. It is instead an instrument designed to preserve life by either altering patient choice or thwarting its expression. And it is dishonest: beyond the misleading "choices" and inflammatory language, the document serves the purposes and aims of an advocacy group more than the needs of a particular person.

Reframing the Government's Interest in These Cases

It is important that we recognize and understand that much of the end-of-life legislation proposed in response to the Schiavo case is part of the larger right-to-life movement. Within this movement, patient choice is intentionally subordinate to the preservation of life. The law of most states already protects an individual's life more than it protects the individual's choice. As we've seen, this is accomplished in many states by requiring clear and convincing evidence of a patient's desire to refuse life-sustaining treatment before it can be withheld or withdrawn. In the 1990 *Browning* case, a Florida appeals court stated, "In making this difficult decision, a surrogate decision-maker should err on the side of life. . . . In cases of doubt, we must assume that a patient would choose to defend life in exercising his or her right to privacy."[4] The Florida District Court of Appeals wrote in 2001, in the first *Schiavo* appeal: "We reconfirm today that a court's default position must favor life."[5] Tipping the scales even further in the direction of the preservation of life will eclipse patient choice, patient interests, and the interests of families in reaching sound and caring decisions for their loved ones.

In chapter 7, I discussed concerns about making quality-of-life evaluations. I mentioned that some courts have accepted, while others have specifically rejected, the idea that the state's interest in life is weakened when the quality of that life is poor. Courts that have accepted the "sliding-scale" approach have adopted it in the context of weighing the state's interest in preserving life against the patient's interest in self-determination. Court declarations that the state's interest in protecting life is low because the quality of life is low seem offensive because the state—and therefore society—appears to be abandoning certain patients.

Is it possible to avoid this offensive conclusion and still let patients in a permanent vegetative state die when there is little or no evidence of what their wishes would be? In other words, as discussed in chapter 7, there may be (and I believe there are) good reasons to keep the presumption in favor of life in cases involving the terminally ill or physical conditions that are not as severe as the permanent vegetative state. But I've also argued for lowering the evidentiary burden about the patient's wishes and in fact changing the presumption to favor withdrawing life support in a permanent vegetative state. In order to do that, does a court or legislature have to indicate that it doesn't have as much interest in the lives of people in a permanent vegetative state?

To some extent, we are stuck with the constitutional law framework of the state's interests versus the individual's right. This is how issues of individual constitutional rights have been framed for many years, and it is unlikely to change in the near future. True, the advocates for continuing to provide artificial nutrition and hydration for Terri Schiavo proposed a different way of viewing these issues—Terri's right to self-determination versus Terri's right to life—but this was effective more as a way of culturally and politically framing the issue than it was in creating a new constitutional framework.

There is, however, an alternative. And that is to understand the state's interest in these cases as *promoting respect and care* for the individual patient rather than as preserving an abstract and broad-brush prolonging of human life. For some patients, respect and care will include efforts to preserve life. For others, however—particularly those in a permanent vegetative state—respect and care will mean a recognition that the patient has no present or future interest in continued life; it means protecting such patients from a perpetuation of biological life merely to satisfy others' interests.

At the heart of the principle of respecting human life is respect for the individual human life, not the biological process of life itself. In other words, it is what has come together to make a living person that must be respected rather than individual living cells. Right-to-life advocates, for example, who object to research on human embryos do not generally object to research on mere cells, even if the cells are living and contain a full set of human DNA. To these advocates, research on adult stem cells is permissible, but research on embryonic stem cells is not, since the latter involves the destruction of a human embryo, which they believe is a person.

It is the individual human life that is endowed with the qualities that command respect as a person. For some people who are religious, this may be connected to the creation of an individual human soul. For those who see the embryo as a person, it is the combination of the genetic material of the gametes that creates the individual human life. But it is not biological life processes themselves that are valued for their own sake. In fact, an earlier encyclical letter of Pope John Paul II lends some support for this view:

> [F]rom the time that the ovum is fertilized, a life is begun which is neither that of the father nor the mother; it is rather the life of a new human being with his own growth. It would never be made human if it were not human already. This has always been clear, and . . . modern genetic science offers clear confirmation. It has demonstrated that from the first instance there is established the program of what this living being will be: a person, this individual person with his characteristic aspects already well determined.[6]

To be sure, Pope John Paul II's pronouncement in the spring of 2004 about the importance of providing artificial nutrition and hydration to patients in a permanent vegetative state received much more attention in relation to the Schiavo case. But there is at least some tension between that pronouncement and this earlier explanation of why human life must be so preciously valued. The pope's encyclical letter emphasizes the *individuality* of every human being.

The individual who was Terri Schiavo had been stripped by medical trauma of all qualities that might matter to her individuality, that might make her a person with individual qualities of any sort, excepting relationships with others. But these relationships with others were no longer *her* relationships, because she could not experience them. The relationships, with family and friends, only benefited others. And the life that they sought to preserve was no longer really hers: she became an argument, an object of memory and affection, and a cause.

10 RESPECT AND CARE
AN ALTERNATIVE FRAMEWORK

If it is the individual human being who is important and to whom our responsibilities are owed—rather than an abstract preservation of life—how do we best respond?

The drama surrounding the battle over Terri Schiavo's feeding tube was rich in visual images. One of the most enduring of these images was that of Terri herself in the videotape that her parents provided to the media—footage that appeared to show Terri responding to her mother's caring inquiries. Even if one understood that expert doctors who had examined Terri had repeatedly confirmed that she was permanently unconscious, that these videotapes were actually consistent with the vegetative state, and that the footage repeatedly shown on television was deliberately edited from hours of videotape that showed no response from Terri, it was hard to escape a nagging feeling of doubt about her condition and its permanence. *Was* she responding? She moved her head to the right as her mother spoke to her from that direction. Could she hear? Did she recognize her mother's voice? Could she see? Was that a *smile* on Terri's lips?

On the one hand, the videotape revealed Terri's utter vulnerability and could evoke feelings of protectiveness toward people who are severely disabled. On the other hand, many people, both in surveys and in casual conversation, revealed that whatever condition Terri was in—even if that *might* have been a slight smile on her face—it would be an intolerable existence for them and they would choose death in that situation over life.

The controversy surrounding the removal of Terri's feeding tube seemed to be in large part about these conflicting reactions—the need to protect vulnerable life and the desire of individuals to choose their own destiny. And our ensconced constitutional framework, which pits the state's interest in preserving life against the individual's right to decide matters affecting his or her body, reinforces this perception of two dominant competing values.

Self-Determination versus Preservation of Life?

But as we've seen, self-determination is not an easy concept to apply when the patient lacks the present ability to exercise it. We may say we're respecting self-determination in these contexts, but often we can only make careful approximations of what the patient would want. Even when people are competent to make their own decisions, we cannot always be confident that the decisions they are making are truly, authentically, and voluntarily their own—because of course they've been influenced by social, cultural, and familial conditions. The problem posed by the formerly competent patient is many times more perplexing, as evidenced in Terri's case.

The idea of protection of human life is similarly attractive in its apparent simplicity and just as elusive in its practical, consistent application. Our society daily ignores or denies the need to protect human life. Our government policies permit the ill health and even death of Americans due to lack of adequate health care. In 2005, the year Terri died, approximately 45 million individuals in the United States lacked health insurance, 8 million of those children. The Institute of Medicine has estimated that 18,000 Americans died in 2000 because of inadequate health care due to their uninsured status. Many of the political leaders and advocacy groups most stridently opposed to removing Terri's feeding tube have expressed no public remorse over the tens of thousands of innocent lives lost in Iraq—few are outright pacifists—nor have they expressed the same degree of public advocacy toward the tens of millions of people worldwide whose lives are in danger from lack of clean water. During the seven years of litigation over the removal of one person's feeding tube, at least 40 million children died from hunger-related causes. I'd wager that not one of them was allotted a feature on the evening news, nor would a visit to the most prominent pro-life Web sites find featured links through which someone can help save these kinds of lives.

Of course, we might well understand that when forced to make direct choices about a particular individual's life support rather than indirect choices about mechanisms to finance care for many people, the moral imperatives are clearer, or at least appear to be more easily identified and defined.

But even in the situation pro-life advocates see as more closely analogous to Terri's situation—that of the protection of the life of embryos and fetuses—values other than the preservation of life come into play. If no values mattered other than the protection of innocent human life, we would either disallow in vitro fertilization practices or impose severe limitations on them (so that no embryos would be created that would be left unimplanted), we would permit no exceptions for abortion in cases of rape or incest, and we would allow no discretion to withhold highly invasive treatment for premature babies or the frail elderly, even when the results are predictably futile. Almost no one would advocate this latter requirement and few the two former. Even pro-life advocates value other things in addition to the mere preservation of all human life.

The temptation here is to try to refine our understanding of patient self-determination, of the protection of human life, and of the scale that we should use to balance the two. And perhaps we could get a bit closer to resolving some of the vexing questions of end-of-life law by more careful study of what constitutes adequate evidence of a person's autonomous wishes—for example, by debating whether we should privilege writings over oral testimony, or listen to a patient's spouse before parents (or vice versa). Perhaps the latter should depend on how long the couple has been married, or on the quality of the relationship between the parents and child, and so on.

The same goes with respect to the protection of human life. The temptation is to think we could get a bit closer to resolving these issues by comparing or contrasting a person in a permanent vegetative state to embryos that might be used in stem cell research, or to prisoners on death row, or to people who have suffered brain death.

Even if we did improve our understanding of the values of self-determination and preservation of life, we would still have to find that elusive scale that would tell us how to balance these two values. This is the hardest part, and at times it just seems like the question is answered according to how liberal a person is (more in favor of self-determination) or how conservative (more in favor of protection of life). That hardly seems satisfactory. We fall along political lines, associating end-of-life law with other liberal and conservative issues. Unfortunately, media and political pressures have led us to too many easy answers, rallying around "right to die" and "right to life" as if these slogans could capture the real values that underpin our appreciation of health and life. If this way of looking at these issues becomes predominant, then we will trail further behind in rather than closer to improving our ethical and legal understanding of how best to make these decisions. We need a new way of talking about these issues. And the Schiavo case is a good place to begin.

Why? Because the next decisions will be *ours* to make—for ourselves, our family members, our clients, our patients, our fellow citizens. We are responsible for these decisions, for the full reach of these decisions, and we owe it to everyone involved to understand the full extent of that responsibility. Whether Terri Schiavo's feeding tube should have been withdrawn was not a question Terri Schiavo could answer. We as a society had to answer it. That doesn't mean that what she might have wanted—if we could have determined that—doesn't matter. Our duties to Terri, what we owed to her, required in part that we try to determine and respect her wishes. But it also meant a lot more.

Responsibility for Respect and Care

Respecting Terri and other patients in end-of-life decision making means that we honor to the extent feasible their own desires regarding life support. In doing so, we respect them as individuals who could once formulate their own values and create their own vision of the world and their place within it.

But respect and care require more as well. Many of those opposed to the removal of Terri Schiavo's feeding tube were focused exclusively on the form of life support to be removed. For them, the provision of artificial nutrition and hydration was a form of "basic care" that could not ever ethically be withdrawn. Yet we've seen that the relationship of care to artificial nutrition and hydration is much more complicated than that. It involves, among other things, a knowledge and appreciation of the condition in which the individual patient is found. It also involves a knowledge and appreciation of the effect that a feeding tube may have on the comfort and health of the patient, which is not always positive. In fact, treating individuals with care and respect will always require particular attention to the unique situation of the individual. The challenge in the law is to fashion rules that are not so broad as to be under- or overinclusive or otherwise inattentive to the individual, but also not so flexible and discretionary as to amount to no rules at all—and allow arbitrary and unreviewable results.

Common ground is possible. For example, it seems obvious that respect and care for people like Terri Schiavo would require respecting their bodily integrity by providing proper hygiene and giving care to their appearance. Prior to a careful determination that a condition of unconsciousness is permanent, aggressive rehabilitation efforts and monitoring are also crucial. We have seen that Terri Schiavo received this kind of care, but other patients, like Terry Wallis, did not.

Proper respect and care for the patient also require that we protect individual patients' medical, physical, and other privacy. We should not allow their bodies to become objects of public display, their medical histories to be open to public scrutiny, the details of their relationships with their spouses, friends, and families to be available for speculation and gossip. It is true that politicians and celebrities are often subjected to such public scrutiny, but unlike them, Terri Schiavo did not choose to become a public figure. Yet that video clip of her was played over and over on television and for a while could be purchased over the Internet (from the Terri Schindler Schiavo Foundation, set up by the Schindler family) for a hundred dollars each.

If there is one thing most of us can probably agree on—and many people in fact said as much at the time—it is that Terri Schiavo would not have wanted *that*.

But what does a duty to respect and care for patients mean in regard to preserving their lives? What does it mean with respect to presumptions and errors? Should they always be made on the side of life, as so far the law has largely done? Some of our current rules have been largely reflexive and the result of too narrow a focus—the focus on the patient's self-determination and the preservation of life. And recent rhetoric in response to the Schiavo case has included calls for an even narrower focus on these two principles. If we step back, to think about respect and care more generally, we arrive at somewhat different answers.

The Terminally Ill or Elderly

For the patient who is terminally ill, or whose body is simply failing because of old age, a reasonable amount of deference should be accorded to the person named by the patient to serve as surrogate or, if no one has been named, to loving family members. Unless given reason not to, we should trust these surrogate decision-makers to honor the patient's wishes, as best they can determine them to be. But as they do so, and as others offer input and advice (like physicians and ethics committees and, as a last resort, courts), translation of the patient's wishes to the situation at hand must not be mechanical. Whether the patient's wishes are in writing, or have been expressed orally, or are merely surmised by the surrogate on the basis of casual conversation or personality, exquisite care must be taken that these perceived wishes truly do meet the situation faced by the patient.

In other words, the possibility of recovery or the likelihood of suffering, the patient's past concern for family members, and many other considerations must be sifted into a rich resolution of the question to continue or discontinue life support. The form of life support—ventilator, artificial nutrition and hydration, antibiotics—should factor into this decision only as it would in the patient's own view and in the context of the burdens and benefits such treatments might offer with respect to comfort, lucidity, prolongation of life, and similar concerns.

Rich resolutions on this order are generally, but not always, possible in the current law of end-of-life decision making as applied to those who are already dying. The standard adopted in many jurisdictions, that life support be removed only on the basis of clear and convincing evidence that it is what the patient would want or when it would be in the patient's best interests, should not pose a barrier, especially since burdensome court review is generally not required. When the law insists, as it does in only a few jurisdictions, that patients have expressly and clearly indicated that they would want life support removed in their current situation, it is erecting unnecessary barriers to caring and respecting for the patients. Requiring stricter reliance on following the letter of living wills (in a misguided pursuit to honor patient self-determination) or stricter evidence for removing artificial nutrition and hydration (in a misguided effort to preserve all life) would upset the wise and generally accepted legal and ethical consensus about how these decisions are best made.

People Who Have Never Been Competent

For a person who has never been competent, such as Sheila Pouliot, we cannot of course honor patient wishes. Instead, we have to look at the burdens and benefits of proposed treatment. In identifying burdens, we have to be careful not to include mere conditions of dependency that more abled people might find "undignified" but that do not cause suffering for the patient. A low level of cognitive function should also not by itself be a reason to discontinue life support or to refuse beneficial treatment. But if a person's lack of ability to understand and therefore cope with certain treatment measures would cause distress or make it difficult to administer treatment in a comfortable way, then that could be taken into consideration.[1] Again, the particulars need careful attention.

If a best interests assessment would warrant removing burdensome or intrusive and nonbeneficial life support from a formerly competent, terminally ill patient, then it should be adequate for the never competent, terminally ill patient as well. If, as I propose, life support could be removed from a formerly competent patient who enters a permanent vegetative state, even without evidence of prior wishes, then the same should be true for the never competent patient who enters a permanent vegetative state. If instead we allow blanket prohibitions against removing life support from never competent patients, or place the requirements for terminating life support impossibly high, then we are not giving them more care because of their vulnerability but less.

The Minimally Conscious State

Trying to figure out general guidelines for approaching the question of continued life support for someone in a minimally conscious state is very, very tough. I think it will—and should—take a number of years of debate, experience, and careful consideration for us to reach any general consensus on what is possible and what is required. As I said earlier, during the Schiavo controversy, I finally executed a living will for myself, and when I did I added to the form a reference to the "minimally conscious state" as a condition in which I would want all life support removed. The impression I got from listening to other people I know talk about Terri Schiavo was that my feelings on this were fairly typical: a number of us think we wouldn't want to live for years with just minimal consciousness and little hope of significant improvement. We wouldn't be ourselves. But then I learned of recent research showing more possibilities for late recovery than doctors have previously supposed, and I had second thoughts with respect to what I would want for myself.

But I also began thinking about the situation more generally and about the responsibilities of others and of us all. Should the fact that I would no longer be "myself" mean that the "altered self" I had become should not live?[2] Should it mean that I ought to be able to ask caregivers to listen to my request made now to deny me beneficial treatment then? This problem was briefly touched on in chapter 7.

How do we weigh the choices someone has made *pre-disability* against the benefits of continued life that the person *post-disability* might enjoy? The person in a minimally conscious state is not aware of and seems to have little connection to those pre-disability choices. If there were burdens to continued living, or if the person were suffering from continued treatment—for example, unable to properly absorb nutrition—then, as with any other person, we could and should take that into account. But the emotional burdens on family members, less so. We shouldn't eliminate a woman's life, for example, because her husband feels he can't move on with his own life if his wife is in a minimally conscious state. He actually does have choices in his life—divorce or counseling, for example. While we should be compassionate about the husband's sorrows and emotional burdens, we can't meet his needs at the cost of someone else's life.

The characterization of artificial nutrition and hydration as "basic care" has more of a ring of truth to it when applied to the minimally conscious patient than the permanently vegetative patient. Recall from chapter 8 the ways in which we might measure how artificial nutrition and hydration may constitute care: by the ends achieved (extending life that can be experienced), or by how the individual receives or perceives the treatment that is given—whether it is "taken in as care" or not. If the person who is minimally conscious can experience positive feelings from having been well nourished or would experience the lack of nourishment in negative ways, or "takes in" artificial nutrition and hydration in a way that is perceived as care, then we would seem obligated to provide it absent a countervailing concern.

But, just as with the person in a permanent vegetative state, we have to realize that we shouldn't require artificial nutrition and hydration simply as a matter of course, or out of abstract notions of these duties, because then we lose sight of the individuals before us and treat them for our own purposes rather than theirs. The obligation to respect the individual person means that we specifically address this person now and his or her needs in particular. Otherwise, we would end up treating minimally conscious patients as we do permanently vegetative patients—as objects rather than as persons—when we presume we must always continue to tube-feed them.

There can also be burdens to continued living that the minimally conscious patient can experience, and careful attention would need to be given to those, as experienced by individual patients. Immobility can cause contractures, recurring infections, and other discomforts or pain; some minimally conscious patients may exhibit frustration and signs of misery.[3] As opposed to permanently vegetative patients, who, because they share a complete loss of awareness, do not need an individualized assessment of the benefits and burdens of treatment and its effects, the minimally conscious patient, in order to be appropriately respected and cared for, requires this sort of inquiry and attention—by surrogates, caregivers, and courts, if necessary.

The toughest question appears to be this: What if the benefits of continued treatment and life for the patient do outweigh the burdens, but the patient made it clear, at one time, that he or she would find life in a condition like this intolerable and would refuse life support?

A number of scholars have considered the ethical and legal parameters of removing life support from severely mentally disabled people who had, when competent, expressed very clear opinions about not wanting to live in similar conditions. (Courts have not directly addressed this question yet.) There is wide disagreement.

Some believe that the pre-disability choices should govern, because a person has a strong interest in living a complete life as the person he or she has chosen to be. It is critically important to who we are as individuals to be able to define our values and what gives our lives meaning and to have some control over who we become and how we will be remembered. According to this view, the mature, competent person must be allowed to identify what states of impairment would be unacceptable and in which they should not be required to continue living.[4] This, I imagine, is a view that a lot of us find compelling.

The problem, though, is the reality: what to do, here and now, for the person in front of us? If she or he is not near a natural end to life and can benefit from nonburdensome life-sustaining treatment in a meaningful way (interaction with others, enjoyment of her environment, and such), then it seems that it would be inhumane not to provide it.

Rebecca Dresser writes, "[T]he ethical and legal responsibilities to protect an incompetent patient ought not be suspended because that person once requested an intervention that would now be inhumane or refused an intervention that now offers clear benefit. If a patient can no longer appreciate the values that motivated the precommitment choice, treatment decisions should take into account what now matters to the patient."[5]

In the few reported court cases that have come close to presenting this type of situation, courts have not been willing to say what Dresser has said. Nevertheless, they have not permitted the withdrawal of life support. Instead, they have continued to trumpet the idea that self-determination is the governing principle but have concluded that the evidence of the person's prior wishes wasn't a specific enough match to the condition in which the person later found himself or herself.

In the 2001 *Wendland* case, the California Supreme Court would not allow the removal of artificial nutrition and hydration from a conscious patient several years after an automobile accident that left him severely impaired. His wife, also his surrogate decision-maker, brought the petition. Robert Wendland possessed some limited physical abilities and some limited cognitive function that allowed him to interact with others, although inconsistently. Sometimes he could answer yes or no questions using a simple keyboard of sorts. One of his doctors testified about asking him a series of questions about his physical state ("Are you sitting up?") to verify his comprehension (he answered them mostly correctly); he then asked him more personal questions, such as whether he felt any pain or was angry. In the middle of this series of questions, the doctor asked him, "Do you want to die?" While Wendland answered the other questions in the series, to this one, he was unresponsive.[6]

The California Supreme Court held that Robert Wendland's statements prior to his automobile accident that he would not want to live as "a vegetable" and the like did not address his current situation, and therefore his feeding tube could not be removed. (Wendland died of other causes prior to this final court review of the case, but as is customary, the court proceeded with the case in order to provide guidance for future cases.)

An earlier Michigan case involving a man named Michael Martin came out very much the same way, although Martin had made more numerous and more specific statements about the kind of condition in which he would want life support removed. As with Wendland, an automobile accident left Martin in a severely impaired but conscious condition in which he was dependent on a feeding tube for nutrition. The medical testimony about the degree of his ability to interact conflicted, but all agreed he was not vegetative. Other witnesses testified as to his ability to engage in some limited interaction with other people and his ability at times to nod his head yes or no to simple questions. His wife petitioned the court for authorization to remove Martin's feeding tube, bringing forward evidence of his pre-accident statements that he would not want to live like a vegetable. Martin's co-workers also testified that he had said he would not want to continue life in a vegetative condition. In addition, his wife, Mary Martin, testified that her husband's statements were not limited to a vegetative condition but were expansive enough to include other states of dependency, for which he had no tolerance. She said they had numerous conversations in which her husband had said that if he were ever in an accident and "could not be the same person," then he would "not want to live that way." In particularly memorable testimony, she stated that he said, "Mary, promise me you wouldn't let me live like that if I can't be the person I am right now, because if you do, believe me I'll haunt you every day of your life."[7]

The court concluded that this evidence did not "constitute clear and convincing evidence of Mr. Martin's preinjury statement of his desire to refuse life-sustaining medical treatment under these specific circumstances."[8] One wonders, as a lone dissenting judge did, what could constitute such level of evidence and how realistic it is to expect more specificity. These are the ways people talk about these things—except that the Martins actually talked about it a lot, seriously and passionately and consistently. The evidence that pre-disability Martin wouldn't want to live in post-disability Martin's condition was really pretty strong.

Something else seems to be going on here. The Michigan Supreme Court did not want to give up its commitment to self-determination, to the ideal that we all have the right to determine our own end-of-life choices, whatever they may be. Yet it seems as though it could not quite face where that path ultimately goes—approving the termination of nonburdensome life-sustaining treatment to a person who is fundamentally changed and has a new place in the world.

And maybe that's right. Maybe the Michigan court wasn't persuasive in how it reached its result, but perhaps there should be limits, as Dresser argues, on what we can precommit our future selves to, especially when we are not dying and not suffering and can engage with the world in some fashion. Or, to put it another way, maybe there are limits on what we can precommit *others* to do on our behalf.

We always ask about the *rights* of those whose life support is at issue. Maybe it also bears asking what those individuals' *responsibilities to others* are, while competent and pre-disability, when they are sitting down to write a living will or telling their loved ones what they wish regarding life support. Is it possible to ask too much? In addition to everything else she'd had to bear because of her husband's accident, is it fair for Mary Martin to be haunted by Michael's request?

It is frankly daunting to consider what this conclusion would mean with respect to our rights to self-determination. It would mean that those rights are limited—that there are limits on what we can ask other people to do for us in the future if we enter this altered state.

I've been assuming in this discussion a patient with some meaningful interaction or potential for meaningful interaction with the world. Wendland and Martin appeared, at least from the reported opinions, to have some. They were both considered by some experts to be in a minimally conscious state, but others disagreed. Certainly they were not vegetative, but, as some physicians have pointed out, while the lower boundary of the minimally conscious state is established at awareness (thus distinguishing this condition from the permanent vegetative state), the upper boundary is not as clear.[9]

What matters for ethical and legal purposes, once consciousness is established, is not so much the diagnostic category of brain damage but the level of meaningful function. But what if there is none? Dresser says we have to do what "now matters to the patient." But what if nothing appears to matter to the minimally conscious patient under consideration? And how are we to know? And how long do we hold out for a late emergence from a minimally conscious state, like that experienced by Terry Wallis?

As I said in the beginning of this section, this issue will take some sorting out over time. We may never get comfortable with it, and we probably never should. But we will see more of these types of cases in the future—especially as people learn to get very specific about the conditions they would want to avoid and include a whole laundry list of them. And there are many more formerly competent people in present states of severe disability (including minimal consciousness) than there are permanently vegetative patients. At the least, we should approach this task with humility rather than certainty that we know all the right answers now.

The Permanent Vegetative State

Finally, for patients in a permanent vegetative state, respect and care means that we do not maintain their bodies just for our sake. It means that we do not presume that they would want to live in a permanent vegetative state, with no hope of recovery, for decades, or even for years. We require vigilance in diagnosis (to avoid mistakes like that which occurred in Haleigh Poutre's and Terry Wallis's cases) and aggressive rehabilitative attempts in the early vegetative period. After a reasonable period of time, when the prognosis of no recovery has reached a very high level of certainty, we should require that continued tube-feeding and other treatment be justified. The surrogate or family members or loved ones of the patient must come forward with evidence that the patient would have wished for treatment to be continued. In the absence of such evidence, family members, spouses, parents, and surrogates would not have to make the argument to anyone, and would not have to recall prior vague comments the patient might have made to support the argument, that the patient would have wished to discontinue treatment. And many of them, I suspect, would feel relieved that they were not made to feel that they were asking for anything extraordinary or morally suspect.

This book seeks to honor what was lost in Terri's life and in the battle over her death. In coming years, we will surely get better at diagnosing, treating, and understanding the condition Terri faced. But no matter how much we learn, we must regard with caution those who claim to have every answer for every person in every condition. We are all subject to mistakes—doctors, lawyers, judges, loved ones, and popes—and often just uncertainty. And yet we must sometimes make decisions about how the most vulnerable among us must live and die. If we approach these decisions with integrity and responsibility and put the value of the person whose life is entrusted to us over that person's value to some cause or use of another, we will make wise decisions. And those wise decisions will be the best decisions we can make: not convinced that we are right but that we are acting responsibly.

THE NATIONAL RIGHT TO LIFE COMMITTEE'S
MODEL STARVATION AND DEHYDRATION OF
PERSONS WITH DISABILITIES PREVENTION ACT

This appendix contains a bill introduced into the Alabama legislature on March 8, 2005 (H.B. 592), which was modeled on the National Right to Life Committee's model act to restrict the withholding or withdrawal of artificial nutrition and hydration. A number of other state legislatures considered a version of the NRLC's model act as well, although to date none have adopted it. The Alabama bill, like many others, died in legislative committee.

A BILL

TO BE ENTITLED

AN ACT

To establish the Alabama Starvation and Dehydration of Persons with Disabilities Prevention Act to provide medical instructions for certain persons in the event none are provided.

BE IT ENACTED BY THE LEGISLATURE OF ALABAMA:

Section 1. This act shall be known and may be cited as the Alabama Starvation and Dehydration of Persons with Disabilities Prevention Act.

Section 2. As used in this act, the following terms shall have the following meanings:

(1) ATTENDING PHYSICIAN. The physician who has primary responsibility for the overall medical treatment and care of a person.

(2) EXPRESS AND INFORMED CONSENT. Consent voluntarily given with sufficient knowledge of the subject matter involved, including a general understanding of the procedure, the medically acceptable alternative procedures or treatments, and the substantial risks and hazards inherent in the proposed treatment or procedures, to enable the person giving consent to make an understanding and enlightened decision without any element of force, fraud, deceit, duress, or other form of constraint or coercion.

(3) HEALTH CARE PROVIDER. A person who is licensed, certified, or otherwise authorized by the law of this state to administer health care in the ordinary course of business or practice of a profession.

(4) NUTRITION. Sustenance administered by way of the gastrointestinal tract.

(5) PERSON LEGALLY INCAPABLE OF MAKING HEALTH CARE DECISIONS. Any person who:

    a. Has been declared legally incompetent to make decisions affecting medical treatment or care.

    b. In the reasonable judgment of the attending physician, is unable to make decisions affecting medical treatment or other health care services.

(6) PHYSICIAN. A doctor of medicine or doctor of osteopathy licensed to practice medicine in the State of Alabama.

(7) REASONABLE MEDICAL JUDGMENT. A medical judgment that would be made by a reasonably prudent physician, knowledgeable about the case and the treatment possibilities with respect to the medical conditions involved.

Section 3. (a) It shall be presumed that every person legally incapable of making health care decisions has directed his or her health care providers to provide him or her with nutrition and hydration to a degree that is sufficient to sustain life.

    (b) No guardian, surrogate, public or private agency, court, or any other person shall have the authority to make a decision on behalf of a person legally incapable of making health care decisions to withhold or withdraw hydration or nutrition from such a person except in the circumstances and under the conditions specifically provided for in Section 4.

Section 4. The presumption pursuant to Section 3 shall not apply in the following:

(1) To the extent that, in reasonable medical judgment:

    a. Provision of nutrition and hydration is not medically possible.

    b. Provision of nutrition and hydration would hasten death.

    c. Because of the medical condition of the person legally incapable of making health care decisions, that person would be incapable of digesting or absorbing the nutrition and hydration so that its provision would not contribute to sustaining the person's life.

(2) If the person executed a directive in accordance with Alabama advance directive laws specifically authorizing the withholding or withdrawal of nutrition or hydration, to the extent that authorization applies.

(3) If there is clear and convincing evidence that the person, when legally capable of making health care decisions, gave express and informed consent to withdrawing or withholding hydration or nutrition in the applicable circumstances.

Section 5. (a) A cause of action for injunctive relief may be maintained against any person who is reasonably believed to be about to violate or who is in the course of violating this act, or to secure a court determination, notwithstanding the position of a guardian or surrogate, whether there is clear and convincing evidence that the person legally incapable of making health care decisions, when legally capable of making such decisions, gave express and informed consent to withdrawing or withholding hydration or nutrition in the applicable circumstances.

(b) The action may be brought by any person who is:

(1) The spouse, parent, child, or sibling of the person.

(2) A current or former health care provider of the person.

(3) A legally appointed guardian of the person.

(4) State department that performs protection and advocacy functions.

(5) A public official with appropriate jurisdiction to prosecute or enforce the laws of this state.

(c) Pending the final determination of the court, it shall direct that nutrition and hydration be provided unless it determines that Section 4 is applicable.

Section 6. This act shall become effective on the first day of the third month following its passage and approval of the Governor, or its otherwise becoming law.

NOTES

INTRODUCTION

1. Smith, "Legacy of Terri Schiavo."
2. As with the other major topics introduced in this chapter, this point is explored more fully later (see chapter 5) with sources cited to support the more developed text.
3. Dresser, "Schiavo's Legacy," 20.
4. "Poll: Keep Feeding Tube Out."
5. ADA Watch et al., "Issues Surrounding Terri Schindler-Schiavo."
6. Shepherd, "In Respect of People."

CHAPTER 1

1. Jennett and Plum, "Persistent Vegetative State."
2. Schiff and Fins, "Hope for 'Comatose' Patients."
3. Ibid.
4. Jennett, *Vegetative State*, 4–5.
5. American Academy of Neurology, "Practice Parameters," 1015.
6. Berube et al., *Mohonk Report*, 10.
7. Fins, Schiff, and Foley, "Late Recovery."
8. Fins, "Rethinking Disorders of Consciousness"; Schiff and Fins, "Hope for 'Comatose' Patients."
9. Groopman, "Silent Minds."
10. Fins, "Minimally Conscious State," 2; see also Fins et al., "Minimally Conscious State."
11. Fins, "Minimally Conscious State," 2.
12. Ibid.
13. Schindler and Schindler, *Life That Matters*, 40.
14. Schiff and Fins, "Hope for 'Comatose' Patients."
15. Fins, "Border Zones of Consciousness," 53.
16. Fritz, "Last Rights."
17. The Uniform Determination of Death Act, adopted in most states, provides that "[a]n individual who has sustained either (1) irreversible cessation of circulatory and respiratory functions, or (2) irreversible cessation of all functions of the entire brain, including the brain stem,

is dead." Two states, New Jersey and New York, allow families to reject a determination of death by neurological function (brain death) if contrary to the patient's religious or moral convictions. See N.J. Stat. Ann. §26:6A-5 (2005); and N.Y. Comp. Codes R. & Regs. tit. 10 §400.16(e)(3)(2006).

18. Multi-Society Task Force, "Medical Aspects of the Persistent Vegetative State, First of Two Parts."
19. Jennett, *Vegetative State*, 8–9.
20. Ibid., 14–15.
21. Ibid., 15.
22. Wolfson, *Report to Governor*, 30.
23. Ibid.
24. Giacino, "Minimally Conscious State," 385.
25. Ibid., 384.
26. Giacino et al., "Minimally Conscious State."
27. Giacino, "Minimally Conscious State," 385.
28. Jennett, *Vegetative State*, 65.
29. Wade and Johnston, "Permanent Vegetative State."
30. *In re Guardianship of Schiavo*, 780 So.2d 176, 178 (Fla. 2d DCA 2001).
31. Thogmartin, "Report of Autopsy"; Fins and Schiff, "After-Life of Terri Schiavo."
32. Jennett, *Vegetative State*, 63.
33. Ibid., 64.
34. Groopman, "Silent Minds."
35. Schiff et al., "Behavioral Improvements."
36. Owen et al., "Detecting Awareness"; see also Owen et al., "Using Functional Magnetic Resonance Imaging."
37. Di et al., "Cerebral Response"; Coleman et al., "Vegetative Patients."
38. Kotchoubey, "Event-Related Potentials," 477.
39. Fins and Schiff, "Shades of Gray."
40. Cranford, "Facts, Lies, and Videotapes," 366.
41. ABC News, "Once in Coma."
42. Fins, Schiff, and Foley, "Late Recovery," 305.

CHAPTER 2

1. Memo to State Attorney Bernie McCabe.
2. Schiavo and Hirsch, *Terri*, 12–13.

3. Goodnough, "Behind Life-and-Death Fight."

4. Wolfson, *Report to Governor*, 11.

5. Didion, "Case of Theresa Schiavo."

6. Wolfson, *Report to Governor*, 11.

7. Ibid., 15.

8. *In re Guardianship of Schiavo*, No. 90-2908-GD-003 (Fla. Cir. Ct. Pinellas Cty. Feb. 11, 2000).

9. Wolfson, *Report to Governor*, 12.

10. Ibid., 13.

11. Pearse, "Report of Guardian Ad Litem," 13.

12. *In re Guardianship of Schiavo*, No. 90-2908-GD-003 (Fla. Cir. Ct. Pinellas Cty. Feb. 11, 2000).

13. Ibid.

14. Ibid.

15. *In re Guardianship of Schiavo*, 792 So.2d 551, 555 (Fla. Dist. Ct. App. 2001).

16. *In re Guardianship of Schiavo*, 800 So.2d 640, 644 (Fla. Dist. Ct. App. 2001).

17. *In re Guardianship of Schiavo*, No. 90-2908-GD-003 (Fla. Cir. Ct. Pinellas Cty. Nov. 22, 2002).

18. *In re Guardianship of Schiavo*, 851 So.2d 182, 185 (Fla. Dist. Ct. App. 2003).

19. 2003 Fla. Laws Ch. 418.

20. Levesque, "Schiavo's Husband."

21. Goodnough, "Governor of Florida."

22. Bousquet, "How Terri's Law Came to Pass."

23. *Bush v. Schiavo*, 885 So.2d 321, 324 (Fla. 2004).

24. Ibid. at 336.

25. Art. I, §23, Fla. Const. (1980).

26. *Schiavo v. Bush*, No. 03-0082120-CI-20 (Fla. Cir. Ct. Pinellas Cty. May 5, 2004).

27. See Fla. Stat. Ann. §825.102(3), which in certain circumstances makes neglect of an elderly or disabled adult a felony and defines neglect to include "[a] caregiver's failure or omission to provide an elderly person or disabled adult with the care, supervision, and services necessary to maintain the elderly person's or disabled adult's physical and mental health, including, but not limited to, food, nutrition, clothing,

shelter, supervision, medicine, and medical services that a prudent person would consider essential for the well-being of the elderly person or disabled adult."

28. The Vatican, "Address."

29. *In re Guardianship of Schiavo*, No. 90-2908-GD-003 (Fla. Cir. Ct. Pinellas Cty. Oct. 22, 2004).

30. *In re Guardianship of Schiavo*, No. 90-2908-GD-003 (Fla. Mar. 18, 2005).

31. Viglucci and Lebowitz, "Legal Experts."

32. An Act for the Relief of the Parents of Theresa Marie Schiavo, Pub. L. No. 109-3, 119 Stat. 15 (2005).

33. *Schiavo ex rel. Schindler v. Schiavo*, 357 F. Supp.2d 1378 (M.D. Fla. 2005). The Schindlers also claimed, unsuccessfully, that Terri was being unlawfully discriminated against on the basis of a disability and that her Eighth Amendment right against cruel and unusual punishment was being violated. *Schiavo ex rel. Schindler v. Schiavo*, 358 F. Supp.2d 1161 (M.D. Fla. 2005).

34. *Schiavo ex rel. Schindler v. Schiavo*, 403 F.3d 1223, 1229 (11th Cir. 2005).

35. Miller, "Terri Schiavo Case."

36. Memo to State Attorney Bernie McCabe.

CHAPTER 3

1. *Washington v. Glucksberg*, 521 U.S. 702 (1997).

2. *Matter of Quinlan*, 348 A.2d 801, 819 (N.J. Super. Ch. 1975).

3. *Matter of Quinlan*, 355 A.2d 647, 663 (N.J. 1976).

4. Ibid. at 659.

5. *Griswold v. Connecticut*, 381 U.S. 479 (1965) (contraception); *Roe v. Wade*, 410 U.S. 113 (1973) (abortion).

6. *Cruzan v. Director, Missouri Dept. of Health*, 497 U.S. 261 (1990).

7. *Compassion in Dying v. Washington*, 79 F.3d 790, 814 (9th Cir. 1996), reversed as *Washington v. Glucksberg*, 521 U.S. 702 (1997).

8. *Washington v. Glucksberg*, 521 U.S. at 725–26.

9. Ibid. at 720.

10. See, for example, *Planned Parenthood v. Casey*, 505 U.S. 833 (1992).

11. Larriviere and Bonnie, "Terminating Artificial Nutrition and Hydration."

12. *Blouin v. Spitzer*, 356 F.3d 348, 351 (2d Cir. 2004).

13. Fla. Stat. Ann. §765.401(3)(1999).

14. Cantor, *Making Medical Decisions*, 122–27.
15. *In re Guardianship of Schiavo*, No. 90-2908-GD-003 (Fla. Cir. Ct. Pinellas Cty. Feb. 11, 2000).
16. *In re Guardianship of Schiavo*, 780 So.2d 176, 179 (Fla. Dist. Ct. App. 2001).
17. Smith, "Consequences of Casual Conversations."
18. See Perry, "Biblical Biopolitics"; and Shepherd, "State Legislative Proposals."
19. See the National Right to Life Committee's model state law, reprinted in appendix.
20. Smith, "Consequences of Casual Conversations."
21. "Questions and Answers on the Revised Model State Starvation and Dehydration of Persons with Disabilities Act," available at <web .archive.org/web/20051105110636/http://www.nrlc.org/euthanasia/ QAModelNH.pdf.> (accessed Nov. 10, 2006).

CHAPTER 4

1. Information about testimony at trial has been taken from the official transcript of the trial. Judge Greer's conclusions drawn from the testimony can be found in *In re Guardianship of Schiavo*, No. 90-2908-GD-003 (Fla. Cir. Ct. Pinellas Cty. Feb. 11, 2000).
2. *In re Guardianship of Schiavo*, 780 So.2d 176, 179 (Fla. Dist. Ct. App. 2001).
3. Snead, "(Surprising) Truth," 400.
4. Jennett, *Vegetative State*, 69.
5. Schiavo and Hirsch, *Terri*, 87–88.
6. Schindler and Schindler, *Life That Matters*, 50–51.
7. Ibid., 77.
8. Rudnick, "My Living Will."
9. Schindler and Schindler, *Life That Matters*, 80.
10. Cantor, "Discarding Substituted Judgment," 1193.
11. *In re Jobes*, 108 N.J. 394, 407–8 (1987) (internal quotations omitted).

CHAPTER 5

1. *In re Jobes*, 108 N.J. 394, 407–8 (1987).
2. SUPPORT Principal Investigators, "Controlled Trial."
3. Cruz and Cruz, "Living Will."

4. Gillick, "Rethinking the Role of Tube Feeding," 208.

5. Blendon, Benson, and Herrmann, "The American Public and the Terri Schiavo Case," 2583.

6. *Harrell v. St. Mary's Hospital, Inc.*, 678 So.2d 455, 456–57 (Fla. 1996).

7. *In re Browning*, 568 So.2d 4, 14 (Fla. 1990).

8. Fagerlin and Schneider, "Enough," 33–35.

9. Lynn, "Why I Don't Have a Living Will," 103.

10. Fla. Stat. Ann. §765.03(3)(1987) ("The term 'life-prolonging procedure' does not include the provision of sustenance or the administration of medication or performance of any medical procedure deemed necessary to provide comfort care or to alleviate pain").

11. *Mack v. Mack*, 618 A.2d 744 (Md. 1993) (Chasanow, J., concurring in part and dissenting in part).

CHAPTER 6

1. *In re Browning*, 568 So.2d 4, 13 (Fla. 1990).

2. *In re Guardianship of Schiavo*, 851 So.2d 182, 186 (Fla. Dist. Ct. App. 2003).

3. Wolfson, *Report to Governor*, 16.

4. *In re Hanford L. Pinette*, No. 48-2004-MH-1519-0 (Fla. Cir. Ct. Orange Cty. Nov. 23, 2004).

5. Colarossi and Harris, "Living-Will Questions Persist."

6. Dresser, "Precommitment," 1832.

7. Orentlicher, "Limitations of Legislation," 1278.

8. Carpenter et al., "In Defense of Living Wills" (reply of Angela Fagerlin and Carl Schneider), 6.

9. Fla. Stat. Ann. §765.404 (1999).

CHAPTER 7

1. ADA Watch et al., "Issues Surrounding Terri Schindler-Schiavo."

2. Brief of Amici Curiae Not Dead Yet et al.

3. Ibid.

4. Lindgren, "Death by Default," 198–99.

5. Gill, "Health Professionals," 530.

6. *Compassion in Dying v. Washington*, 79 F.3d 790, 814 (9th Cir. 1996).

7. *Bouvia v. Superior Court*, 179 Cal. App.3d 1127, 1143 (1986).

8. *Bush v. Schiavo*, 885 So.2d 321, 325 (Fla. 2004).

9. At the time this book went to press, videos of Terri Schiavo could still be viewed on the Web site of the Terri Schindler Schiavo Foundation, established by the Schindler family. See <http://www.terrisfight.org>.

10. *Cruzan v. Director, Missouri Dept. of Health*, 497 U.S. 261, 262 (1990).

11. *Washington v. Glucksberg*, 521 U.S. 702, 729 (1997).

12. *Matter of Quinlan*, 355 A.2d 647, 664 (N.J. 1976).

13. *Compassion in Dying v. Washington*, 79 F.3d 790, 817 (9th Cir. 1996).

14. *In re Wendland*, 28 P.3d 151, 170 (Cal. 2001).

15. Dworkin, *Life's Dominion*, 213.

16. Buchanan and Brock, *Deciding for Others*, 129.

17. Cantor, "Permanently Unconscious Patient," 414–15.

18. Dresser, "Precommitment."

CHAPTER 8

1. The Vatican, "Address."

2. The Vatican, "Responses to Certain Questions."

3. *Cruzan v. Director, Missouri Dept. of Health*, 497 U.S. 261, 308 (1990) (O'Connor, J., concurring).

4. Goodman, *Florida Bioethics Newsletter*, 11.

5. For example, Delaware's statute, which reads, "'Artificial nutrition and hydration' means supplying food and water through a conduit, such as a tube or intravenous line where the recipient is not required to chew or swallow voluntarily, including, but not limited to, nasogastric tubes, gastrostomies, jejunostomies and intravenous infusions. Artificial nutrition and hydration does not include assisted feeding, such as spoon or bottle feeding." 16 Del. C. §2501(c)(2008).

6. Cranford, "Facts, Lies, and Videotapes," 368.

7. *Cruzan v. Director, Missouri Dept. of Health*, 497 U.S. at 269.

8. *Union Pacific Railway Co. v. Botsford*, 141 U.S. 250, 251 (1891).

9. *Cruzan v. Director, Missouri Dept. of Health*, 497 U.S. at 269.

10. *Schloendorff v. Society of New York Hospital*, 105 N.E. 92, 93 (N.Y. 1914).

11. Bernat, Gert, and Mogielnicki, "Patient Refusal," 2723.

12. Terman, *Best Way to Say Goodbye*.

13. Cranford, "Facts, Lies, and Videotapes," 368.

14. Gillick, "Rethinking the Role of Tube Feeding."

15. Casarett, Kapo, and Caplan, "Appropriate Use," 2608 (citing studies).

16. Van Rosendaal and Verhoef, "Difficult Decisions"; Brody et al., "Withdrawing Intensive Life-Sustaining Treatment."

17. Orentlicher and Callahan, "Feeding Tubes"; Gillick, "Rethinking the Role of Tube Feeding."
18. O'Brien et al., "Nursing Home Residents' Preferences"; O'Brien et al., "Tube Feeding Preferences."
19. CNN News, "Federal Judge Hears Terri Schiavo Case."
20. Brody et al., "Withdrawing Intensive Life-Sustaining Treatment"; Gillick, "Rethinking the Role of Tube Feeding."
21. McCann, Hall, and Groth-Juncker, "Comfort Care."
22. Ouellette, "Vitalism," 17 (emphasis added).
23. National Council on Independent Living, "Rights of People."
24. See, for example, Center on Human Policy, "Statement of Common Principles."

CHAPTER 9

1. *Gonzales v. Carhart*, 127 S. Ct. 1610 (2007).
2. Dolgin, "New Terms."
3. For information on the Will to Live, see <http://www.nrlc.org/euthanasia/willtolive/index.html> (accessed Sept. 17, 2008).
4. *In re Browning*, 543 So.2d 258, 273 (Fla. Dist. Ct. App. 1989).
5. *In re Guardianship of Schiavo*, 780 So.2d 176, 179 (Fla. Dist. Ct. App. 2001).
6. John Paul II, "Evangelium Vitae" (omitting internal quotations and citations).

CHAPTER 10

1. *Superintendent of Belchertown State School v. Saikewicz*, 370 N.E.2d 417 (Mass. 1977).
2. Dresser and Robertson, "Quality of Life"; Dresser, "Precommitment."
3. Nelson and Cranford, "Michael Martin and Robert Wendland."
4. Dworkin, *Life's Dominion*, 199–237.
5. Dresser, "Precommitment," 1840.
6. *In re Wendland*, 28 P.3d 151, 156–57 (Cal. 2001).
7. *In re Martin*, 538 N.W.2d 399, 412 (Mich. 1995).
8. Ibid. at 413.
9. See, e.g., Bernat, "Questions Remaining."

BIBLIOGRAPHY

A very useful Web site, containing many of the key legal documents in the dispute concerning Terri Schiavo as well as a helpful time line, has been created through a joint project of the University of Miami Ethics Programs and the Shepard Broad Law Center at Nova Southeastern University. The primary authors of the Web site are Kathy Cerminara and Kenneth Goodman. See <http://www6.miami.edu/ethics/schiavo/terri_schiavo_timeline.html>.

LEGAL MATERIALS

16 Del. C. §2501(c)(2008).

2003 Fla. Laws Ch. 418 (Terri's Law).

An Act for the Relief of the Parents of Theresa Marie Schiavo, Pub. L. No. 109-3, 119 Stat. 15 (2005) (federal law allowing federal review of order to remove feeding tube).

Art. I, §23, Fla. Const. (1980) (Florida's constitutional right to privacy).

Blouin v. Spitzer, 356 F.3d 348 (2d Cir. 2004) (federal suit against the New York attorney general's office for interference in the treatment of Sheila Pouliot).

Bouvia v. Superior Court, 179 Cal. App. 3d 1127 (1986).

Brief of Amici Curiae Not Dead Yet et al. in Support of Appellant and Requesting Reversal, *Bush v. Schiavo* (filed July 12, 2004) (brief of disability rights groups).

In re Browning, 543 So.2d 258 (Fla. Dist. Ct. App. 1989) (lower appellate court decision in Florida case on right to refuse life-sustaining treatment).

In re Browning, 568 So.2d 4 (Fla. 1990) (landmark Florida Supreme Court case on the right to refuse life-sustaining treatment).

Bush v. Schiavo, 885 So.2d 321 (Fla. 2004) (Florida Supreme Court decision striking down Terri's Law).

Compassion in Dying v. Washington, 79 F.3d 790 (9th Cir. 1996), reversed as *Washington v. Glucksberg*, 521 U.S. 702 (1997) (court of appeals' decision finding constitutional right to physician aid in dying).

Cruzan by Cruzan v. Harmon, 760 S.W.2d 408 (Mo. 1988) (Missouri Supreme

Court decision reversing trial court's approval of withdrawing artificial nutrition and hydration from Nancy Cruzan).

Cruzan v. Director, Missouri Dept. of Health, 497 U.S. 261 (1990) (U.S. Supreme Court decision upholding Missouri's requirement that Nancy Cruzan's wishes be proved by clear and convincing evidence of her prior expressions).

Fla. Stat. Ann. §765.03(3)(1987).

Fla. Stat. Ann. §§765.101–404(1999) (Florida statutes relating to withdrawal of life-sustaining treatment).

Fla. Stat. Ann. §825.102(3)(2000).

Gonzales v. Carhart, 127 S. Ct. 1610 (2007) (U.S. Supreme Court decision upholding federal Partial-Birth Abortion Ban Act).

Griswold v. Connecticut, 381 U.S. 479 (1965) (right to contraception).

Harrell v. St. Mary's Hospital, Inc., 678 So.2d 455 (Fla. 1996).

In re Jobes, 108 N.J. 394 (1987).

In re Estate of Longeway v. Cmty. Convalescent Ctr., 549 N.E.2d 292 (Ill. 1989) (end-of-life case discussing hand-feeding).

Mack v. Mack, 618 A.2d 744 (Md. 1993).

In re Martin, 538 N.W.2d 399 (Mich. 1995) (decision refusing to allow termination of life support for severely disabled or minimally conscious patient).

Memo to State Attorney Bernie McCabe from Prosecutors Doug Crow and Bob Lewis, June 25, 2005, <http://www6.miami.edu/ethics/schiavo/pdf_files/070705-Crow-Lewis-to-McCabe.pdf> (accessed July 20, 2008).

N.J. Stat. Ann. §26:6A-5 (2005) (New Jersey Declaration of Death Act).

N.Y. Comp. Codes R. & Regs. tit. 10 §400.16(e)(3)(2006).

Pearse, Richard L., Jr. "Report of Guardian Ad Litem," December 29, 1998, <http://www6.miami.edu/ethics/schiavo/pdf_files/122998_Schiavo_Richard_Pearse_GAL_report.pdf> (accessed September 15, 2008).

In re Hanford L. Pinette, No. 48-2004-MH-1519-0 (Fla. Cir. Ct. Orange Cty. November 23, 2004) (order granting hospital authority to comply with living will over objection of patient's proxy).

Planned Parenthood v. Casey, 505 U.S. 833 (1992).

Matter of Quinlan, 348 A.2d 801 (N.J. Super. Ch. 1975) (lower court opinion regarding Karen Ann Quinlan).

Matter of Quinlan, 355 A.2d 647 (N.J. 1976) (New Jersey Supreme Court decision in Karen Ann Quinlan case).

Roe v. Wade, 410 U.S. 113 (1973) (right to abortion).

In re Guardianship of Schiavo, No. 90-2908-GD-003 (Fla. Cir. Ct. Pinellas Cty. February 11, 2000) (original order of Judge Greer to remove feeding tube).

In re Guardianship of Schiavo, 780 So.2d 176 (Fla. Dist. Ct. App. 2001) (affirming original trial court order to remove feeding tube).

In re Guardianship of Schiavo, 792 So.2d 551 (Fla. Dist. Ct. App. 2001) (addressing various issues of process).

In re Guardianship of Schiavo, 800 So.2d 640 (Fla. Dist. Ct. App. 2001) (ordering new hearing to determine if there was new evidence of treatment possibilities).

In re Guardianship of Schiavo, No. 90-2908-GD-003 (Fla. Cir. Ct. Pinellas Cty. November 22, 2002) (second order of Judge Greer to remove feeding tube following extensive hearing on treatment possibilities).

In re Guardianship of Schiavo, 851 So.2d 182 (Fla. Dist. Ct. App. 2003) (affirming trial court's second order to remove feeding tube).

In re Guardianship of Schiavo, No. 90-2908-GD-003 (Fla. Cir. Ct. Pinellas Cty. October 22, 2004) (order denying motions for relief from judgment and reconsideration on the basis that Terri Schiavo would have "changed her mind about dying" after the March 2004 statement of Pope John Paul II).

In re Guardianship of Schiavo, No. 90-2908-GD-003 (Fla. Cir. Ct. Pinellas Cty. March 9, 2005) (order denying Schindlers' petition for swallowing tests and swallowing therapy).

In re Guardianship of Schiavo, No. 90-2908-GD-003 (Fla. Cir. Ct. Pinellas Cty. March 18, 2005) (emergency all-writs petition by the Committee on Government Reform of the House of Representatives relating to subpoenas).

In re Guardianship of Schiavo, No. 90-2908-GD-003 (Fla. Cir. Ct. Pinellas Cty. March 23, 2005) (restraining order against Florida Department of Children and Families).

Schiavo v. Bush, No. 03-0082120-CI-20 (Fla. Cir. Ct. Pinellas Cty. May 5, 2004) (circuit court decision striking down Terri's Law).

Schiavo ex rel. Schindler v. Schiavo, 357 F. Supp. 2d 1378 (M.D. Fla. 2005) (federal court decision denying injunctive relief under federal Act for the Relief of the Parents of Theresa Marie Schiavo).

Schiavo ex rel. Schindler v. Schiavo, 358 F. Supp. 2d 1161 (M.D. Fla. 2005) (federal court decision denying injunctive relief under an amended motion for relief under federal Act for the Relief of the Parents of Theresa Marie Schiavo).

Schiavo ex rel. Schindler v. Schiavo, 403 F.3d 1223 (11th Cir. 2005), *reh'g en banc denied*, 403 F.3d 1261 (11th Cir. 2005) (federal court of appeals' decision affirming lower court's denial of injunctive relief under federal Act for the Relief of the Parents of Theresa Marie Schiavo).

Schloendorff v. Society of New York Hospital, 105 N.E.92 (N.Y. 1914).

Superintendent of Belchertown State School v. Saikewicz, 370 N.E.2d 417 (Mass. 1977).

Thogmartin, Jon R., District Six Medical Examiner's Office. "Report of Autopsy for Theresa Schiavo (2005)," <http://www6.miami.edu/ethics/schiavo/pdf_files/061505-autopsy.pdf> (accessed July 23, 2008).

Transcript, *In re Guardianship of Schiavo*, No. 90-2908-GB-003 (Fla. Cir. Ct. Pinellas Cty.) (trial transcript from 2000 hearing).

Uniform Determination of Death Act §1 (1980), 12A U.L.A. 593 (1996).

Union Pacific Railway Co. v. Botsford, 141 U.S. 250 (1891).

Washington v. Glucksberg, 521 U.S. 702 (1997) (U.S. Supreme Court decision rejecting claim of constitutional right of physician aid in hastening death).

In re Wendland, 28 P.3d 151 (Cal. 2001) (decision refusing to allow termination of artificial nutrition and hydration for severely disabled or minimally conscious patient).

Wolfson, Jay. "A Report to Governor Jeb Bush and the 6th Judicial Circuit in the Matter of Theresa Marie Schiavo (2003)," <http://abstractappeal.com/schiavo/WolfsonReport.pdf> (accessed July 23, 2008).

OTHER SOURCES

ABC News. "Once in Coma, Girl May Testify against Alleged Attacker," March 14, 2008, <http://abcnews.go.com/TheLaw/story?id=4375206> (Haleigh Poutre case).

ADA Watch et al. "Issues Surrounding Terri Schindler-Schiavo Are Disability Rights Issues, Say National Disability Organizations." *Ragged Edge Online*, October 27, 2003, <http://www.raggededgemagazine.com/schiavostatement.html> (accessed July 23, 2008).

American Academy of Neurology. "Practice Parameters: Assessment and Management of Patients in the Persistent Vegetative State: Report of the Quality Standards Subcommittee of the American Academy of Neurology (1994)." *Neurology* 45 (1995): 1015–18.

Annas, George J. "'Culture of Life' Politics at the Bedside—The Case of Terri Schiavo." *New England Journal of Medicine* 352 (2005): 1710–15.

———. "'I Want to Live': Medicine Betrayed by Ideology in the Political Debate over Terri Schiavo." *Stetson Law Review* 35 (2005): 49–80.

Bach, C. A., and R. W. McDaniel. "Quality of Life in Quadriplegic Adults: A Focus Group Study." *Rehabilitation Nursing* 18, no. 6 (1993): 364–67.

Bernat, James L. "Questions Remaining about the Minimally Conscious State." *Neurology* 58 (2002): 337–38.

Bernat, James L., Bernard Gert, and R. Peter Mogielnicki. "Patient Refusal of Hydration and Nutrition." *Archives of Internal Medicine* 153 (1993): 2723–28.

Berube, Jean, Joseph Fins, Joseph Giacino, Douglas Katz, Jean Langlois, John Whyte, and George A. Zignay. *The Mohonk Report: A Report to Congress, Disorders of Consciousness: Assessment, Treatment and Research Needs*, 2006, <http://www.northeastcenter.com/the-mohonk-report-disorders-of-consciousness-assessment-treatment-research-needs.pdf>.

Blendon, Robert J., John M. Benson, and Melissa J. Herrmann. "The American Public and the Terri Schiavo Case." *Archives of Internal Medicine* 165 (2005): 2580–84.

Bousquet, Steve. "How Terri's Law Came to Pass." *St. Petersburg Times*, November 2, 2003.

Branom, Mike. "Judge Upholds Living Will." *Tallahassee Democrat*, November 24, 2004.

Brody, Howard, Margaret C. Campbell, Kathy Faber-Langendoen, and Karen S. Ogle. "Withdrawing Intensive Life-Sustaining Treatment—Recommendations for Compassionate Clinical Management." *New England Journal of Medicine* 336 (1997): 652–57.

Buchanan, Allen E., and Dan W. Brock. *Deciding for Others: The Ethics of Surrogate Decision Making*. Cambridge: Cambridge University Press, 1989.

Byrd, Johnnie. Interview by Ray Suarez. "The Right to Live or Die." *NewsHour with Jim Lehrer*. PBS, October 22, 2003, <www.pbs.org/newshour/bb/law/july-dec03/lifesupport_10-22.html> (accessed February 27, 2006).

Cantor, Norman L. "Discarding Substituted Judgment and Best Interests: Toward a Constructive Preference Standard for Dying, Previously

Competent Patients without Advance Directives." *Rutgers Law Review* 48 (1996): 1193–1272.

———. *Making Medical Decisions for the Profoundly Mentally Disabled.* Cambridge, Mass.: MIT Press, 2005.

———. "The Permanently Unconscious Patient, Non-Feeding and Euthanasia." *American Journal of Law and Medicine* 15 (1989): 381–438.

Caplan, Arthur L., James J. McCartney, and Dominic A. Sisti, eds. *The Case of Terri Schiavo.* Amherst, N.Y.: Prometheus Books, 2006.

Carpenter, Allen F., John O. Neher, Betsy Carpenter, Angela Fagerlin, and Carl Schneider. "In Defense of Living Wills." *Hastings Center Report* 34 (2004): 5–6.

Casarett, David, Jennifer Kapo, and Arthur Caplan. "Appropriate Use of Artificial Nutrition and Hydration—Fundamental Principles and Recommendations." *New England Journal of Medicine* 353 (2005): 2607–12.

Center on Human Policy. "A Statement of Common Principles on Life-Sustaining Care and Treatment of People with Disabilities," August 24, 2005, <http://thechp.syr.edu/endorse/> (accessed February 27, 2006).

Cerminara, Kathy L. "Critical Essay: Musings on the Need to Convince Some People with Disabilities That End-of-Life Decision-Making Advocates Are Not Out to Get Them." *Loyola University Chicago Law Journal* 37 (2006): 379–81.

Clark, Annette E. "The Right to Die: The Broken Road from Quinlan to Schiavo." *Loyola University Chicago Law Journal* 37 (2006): 385–405.

Colarossi, Anthony, and Melissa Harris. "Living-Will Questions Persist: A Lake Case Causes Some to Wonder if Their Wishes Will Be Followed." *Orlando Sentinel*, November 25, 2004.

Colby, William H. *Long Goodbye: The Deaths of Nancy Cruzan.* Carlsbad, Calif.: Hay House, 2002.

———. *Unplugged: Reclaiming Our Right to Die in America.* New York: AMACOM, 2006.

Coleman, Martin R., et al. "Do Vegetative Patients Retain Aspects of Language Comprehension? Evidence from fMRI." *Brain* 130 (2007): 2494–2509.

Combs, Mary. "Schiavo: The Road Not Taken." *University of Miami Law Review* 61 (2007): 539–94.

CNN News. "Federal Judge Hears Terri Schiavo Case," March 21, 2005, <http://transcripts.cnn.com/TRANSCRIPTS/0503/21/ltm.01.html>

(accessed July 23, 2008) (transcript of video clip of Representative Tom DeLay).

Cranford, Ronald. "Facts, Lies, and Videotapes: The Permanent Vegetative State and the Sad Case of Terri Schiavo." *Journal of Law, Medicine and Ethics* 33 (2005): 363–71.

Cruz, Humberto, and Georgina Cruz. "Living Will Provides Direction When You Can't." *South Florida Sun-Sentinel*, December 7, 2003.

Di, H. B., et al. "Cerebral Response to Patient's Own Name in the Vegetative and Minimally Conscious States." *Neurology* 68 (2007): 895–99.

Didion, Joan. "The Case of Theresa Schiavo." *New York Review of Books*, June 9, 2005, <http://www.nybooks.com/articles/18050>.

Dolgin, Janet. "New Terms for an Old Debate: Embryos, Dying, and the 'Culture Wars.'" *Houston Journal of Health Law and Policy* 6 (2006): 249–73.

Dresser, Rebecca. "Life, Death, and Incompetent Patients: Conceptual Infirmities and Hidden Values in the Law." *Arizona Law Review* 28 (1986): 373–405.

———. "Precommitment: A Misguided Strategy for Securing Death with Dignity." *Texas Law Review* 81 (2003): 1823–47.

———. "Schiavo's Legacy: The Need for an Objective Standard." *Hastings Center Report* 35 (2005): 20–22.

Dresser, Rebecca S., and John A. Robertson. "Quality of Life and Nontreatment Decisions for Incompetent Patients: A Critique of the Orthodox Approach." *Law, Medicine and Health Care* 17 (1989): 234–44.

Dworkin, Ronald. *Life's Dominion: An Argument about Abortion, Euthanasia, and Individual Freedom.* London: HarperCollins, 1993.

Eisenberg, Jon B. *Using Terri: The Religious Right's Conspiracy to Take Away Our Rights.* San Francisco: HarperSanFrancisco, 2005.

Fagerlin, Angela, and Carl Schneider. "Enough: The Failure of the Living Will." *Hastings Center Report* 34 (2004): 30–42.

Fins, Joseph J. "Border Zones of Consciousness: Another Immigration Debate?" *American Journal of Bioethics* 7 (2007): 51–54.

———. "The Minimally Conscious State: Ethics and Diagnostic Nosology." *Lahey Clinic Medical Ethics* 14, no. 3 (Fall 2007): 1–2, <http://www.lahey.org/Pdf/Ethics/Ethics_Fall_2007.pdf> (accessed July 28, 2008).

———. "Rethinking Disorders of Consciousness: New Research and Its Implications." *Hastings Center Report* 35 (2005): 22–24.

Fins, Joseph J., Maria G. Master, Linda M. Gerber, and Joseph T. Giacino. "Minimally Conscious State: A Diagnosis in Search of an Epidemiology." *Archives of Neurology* 64 (2007): 1400–1405.

Fins, Joseph J., and Nicholas D. Schiff. "The After-Life of Terri Schiavo." *Hastings Center Report* 35 (2005): 8.

———. "Shades of Gray: New Insights into the Vegetative State." *Hastings Center Report* 36 (2006): 8.

Fins, Joseph J., Nicholas D. Schiff, and Kathleen M. Foley. "Late Recovery from the Minimally Conscious State: Ethical and Policy Implications." *Neurology* 68 (2007): 304–7.

Fritz, Mark. "Last Rights: How a Simple Device Set Off a Fight over Elderly Care." *Wall Street Journal* (eastern edition), December 8, 2005.

Gerhart, K. A., J. Joziol-McLain, S. R. Lowenstein, and G. G. Whiteneck. "Quality of Life Following Spinal Cord Injury: Knowledge and Attitudes of Emergency Care Providers." *Annals of Emergency Medicine* 23 (1994): 807–12.

Giacino, J. T. "The Minimally Conscious State: Defining the Borders of Consciousness." *Progress in Brain Research* 150 (2005): 381–95.

Giacino, J. T., S. Ashwal, N. Childs, R. Cranford, B. Jennett, D. I. Katz, J. P. Kelly, et al. "The Minimally Conscious State: Definition and Diagnostic Criteria." *Neurology* 58 (2002): 349–53.

Gill, Carol J. "Health Professionals, Disability, and Assisted Suicide." *Psychology, Public Policy and Law* 56 (2000): 526–45.

Gillick, Muriel R. "Advance Care Planning." *New England Journal of Medicine* 350 (2004): 7–8.

———. "Rethinking the Role of Tube Feeding in Patients with Advanced Dementia." *New England Journal of Medicine* 342 (2000): 206–10.

Goodman, Kenneth. *Florida Bioethics Newsletter*, July 2005.

Goodnough, Abby. "Behind Life-and-Death Fight, a Rift That Began Years Ago." *New York Times*, March 26, 2005.

———. "Governor of Florida Orders Woman Fed in Right-to-Die Case." *New York Times*, October 22, 2003.

Groopman, Jerome. "Silent Minds." *New Yorker*, October 15, 2007, 38–43.

Haley, William E., Rebecca S. Allen, Sandra Reynolds, Hongbin Chen, Allison Burton, and Dolores Gallagher-Thompson. "Family Issues in

End-of-Life Decision Making and End-of-Life Care." *American Behavioral Scientist* 46, no. 2 (2002): 284–98.

Hamel, Ronald P., and James J. Walter, eds. *Artificial Nutrition and Hydration and the Permanently Unconscious Patient: The Catholic Debate*. Washington, D.C.: Georgetown University Press, 2007.

Hensel, William A. "My Living Will: A Piece of My Mind." *Journal of the American Medical Association* 275 (1996): 588.

Hickman, Susan E., Charles P. Sabatino, Alvin H. Moss, and Jessica Wehrle Nester. "The POLST (Physician Orders for Life-Sustaining Treatment) Paradigm to Improve End-of-Life Care: Potential State Legal Barriers to Implementation." *Journal of Law, Medicine and Ethics* 36 (2008): 119–40.

Jennett, Bryan. *The Vegetative State: Medical Facts, Ethical and Legal Dilemmas*. Cambridge: Cambridge University Press, 2002.

Jennett, Bryan, and Fred Plum. "Persistent Vegetative State after Brain Damage: A Syndrome in Search of a Name." *Lancet*, 1972, 734–37.

John Paul II. "Evangelium Vitae (The Gospel of Life)." Encyclical Letter of John Paul II, March 25, 1995, <http://www.vatican.va/holy_father/john_paul_ii/encyclicals/documents/hf_jp-ii_enc_25031995_evangelium-vitae_en.html>.

Kotchoubey, Boris. "Event-Related Potentials Predict the Outcome of the Vegetative State." *Clinical Neurophysiology* 118 (2007): 477–79.

Larriviere, Dan, and Richard J. Bonnie. "Terminating Artificial Nutrition and Hydration in Persistent Vegetative State Patients: Current and Proposed State Laws." *Neurology* 66 (2006): 1624–28.

Levesque, William R. "Quiet Judge Persists in Schiavo Maelstrom." *Tampabay.com*, March 6, 2000, <http://www.sptimes.com/2005/03/06/Tampabay/Quiet_judge_persists_.shtml>.

——. "Schiavo's Husband Says He'll Fight Back." *St. Petersburg Times*, October 24, 2003.

Lindgren, James. "Death by Default." *Law and Contemporary Problems* 56 (1993): 186–254.

Lynn, Joanne. "Why I Don't Have a Living Will." *Law, Medicine, and Health Care* 19 (1991): 101–4.

McCann, R. M., W. J. I. Hall, and A. Groth-Juncker. "Comfort Care for Terminally Ill Patients: The Appropriate Use of Nutrition and Hydration." *Journal of the American Medical Association* 272 (1994): 1263–66.

Meisel, Alan. "Barriers to Forgoing Nutrition and Hydration in Nursing Homes." *American Journal of Law and Medicine* 21 (1995): 335–82.

————. "Suppose the Schindlers Had Won the Schiavo Case." *University of Miami Law Review* 61 (2007): 733–62.

Meisel, Alan, and Kathy Cerminara. *The Right to Die: The Law of End-of-Life Decisionmaking.* 3rd ed. New York: Aspen Publishers, 2004.

Miller, Carol Marbin. "Terri Schiavo Case: Plan to Seize Schiavo Fizzles." *Miami Herald,* March 26, 2005.

The Multi-Society Task Force on PVS. "Medical Aspects of the Persistent Vegetative State, First of Two Parts." *New England Journal of Medicine* 330 (1994): 1499–1508, <http://content.nejm.org/cgi/content/full/330/21/1499> (accessed July 28, 2008).

————. "Medical Aspects of the Persistent Vegetative State, Second of Two Parts." *New England Journal of Medicine* 330 (1994): 1572–79, <http://content.nejm.org/cgi/content/short/330/22/1572> (accessed July 28, 2008).

National Council on Independent Living. "Rights of People with Disabilities to Food and Water Resolution," July 14, 2005, <http://www.notdeadyet.org/docs/ncilreso705.html> (accessed February 27, 2006).

Nelson, Lawrence J., and Ronald E. Cranford. "Michael Martin and Robert Wendland: Beyond the Vegetative State." *Journal of Contemporary Health Law and Policy* 15 (1999): 427–53.

Noah, Barbara A. "Politicizing the End of Life: Lessons from the Schiavo Controversy." *University of Miami Law Review* 59 (2004): 107–34.

————. "The Role of Religion in the Schiavo Controversy." *Houston Journal of Health Law and Policy* 6 (2006): 319–46.

O'Brien, Linda A., Jeane Ann Grisso, Greg Maislin, Karin LaPann, P. J. Greco, E. A. Siegert, and Lois K. Evans. "Nursing Home Residents' Preferences for Life-Sustaining Treatments." *Journal of the American Medical Association* 274 (1995): 1775–79.

O'Brien, Linda A., E. A. Siegert, Jeane Ann Grisso, Greg Maislin, Karin LaPann, Lois K. Evans, and Karol P. Krotki. "Tube Feeding Preferences among Nursing Home Residents." *Journal of General Internal Medicine* 12 (1997): 364–71.

Orentlicher, David. "The Limitations of Legislation." *Maryland Law Review* 53 (1994): 1255–1305.

Orentlicher, David, and Christopher M. Callahan. "Feeding Tubes, Slippery Slopes, and Physician-Assisted Suicide." *Journal of Legal Medicine* 25 (2004): 389–409.

Ouellette, Alicia. "When Vitalism Is Dead Wrong: The Discrimination against and Torture of Incompetent Patients by Compulsory Life-Sustaining Treatment." *Indiana Law Journal* 79 (2004): 1–48.

Owen, Adrian M., Martin R. Coleman, Melanie Boly, Matthew H. Davis, Steven Laureys, and John D. Pickard. "Detecting Awareness in the Vegetative State." *Science* 313 (2006): 1402.

———. "Using Functional Magnetic Resonance Imaging to Detect Covert Awareness in the Vegetative State." *Archives of Neurology* 64 (2007): 1098–1102.

Perry, Joshua L. "Biblical Biopolitics: Judicial Process, Religious Rhetoric, Terri Schiavo and Beyond." *Health Matrix* 16 (2006): 553–629.

"Poll: Keep Feeding Tube Out." *CBS News.com*, March 23, 2005, <http://www.cbsnews.com/stories/2005/03/23/opinion/polls/main682674.shtml>.

Robertson, John A. "*Schiavo* and Its (In)Significance." *Stetson Law Review* 35 (2005): 101–21.

Rosenfeld, Kenneth E., Neil S. Wenger, and Marjorie Kagawa-Singer. "End-of-Life Decision Making: A Qualitative Study of Elderly Individuals." *Journal of General Internal Medicine* 15 (2000): 620–25.

Rudnick, Paul. "My Living Will." *New Yorker*, April 25, 2005, <http://www.newyorker.com/archive/2005/04/25/050425sh_shouts>.

Schiavo, Michael, and Michael Hirsch. *Terri: The Truth.* New York: Dutton, 2006.

Schiff, Nicholas D., and Joseph F. Fins. "Hope for 'Comatose' Patients." *Cerebrum* 5 (2003): 7–24, <http://www.dana.org/news/cerebrum/detail.aspx?id=1274> (accessed July 28, 2008).

Schiff, Nicholas D., Joseph T. Giacino, K. Kalmar, J. D. Victor, K. Baker, M. Gerber, B. Fritz, B. Eisenberg, J. O'Connor, E. J. Kobylarz, S. Farris, A. Machado, C. McCagg, Fred Plum, Joseph J. Fins, and A. R. Rezai. "Behavioral Improvements with Thalamic Stimulation after Severe Traumatic Brain Injury." *Nature* 448 (2007): 600–604.

Schindler, Mary, and Robert Schindler. *A Life That Matters: The Legacy of Terri Schiavo—A Lesson for Us All.* New York: Warner Books, 2006.

Sehgal, Ashwini, A. Galbraith, M. Chesney, P. Schoenfeld, G. Charles, and B. Lo. "How Strictly Do Dialysis Patients Want Their Advance Directives Followed?" *Journal of American Medical Association* 267 (1992): 59–63.

Shepherd, Lois. "In Respect of People Living in a Permanent Vegetative State—and Allowing Them to Die." *Health Matrix* 16 (2006): 631–91.

———. "State Legislative Proposals Following Schiavo: What Are They Thinking?" *Temple Political and Civil Rights Law Review* 15 (2006): 361–87.

———. "Terri Schiavo and the Disability Rights Community: A Cause for Concern." *University of Chicago Legal Forum* (2006): 253–73.

Smith, Wesley. "The Consequences of Casual Conversations." *Daily Standard*, October 27, 2003, <http://www.weeklystandard.com/Content/Public/Articles/000/000/003/304rgjad.asp> (accessed July 23, 2008).

———. "The Legacy of Terri Schiavo." *Weekly Standard*, April 11, 2005, <http://www.weeklystandard.com/Utilities/printer_preview.asp?idArticle=5443&R=EE5B89> (accessed July 23, 2008).

Snead, O. Carter. "The (Surprising) Truth about Schiavo: A Defeat for the Cause of Autonomy." *Constitutional Commentary* 22 (2005): 383–404.

SUPPORT Principal Investigators. "A Controlled Trial to Improve Care for Seriously Ill Hospitalized Patients." *Journal of the American Medical Association* 274 (1995): 1591–98.

Terman, Stanley A. *The Best Way to Say Goodbye: A Legal Peaceful Choice at the End of Life.* Carlsbad, Calif.: Life Transitions Publications, 2007.

Thompson, Jamie. "She's the Other Woman in Michael Schiavo's Heart." *St. Petersburg Times Online Tampa Bay*, March 26, 2005, <http://www.sptimes.com/2005/03/26/news_pf/Tampabay/She_s_the_other_woman.shtml> (accessed January 1, 2008).

Trachtman, Howard. "Death Be Not Political." *American Journal of Bioethics* 3 (2004): 31.

Van Rosendaal, Guido, and Marja J. Verhoef. "Difficult Decisions for Longterm Tube-Feeding." *CMAJ* 161 (1999): 798.

The Vatican. "Address to the Participants in the International Congress: Life-Sustaining Treatments and Vegetative State: Scientific Advances and Ethical Dilemmas," March 20, 2004, <http://www.vatican.va/holy_father/john_paul_ii/speeches/2004/march/documents/hf_jp-ii_spe_20040320_congress-fiamc_en.html> (accessed January 1, 2008).

———. Congregation for the Doctrine of the Faith. "Responses to Certain Questions of the United States Conference of Catholic Bishops Concerning Artificial Nutrition and Hydration," June 29, 2007, <http://www.vatican.va/roman_curia/congregations/cfaith/documents/rc_con_cfaith_doc_20070801_risposte-usa_en.html> (accessed January 1, 2008).

Veatch, Robert M. "Brain Death and Slippery Slopes." *Journal of Clinical Ethics* 3, no. 3 (1992): 181–87.

———. "The Dead Donor Rule: True by Definition." *American Journal of Bioethics* 3 (2004): 10–11.

———. "The Whole-Brain-Oriented Concept of Death: An Outmoded Philosophical Formulation." *Journal of Thanatology* 3 (1975): 13–30.

Viglucci, Andres, and Larry Lebowitz. "Legal Experts Call House Action Unprecedented and Illegal." *Miami Herald*, March 19, 2005.

Wade, Derick T., and Claire Johnston. "The Permanent Vegetative State: Practical Guidance on Diagnosis and Management." *British Medical Journal* 319 (1999): 841–44.

Waldman, Diane. "Timely Triage: Schiavo Videos—Context and Reception." *Jumpcut* 48 (Winter 2006), <http://www.ejumpcut.org/currentissue/SchiavoWaldman/index.html> (accessed April 26, 2006).

Winick, Bruce. "A Legal Autopsy of the Lawyering in *Schiavo*: A Therapeutic Jurisprudence/Preventive Law Rewind Exercise." *University of Miami Law Review* 61 (2007): 595–664.

INDEX

STUDIES IN SOCIAL MEDICINE

Nancy M. P. King, Gail E. Henderson, and Jane Stein, eds., *Beyond Regulations: Ethics in Human Subjects Research* (1999).

Laurie Zoloth, *Health Care and the Ethics of Encounter: A Jewish Discussion of Social Justice* (1999).

Susan M. Reverby, ed., *Tuskegee's Truths: Rethinking the Tuskegee Syphilis Study* (2000).

Beatrix Hoffman, *The Wages of Sickness: The Politics of Health Insurance in Progressive America* (2000).

Margarete Sandelowski, *Devices and Desires: Gender, Technology, and American Nursing* (2000).

Keith Wailoo, *Dying in the City of the Blues: Sickle Cell Anemia and the Politics of Race and Health* (2001).

Judith Andre, *Bioethics as Practice* (2002).

Chris Feudtner, *Bittersweet: Diabetes, Insulin, and the Transformation of Illness* (2003).

Ann Folwell Stanford, *Bodies in a Broken World: Women Novelists of Color and the Politics of Medicine* (2003).

Lawrence O. Gostin, *The AIDS Pandemic: Complacency, Injustice, and Unfulfilled Expectations* (2004).

Arthur A. Daemmrich, *Pharmacopolitics: Drug Regulation in the United States and Germany* (2004).

Carl Elliott and Tod Chambers, eds., *Prozac as a Way of Life* (2004).

Steven M. Stowe, *Doctoring the South: Southern Physicians and Everyday Medicine in the Mid-Nineteenth Century* (2004).

Arleen Marcia Tuchman, *Science Has No Sex: The Life of Marie Zakrzewska, M.D.* (2006).

Michael H. Cohen, *Healing at the Borderland of Medicine and Religion* (2006).

Keith Wailoo, Julie Livingston, and Peter Guarnaccia, eds., *A Death Retold: Jesica Santillan, the Bungled Transplant, and Paradoxes of Medical Citizenship* (2006).

Michelle T. Moran, *Colonizing Leprosy: Imperialism and the Politics of Public Health in the United States* (2007).

Karey Harwood, *The Infertility Treadmill: Feminist Ethics, Personal Choice, and the Use of Reproductive Technologies* (2007).

Samuel Kelton Roberts Jr. *Infectious Fear: Politics, Disease, and the Health Effects of Segregation* (2008).

Lois Shepherd. *If That Ever Happens to Me: Making Life and Death Decisions after Terri Schiavo* (2008).